Compiled from Billboard's pop singles charts, 1955-1985

Record Research Inc.
P.O. Box 200
Menomonee Falls, Wisconsin 53051

ISBN 0-89820-056-3

Published by Record Research Inc.
P.O. Box 200, Menomonee Falls, Wisconsin 53051

CONTENTS

Author's Notes **5**

The Ranking System **7**

THE TOP 2000 RANKING **9**

A listing of the Top 2000 hits, in rank order, from 1955-1985.

THE ARTISTS **67**

An alphabetical listing, by artist name, of the Top 2000 hits.

THE SONG TITLES **103**

An alphabetical listing, by song title, of the Top 2000 hits.

Miscellaneous

The Top 50 Artists Of The Top 2000 .... **135**

Songs With More Than One Hit Version **136**

Same Song Titles But Different Songs **138**

Re-Charted Singles **139**

The Twist **140**

2-Sided Hits **140**

Breakdown By Year **140**

AUTHOR'S NOTES

It is with a wonderful feeling of bliss that I welcome you to a fantastic trip down memory lane. From early summer of 1955 when *ROCK AROUND THE CLOCK* by Bill Haley and His Comets burst through as the nation's first #1 rock hit, to late summer of 1985 when Huey Lewis and The News took us "back to the future" with *THE POWER OF LOVE,* these are the 2000 most played and most purchased records of the rock era.

Here, indeed, are the ultimate greatest hits of the past 30 years...the music and sounds that bring back a moment as only a song can. Songs like *SILHOUETTES, MY TRUE LOVE, LITTLE RED CORVETTE, BLUE MOON* and *BAD MOON RISING*...artists like Ral Donner, The Ronettes, Men At Work, Buddy Knox and Buddy Holly...all part of 2000 sweet and bittersweet memories.

The number 2000 may seem like a huge number of titles, however, it represents only slightly more than 1% of the total 45 RPM records released during the past 30 years. When you're dealing with the top 1% of anything, it surely represents the very best you have to offer, and this is exactly what this book is all about. These are the top pop songs, honored for achieving the highest rankings on *BILLBOARD'S* national pop singles charts. These are the songs that climbed the chart ladder to its highest rungs.

As you browse through the list or as you count down the Top 100, Top 1000, or the entire list, do it slowly and lovingly. Remember, these are America's favorite songs from the past several exciting and turbulent decades. These are the songs we listened to while wading through Watergate, Vietnam, seven presidential eras and many cultural changes; in addition, to laughing and crying through millions of weddings, births and graduations. These are the songs that gave us euphoria as high as the sky and sorrow as deep as the ocean...the songs that bring memories of heartbreak and of genuine love.

So, whether you're a fan of Melanie or Madonna, or whether your favorite song is *LOUIE LOUIE* or *LONG TALL SALLY, you're sure to find your favorite artists and songs among those listed herein. And whether you own all 2000 of these hits or just 20 of them, it's fascinating to see exactly where their slot in music history lies. Did THE PIED PIPER* win over *LADY MADONNA*...did *DRIVE* outrun *STRAY CAT STRUT*...did *SUMMER BREEZE* blow over *FIRE LAKE?* For these answers and thousands more, simply turn the pages..."memories are made of this".

JOEL WHITBURN

THE RANKING SYSTEM

The basic concept for ranking 30 years of hits is a logical and simple one based on the principle that the highest position at which a record peaks is the single most important factor during its chart life. Climbing and inching its way to the upper echelons of the chart is a battle each hit record wages in the never ending race for chart superiority. And when the dust has settled and each record has ended its chart run, the record's peak position is the primary statistic used in the rankings for this book. All records that peaked at position #1 through #6 plus a few that peaked at #7 were needed to fill out this Top 2000 ranking. In a nutshell, records that peaked at #2 will never be ranked over records that peaked at #1, #3 records will never be ranked over those peaking at #2, etc.

Following is the chronology used in ranking the Top 2000 hits:

1) Peak position

a) All records peaking at #1 are listed first, followed by records peaking at #2, etc.

b) Ties among each highest position grouping are broken as follows:

2) Total weeks record held its peak position

3) Total weeks charted

4) Total weeks charted in Top 40

5) Total weeks charted in Top 10

If there are still ties, the records are ranked alphabetically by artist.

The *BILLBOARD* charts were used exclusively in compiling this data. For the years 1955-1958, the following *Billboard* pop charts were researched, with each record's highest position taken from whichever chart it attained a higher ranking: "Top 100", "Best Sellers", "Most Played by Jockeys" and "Most Played in Juke Boxes". From 1958 to the present, the sole all-encompassing pop chart used was *Billboard's* "Hot 100 Singles".

THE TOP 2000 RANKING

This section lists, in rank order, the Top 2000 hits from 1955-1985. The peak position and the total weeks at the peak position are shown in a shaded box above the corresponding titles. The shaded box is shown at the top of each new page whether or not there is a change in peak position/peak weeks.

Columnar headings show the following data:

YR: Year record reached its peak position
T 10: Total weeks charted in the Top 10
T 40: Total weeks charted in the Top 40
CHR: Total weeks charted
RNK: Top 2000 ranking (highlighted in dark type)

YR	WEEKS T 10	T 40	CHR	RNK	Title ... Artist
					Peak Pos **1** Peak Wks **11**
56	21	24	28	**1**	☐ **Don't Be Cruel/Hound Dog** ... Elvis Presley
					Peak Pos **1** Peak Wks **10**
56	17	22	26	**2**	☐ **Singing The Blues** ... Guy Mitchell
81	15	21	26	**3**	☐ **Physical** ... Olivia Newton-John
77	14	21	25	**4**	☐ **You Light Up My Life** ... Debby Boone
					Peak Pos **1** Peak Wks **9**
57	15	22	30	**5**	☐ **All Shook Up** ... Elvis Presley
81	13	19	27	**6**	☐ **Endless Love** ... Diana Ross & Lionel Richie
59	16	22	26	**7**	☐ **Mack The Knife** ... Bobby Darin
81	14	20	26	**8**	☐ **Bette Davis Eyes** ... Kim Carnes
60	12	17	21	**9**	☐ **The Theme From "A Summer Place"** ... Percy Faith
68	14	19	19	**10**	☐ **Hey Jude** ... The Beatles
					Peak Pos **1** Peak Wks **8**
55	19	25	38	**11**	☐ **Rock Around The Clock** ... Bill Haley & His Comets
56	16	22	37	**12**	☐ **The Wayward Wind** ... Gogi Grant
56	15	22	27	**13**	☐ **Heartbreak Hotel** ... Elvis Presley
76	11	17	23	**14**	☐ **Tonight's The Night (Gonna Be Alright)** ... Rod Stewart
83	13	20	22	**15**	☐ **Every Breath You Take** ... The Police
55	16	19	22	**16**	☐ **Sixteen Tons** ... Tennessee Ernie Ford
78	13	18	20	**17**	☐ **Night Fever** ... Bee Gees
					Peak Pos **1** Peak Wks **7**
57	17	24	34	**18**	☐ **Love Letters In The Sand** ... Pat Boone
57	15	19	27	**19**	☐ **Jailhouse Rock** ... Elvis Presley
78	12	19	25	**20**	☐ **Shadow Dancing** ... Andy Gibb
57	14	18	25	**21**	☐ **(Let Me Be Your) Teddy Bear** ... Elvis Presley
83	11	17	24	**22**	☐ **Billie Jean** ... Michael Jackson
61	12	17	23	**23**	☐ **Tossin' And Turnin'** ... Bobby Lewis
58	12	18	21	**24**	☐ **At The Hop** ... Danny & The Juniors
82	12	16	20	**25**	☐ **I Love Rock 'N Roll** ... Joan Jett & The Blackhearts
82	12	15	19	**26**	☐ **Ebony And Ivory** ... Paul McCartney & Stevie Wonder
68	11	15	15	**27**	☐ **I Heard It Through The Grapevine** ... Marvin Gaye
64	12	14	15	**28**	☐ **I Want To Hold Your Hand** ... The Beatles
66	12	13	15	**29**	☐ **I'm A Believer** ... The Monkees
					Peak Pos **1** Peak Wks **6**
57	14	19	26	**30**	☐ **April Love** ... Pat Boone
56	16	20	25	**31**	☐ **Rock And Roll Waltz** ... Kay Starr
83	14	20	25	**32**	☐ **Flashdance...What A Feeling** ... Irene Cara
82	12	20	25	**33**	☐ **Centerfold** ... The J. Geils Band
78	15	19	25	**34**	☐ **Le Freak** ... Chic

YR	WEEKS T 10	WEEKS T 40	WEEKS CHR	RNK	Title . . . Artist
					Peak Pos 1 Peak Wks 6
80	13	19	25	**35**	☐ **Lady** . . . Kenny Rogers
80	12	19	25	**36**	☐ **Call Me** . . . Blondie
82	15	18	25	**37**	☐ **Eye Of The Tiger** . . . Survivor
56	15	20	24	**38**	☐ **The Poor People Of Paris** . . . Les Baxter
56	15	19	24	**39**	☐ **Memories Are Made Of This** . . . Dean Martin
58	12	19	22	**40**	☐ **It's All In The Game** . . . Tommy Edwards
83	13	18	22	**41**	☐ **Say Say Say** . . . Paul McCartney & Michael Jackson
79	12	16	22	**42**	☐ **My Sharona** . . . The Knack
55	17	21	21	**43**	☐ **Love Is A Many-Splendored Thing** . . . Four Aces
59	13	18	21	**44**	☐ **The Battle Of New Orleans** . . . Johnny Horton
57	13	17	21	**45**	☐ **Young Love** . . . Tab Hunter
55	16	19	19	**46**	☐ **The Yellow Rose Of Texas** . . . Mitch Miller
84	9	14	19	**47**	☐ **Like A Virgin** . . . Madonna
72	11	15	18	**48**	☐ **The First Time Ever I Saw Your Face** . . . Roberta Flack
72	11	15	18	**49**	☐ **Alone Again (Naturally)** . . . Gilbert O'Sullivan
69	11	16	17	**50**	☐ **Aquarius/Let The Sunshine In** . . . The 5th Dimension
71	11	15	17	**51**	☐ **Joy To The World** . . . Three Dog Night
60	11	14	16	**52**	☐ **Are You Lonesome To-night?** . . . Elvis Presley
58	10	14	14	**53**	☐ **The Purple People Eater** . . . Sheb Wooley
70	10	13	14	**54**	☐ **Bridge Over Troubled Water** . . . Simon & Garfunkel
69	9	12	12	**55**	☐ **In The Year 2525** . . . Zager & Evans
					Peak Pos 1 Peak Wks 5
57	16	23	31	**56**	☐ **Tammy** . . . Debbie Reynolds
56	14	20	23	**57**	☐ **My Prayer** . . . The Platters
56	15	19	23	**58**	☐ **Love Me Tender** . . . Elvis Presley
77	12	17	23	**59**	☐ **Best Of My Love** . . . Emotions
80	14	19	22	**60**	☐ **(Just Like) Starting Over** . . . John Lennon
84	11	16	21	**61**	☐ **When Doves Cry** . . . Prince
84	10	15	21	**62**	☐ **Jump** . . . Van Halen
60	11	16	20	**63**	☐ **It's Now Or Never** . . . Elvis Presley
58	10	16	20	**64**	☐ **Don't** . . . Elvis Presley
79	10	15	20	**65**	☐ **Bad Girls** . . . Donna Summer
58	12	16	19	**66**	☐ **All I Have To Do Is Dream** . . . The Everly Brothers
58	11	16	19	**67**	☐ **Tequila** . . . The Champs
76	11	15	19	**68**	☐ **Silly Love Songs** . . . Wings
68	10	15	18	**69**	☐ **Love Is Blue** . . . Paul Mauriat
62	11	14	18	**70**	☐ **I Can't Stop Loving You** . . . Ray Charles
71	11	15	17	**71**	☐ **Maggie May** . . . Rod Stewart
71	10	15	17	**72**	☐ **It's Too Late** . . . Carole King
67	9	15	17	**73**	☐ **To Sir With Love** . . . Lulu
59	10	14	17	**74**	☐ **Venus** . . . Frankie Avalon

YR	WEEKS T 10	WEEKS T 40	WEEKS CHR	RNK	Title . . . Artist
					Peak Pos 1 / Peak Wks 5
60	9	13	17	75	☐ **Cathy's Clown** . . . The Everly Brothers
70	11	16	16	76	☐ **I'll Be There** . . . The Jackson 5
62	10	14	16	77	☐ **Big Girls Don't Cry** . . . The 4 Seasons
61	10	13	16	78	☐ **Big Bad John** . . . Jimmy Dean
58	10	13	16	79	☐ **Nel Blu Dipinto Di Blu (Volare)** . . . Domenico Modugno
73	9	13	16	80	☐ **Killing Me Softly With His Song** . . . Roberta Flack
63	10	13	15	81	☐ **Sugar Shack** . . . Jimmy Gilmer & The Fireballs
68	10	13	15	82	☐ **Honey** . . . Bobby Goldsboro
71	9	12	15	83	☐ **One Bad Apple** . . . The Osmonds
68	9	13	14	84	☐ **People Got To Be Free** . . . The Rascals
62	7	12	14	85	☐ **Sherry** . . . The 4 Seasons
66	9	11	13	86	☐ **The Ballad Of The Green Berets** . . . SSgt Barry Sadler
69	9	12	12	87	☐ **Get Back** . . . The Beatles
64	6	9	10	88	☐ **Can't Buy Me Love** . . . The Beatles
					Peak Pos 1 / Peak Wks 4
77	16	23	31	89	☐ **I Just Want To Be Your Everything** . . . Andy Gibb
56	17	24	29	90	☐ **Lisbon Antigua** . . . Nelson Riddle
83	11	18	29	91	☐ **Total Eclipse Of The Heart** . . . Bonnie Tyler
80	14	17	29	92	☐ **Upside Down** . . . Diana Ross
57	13	23	28	93	☐ **Honeycomb** . . . Jimmie Rodgers
58	6	13	28	94	☐ **The Chipmunk Song** . . . The Chipmunks
78	13	22	27	95	☐ **Stayin' Alive** . . . Bee Gees
55	18	26	26	96	☐ **Autumn Leaves** . . . Roger Williams
57	11	20	26	97	☐ **Wake Up Little Susie** . . . The Everly Brothers
80	12	19	25	98	☐ **Another Brick In The Wall (Part II)** . . . Pink Floyd
83	10	19	25	99	☐ **Down Under** . . . Men At Work
80	9	19	24	100	☐ **Rock With You** . . . Michael Jackson
83	13	17	24	101	☐ **All Night Long (All Night)** . . . Lionel Richie
56	14	19	23	102	☐ **I Almost Lost My Mind** . . . Pat Boone
58	12	19	23	103	☐ **Sugartime** . . . The McGuire Sisters
78	13	17	23	104	☐ **Kiss You All Over** . . . Exile
82	13	17	23	105	☐ **Maneater** . . . Daryl Hall & John Oates
73	11	17	23	106	☐ **Tie A Yellow Ribbon Round The Ole Oak Tree** . . . Dawn featuring Tony Orlando
80	9	16	23	107	☐ **Magic** . . . Olivia Newton-John
75	6	16	23	108	☐ **Love Will Keep Us Together** . . . The Captain & Tennille
79	10	15	23	109	☐ **Reunited** . . . Peaches & Herb
80	9	15	23	110	☐ **Funkytown** . . . Lipps, Inc.
70	13	19	22	111	☐ **Raindrops Keep Fallin' On My Head** . . . B.J. Thomas
69	12	18	22	112	☐ **Sugar, Sugar** . . . The Archies
80	12	17	22	113	☐ **Crazy Little Thing Called Love** . . . Queen
82	10	17	22	114	☐ **Jack & Diane** . . . John Cougar

YR	WEEKS T 10	WEEKS T 40	WEEKS CHR	RNK	Title . . . Artist
					Peak Pos **1** / Peak Wks **4**
79	12	18	21	**115**	☐ **Da Ya Think I'm Sexy?** . . . Rod Stewart
59	10	15	21	**116**	☐ **Stagger Lee** . . . Lloyd Price
76	8	15	20	**117**	☐ **Don't Go Breaking My Heart** . . . Elton John & Kiki Dee
72	8	14	20	**118**	☐ **I Can See Clearly Now** . . . Johnny Nash
67	9	12	20	**119**	☐ **Ode To Billie Joe** . . . Bobbie Gentry
72	11	17	19	**120**	☐ **American Pie - Parts I & II** . . . Don McLean
58	9	14	19	**121**	☐ **He's Got The Whole World (In His Hands)** . . . Laurie London
72	9	14	19	**122**	☐ **Without You** . . . Nilsson
69	9	14	19	**123**	☐ **Everyday People** . . . Sly & The Family Stone
76	8	13	19	**124**	☐ **Disco Lady** . . . Johnnie Taylor
73	9	15	18	**125**	☐ **My Love** . . . Paul McCartney & Wings
85	8	12	18	**126**	☐ **We Are The World** . . . USA for Africa
70	11	15	17	**127**	☐ **(They Long To Be) Close To You** . . . Carpenters
59	10	14	17	**128**	☐ **The Three Bells** . . . The Browns
61	9	12	17	**129**	☐ **Runaway** . . . Del Shannon
68	11	14	16	**130**	☐ **(Sittin' On) The Dock Of The Bay** . . . Otis Redding
60	10	13	16	**131**	☐ **Stuck On You** . . . Elvis Presley
67	8	13	16	**132**	☐ **The Letter** . . . The Box Tops
59	8	12	16	**133**	☐ **Come Softly To Me** . . . Fleetwoods
69	11	14	15	**134**	☐ **Honky Tonk Women** . . . The Rolling Stones
59	10	14	15	**135**	☐ **Lonely Boy** . . . Paul Anka
71	10	14	15	**136**	☐ **How Can You Mend A Broken Heart** . . . The Bee Gees
62	10	13	15	**137**	☐ **Roses Are Red (My Love)** . . . Bobby Vinton
69	9	13	15	**138**	☐ **Dizzy** . . . Tommy Roe
63	9	12	15	**139**	☐ **He's So Fine** . . . The Chiffons
70	10	13	14	**140**	☐ **My Sweet Lord** . . . George Harrison
67	9	13	14	**141**	☐ **Windy** . . . The Association
65	9	12	14	**142**	☐ **(I Can't Get No) Satisfaction** . . . The Rolling Stones
68	8	12	14	**143**	☐ **This Guy's In Love With You** . . . Herb Alpert
63	9	12	13	**144**	☐ **Dominique** . . . The Singing Nun
64	9	12	13	**145**	☐ **There! I've Said It Again** . . . Bobby Vinton
64	8	12	13	**146**	☐ **Baby Love** . . . The Supremes
67	9	11	13	**147**	☐ **Groovin'** . . . The Young Rascals
67	9	11	13	**148**	☐ **Somethin' Stupid** . . . Nancy Sinatra & Frank Sinatra
67	10	12	12	**149**	☐ **Daydream Believer** . . . The Monkees
65	6	9	11	**150**	☐ **Yesterday** . . . The Beatles
					Peak Pos **1** / Peak Wks **3**
60	25	33	39	**151**	☐ **The Twist** . . . Chubby Checker
77	17	26	33	**152**	☐ **How Deep Is Your Love** . . . Bee Gees

YR	WEEKS T 10	WEEKS T 40	WEEKS CHR	RNK	Title . . . Artist
					Peak Pos **1** — Peak Wks **3**
78	10	16	32	**153**	☐ **Baby Come Back** . . . Player
80	15	21	31	**154**	☐ **Another One Bites The Dust** . . . Queen
82	12	21	28	**155**	☐ **Don't You Want Me** . . . The Human League
84	10	18	28	**156**	☐ **What's Love Got To Do With It** . . . Tina Turner
56	15	22	27	**157**	☐ **Moonglow and Theme From "Picnic"** . . . Morris Stoloff
79	13	17	27	**158**	☐ **I Will Survive** . . . Gloria Gaynor
76	6	15	27	**159**	☐ **December, 1963 (Oh, What a Night)** . . . The Four Seasons
60	10	14	27	**160**	☐ **Running Bear** . . . Johnny Preston
56	18	22	26	**161**	☐ **The Green Door** . . . Jim Lowe
57	13	17	26	**162**	☐ **You Send Me** . . . Sam Cooke
84	10	15	26	**163**	☐ **I Just Called To Say I Love You** . . . Stevie Wonder
77	13	18	25	**164**	☐ **Love Theme From "A Star Is Born" (Evergreen)** . . . Barbra Streisand
83	10	18	25	**165**	☐ **Beat It** . . . Michael Jackson
76	10	18	25	**166**	☐ **Play That Funky Music** . . . Wild Cherry
80	11	19	24	**167**	☐ **Woman In Love** . . . Barbra Streisand
81	12	17	24	**168**	☐ **Arthur's Theme (Best That You Can Do)** . . . Christopher Cross
84	10	16	24	**169**	☐ **Against All Odds (Take A Look At Me Now)** . . . Phil Collins
84	8	14	24	**170**	☐ **Wake Me Up Before You Go-Go** . . . Wham!
60	11	18	23	**171**	☐ **I'm Sorry** . . . Brenda Lee
58	11	18	23	**172**	☐ **To Know Him, Is To Love Him** . . . The Teddy Bears
78	12	17	23	**173**	☐ **Boogie Oogie Oogie** . . . A Taste Of Honey
74	9	17	23	**174**	☐ **The Way We Were** . . . Barbra Streisand
81	8	17	23	**175**	☐ **Kiss On My List** . . . Daryl Hall & John Oates
84	11	16	23	**176**	☐ **Footloose** . . . Kenny Loggins
82	7	15	23	**177**	☐ **Up Where We Belong** . . . Joe Cocker & Jennifer Warnes
67	9	14	23	**178**	☐ **Light My Fire** . . . The Doors
84	9	16	22	**179**	☐ **Karma Chameleon** . . . Culture Club
79	14	17	21	**180**	☐ **Hot Stuff** . . . Donna Summer
85	9	17	21	**181**	☐ **Careless Whisper** . . . Wham! featuring George Michael
80	11	16	21	**182**	☐ **Coming Up (Live at Glasgow)** . . . Paul McCartney & Wings
79	9	16	21	**183**	☐ **Escape (The Pina Colada Song)** . . . Rupert Holmes
72	7	16	21	**184**	☐ **The Candy Man** . . . Sammy Davis, Jr.
74	8	15	21	**185**	☐ **Seasons In The Sun** . . . Terry Jacks
84	10	14	21	**186**	☐ **Ghostbusters** . . . Ray Parker Jr.
78	9	15	20	**187**	☐ **MacArthur Park** . . . Donna Summer
57	10	14	20	**188**	☐ **Butterfly** . . . Andy Williams

YR	WEEKS T 10	WEEKS T 40	WEEKS CHR	RNK	Title . . . Artist
					Peak Pos 1 / Peak Wks 3
58	12	18	19	189	☐ **Witch Doctor** . . . David Seville
70	11	16	19	190	☐ **I Think I Love You** . . . The Partridge Family
59	10	16	19	191	☐ **Smoke Gets In Your Eyes** . . . The Platters
72	7	14	19	192	☐ **Lean On Me** . . . Bill Withers
85	7	13	19	193	☐ **Shout** . . . Tears For Fears
71	11	16	18	194	☐ **Knock Three Times** . . . Dawn
62	11	14	18	195	☐ **Peppermint Twist - Part I** . . . Joey Dee & the Starliters
71	10	14	18	196	☐ **Brand New Key** . . . Melanie
60	9	14	18	197	☐ **Save The Last Dance For Me** . . . The Drifters
85	8	14	18	198	☐ **Can't Fight This Feeling** . . . REO Speedwagon
72	9	13	18	199	☐ **Baby Don't Get Hooked On Me** . . . Mac Davis
61	10	15	17	200	☐ **Wonderland By Night** . . . Bert Kaempfert
73	11	14	17	201	☐ **You're So Vain** . . . Carly Simon
73	9	14	17	202	☐ **Crocodile Rock** . . . Elton John
57	9	14	17	203	☐ **Too Much** . . . Elvis Presley
77	8	13	17	204	☐ **Sir Duke** . . . Stevie Wonder
75	7	13	17	205	☐ **Fly, Robin, Fly** . . . Silver Convention
76	6	13	17	206	☐ **50 Ways To Leave Your Lover** . . . Paul Simon
74	8	12	17	207	☐ **The Streak** . . . Ray Stevens
61	8	14	16	208	☐ **Pony Time** . . . Chubby Checker
72	8	14	16	209	☐ **Me And Mrs. Jones** . . . Billy Paul
62	8	13	16	210	☐ **Telstar** . . . The Tornadoes
69	8	14	15	211	☐ **Wedding Bell Blues** . . . The 5th Dimension
70	8	14	15	212	☐ **American Woman** . . . The Guess Who
64	8	14	15	213	☐ **Oh, Pretty Woman** . . . Roy Orbison
66	10	13	15	214	☐ **Winchester Cathedral** . . . The New Vaudeville Band
71	9	13	15	215	☐ **Go Away Little Girl** . . . Donny Osmond
70	8	13	15	216	☐ **War** . . . Edwin Starr
61	8	13	15	217	☐ **The Lion Sleeps Tonight** . . . The Tokens
63	9	12	15	218	☐ **Hey Paula** . . . Paul & Paula
67	9	12	15	219	☐ **Happy Together** . . . The Turtles
62	8	12	15	220	☐ **Hey! Baby** . . . Bruce Channel
63	8	12	15	221	☐ **Blue Velvet** . . . Bobby Vinton
75	7	12	15	222	☐ **Island Girl** . . . Elton John
63	7	12	15	223	☐ **Fingertips - Pt 2** . . . Little Stevie Wonder
62	8	11	15	224	☐ **Duke Of Earl** . . . Gene Chandler
61	7	11	15	225	☐ **Take Good Care Of My Baby** . . . Bobby Vee
74	6	11	15	226	☐ **(You're) Having My Baby** . . . Paul Anka
70	9	13	14	227	☐ **Ain't No Mountain High Enough** . . . Diana Ross
71	9	13	14	228	☐ **Family Affair** . . . Sly & The Family Stone
62	8	13	14	229	☐ **Soldier Boy** . . . The Shirelles
72	10	12	14	230	☐ **A Horse With No Name** . . . America

YR	WEEKS T 10	WEEKS T 40	WEEKS CHR	RNK	Title . . . Artist
					Peak Pos 1 · Peak Wks 3
63	9	12	14	231	☐ **My Boyfriend's Back** . . . The Angels
63	8	12	14	232	☐ **Sukiyaki** . . . Kyu Sakamoto
66	6	12	14	233	☐ **Cherish** . . . The Association
75	5	12	14	234	☐ **Bad Blood** . . . Neil Sedaka
65	8	11	14	235	☐ **Turn! Turn! Turn!** . . . The Byrds
61	8	11	14	236	☐ **Blue Moon** . . . The Marcels
63	8	11	14	237	☐ **I Will Follow Him** . . . Little Peggy March
65	7	10	14	238	☐ **I Got You Babe** . . . Sonny & Cher
75	6	10	14	239	☐ **He Don't Love You (Like I Love You)** . . . Tony Orlando & Dawn
63	7	12	13	240	☐ **Walk Like A Man** . . . The 4 Seasons
68	7	12	13	241	☐ **Mrs. Robinson** . . . Simon & Garfunkel
65	6	12	13	242	☐ **Help!** . . . The Beatles
66	8	11	13	243	☐ **(You're My) Soul And Inspiration** . . . The Righteous Brothers
64	7	11	13	244	☐ **Chapel Of Love** . . . The Dixie Cups
66	7	11	12	245	☐ **We Can Work It Out** . . . The Beatles
66	8	10	12	246	☐ **Monday, Monday** . . . The Mama's & The Papa's
64	7	11	11	247	☐ **I Feel Fine** . . . The Beatles
65	7	11	11	248	☐ **Mrs. Brown You've Got A Lovely Daughter** . . . Herman's Hermits
64	8	10	11	249	☐ **The House Of The Rising Sun** . . . The Animals
67	8	10	11	250	☐ **Hello Goodbye** . . . The Beatles
66	7	10	11	251	☐ **Summer In The City** . . . The Lovin' Spoonful
					Peak Pos 1 · Peak Wks 2
62	8	24	37	252	☐ **Monster Mash** . . . Bobby "Boris" Pickett & The Crypt-Kickers
81	12	22	32	253	☐ **Jessie's Girl** . . . Rick Springfield
83	9	18	32	254	☐ **Baby, Come To Me** . . . Patti Austin & James Ingram
81	7	21	30	255	☐ **Celebration** . . . Kool & The Gang
78	11	22	29	256	☐ **(Love Is) Thicker Than Water** . . . Andy Gibb
57	14	19	29	257	☐ **Round And Round** . . . Perry Como
81	9	18	28	258	☐ **I Love A Rainy Night** . . . Eddie Rabbitt
81	9	18	26	259	☐ **9 To 5** . . . Dolly Parton
76	9	17	26	260	☐ **Kiss And Say Goodbye** . . . Manhattans
84	7	15	26	261	☐ **Caribbean Queen (No More Love On The Run)** . . . Billy Ocean
82	14	19	25	262	☐ **Abracadabra** . . . The Steve Miller Band
83	12	18	25	263	☐ **Islands In The Stream** . . . Kenny Rogers & Dolly Parton
79	9	15	25	264	☐ **Rise** . . . Herb Alpert
56	14	19	24	265	☐ **The Great Pretender** . . . The Platters

YR	WEEKS T 10	WEEKS T 40	WEEKS CHR	RNK	Title . . . Artist
					Peak Pos **1** / Peak Wks **2**
82	12	18	24	**266**	☐ **Hard To Say I'm Sorry** . . . Chicago
84	10	17	24	**267**	☐ **Hello** . . . Lionel Richie
85	7	14	24	**268**	☐ **Everybody Wants To Rule The World** . . . Tears For Fears
75	9	18	23	**269**	☐ **Rhinestone Cowboy** . . . Glen Campbell
84	10	17	23	**270**	☐ **Owner Of A Lonely Heart** . . . Yes
81	9	17	23	**271**	☐ **Private Eyes** . . . Daryl Hall & John Oates
84	9	16	23	**272**	☐ **Out Of Touch** . . . Daryl Hall & John Oates
74	5	10	23	**273**	☐ **I Honestly Love You** . . . Olivia Newton-John
73	6	17	22	**274**	☐ **The Most Beautiful Girl** . . . Charlie Rich
77	10	16	22	**275**	☐ **Torn Between Two Lovers** . . . Mary MacGregor
60	9	16	22	**276**	☐ **El Paso** . . . Marty Robbins
83	9	16	22	**277**	☐ **Maniac** . . . Michael Sembello
73	8	16	22	**278**	☐ **Bad, Bad Leroy Brown** . . . Jim Croce
78	8	15	22	**279**	☐ **Grease** . . . Frankie Valli
73	8	14	22	**280**	☐ **Will It Go Round In Circles** . . . Billy Preston
55	18	21	21	**281**	☐ **Learnin' The Blues** . . . Frank Sinatra
80	11	19	21	**282**	☐ **It's Still Rock And Roll To Me** . . . Billy Joel
58	10	17	21	**283**	☐ **It's Only Make Believe** . . . Conway Twitty
79	9	17	21	**284**	☐ **Too Much Heaven** . . . Bee Gees
76	9	17	21	**285**	☐ **If You Leave Me Now** . . . Chicago
75	9	17	21	**286**	☐ **Philadelphia Freedom** . . . The Elton John Band
85	8	16	21	**287**	☐ **I Want To Know What Love Is** . . . Foreigner
79	11	15	21	**288**	☐ **Ring My Bell** . . . Anita Ward
84	8	15	21	**289**	☐ **The Reflex** . . . Duran Duran
81	6	15	21	**290**	☐ **Morning Train (Nine To Five)** . . . Sheena Easton
75	6	14	21	**291**	☐ **Fame** . . . David Bowie
55	15	20	20	**292**	☐ **Ain't That A Shame** . . . Pat Boone
78	11	16	20	**293**	☐ **Three Times A Lady** . . . Commodores
59	10	16	20	**294**	☐ **Heartaches By The Number** . . . Guy Mitchell
73	8	16	20	**295**	☐ **Top Of The World** . . . Carpenters
84	9	14	20	**296**	☐ **Time After Time** . . . Cyndi Lauper
81	8	14	20	**297**	☐ **Rapture** . . . Blondie
73	8	14	20	**298**	☐ **Half-Breed** . . . Cher
76	8	14	20	**299**	☐ **Afternoon Delight** . . . Starland Vocal Band
73	7	14	20	**300**	☐ **The Night The Lights Went Out In Georgia** . . . Vicki Lawrence
74	6	14	20	**301**	☐ **The Loco-Motion** . . . Grand Funk
77	6	14	20	**302**	☐ **Rich Girl** . . . Daryl Hall & John Oates
85	6	14	20	**303**	☐ **Everything She Wants** . . . Wham!
79	9	13	20	**304**	☐ **Tragedy** . . . Bee Gees
77	6	13	20	**305**	☐ **Star Wars Theme/Cantina Band** . . . Meco

YR	WEEKS T 10	WEEKS T 40	WEEKS CHR	RNK	Title . . . Artist
					Peak Pos 1 — Peak Wks 2
73	13	17	19	306	☐ **Let's Get It On** . . . Marvin Gaye
73	10	16	19	307	☐ **Keep On Truckin' (Part 1)** . . . Eddie Kendricks
73	9	16	19	308	☐ **Midnight Train To Georgia** . . . Gladys Knight & The Pips
85	8	15	19	309	☐ **The Power Of Love** . . . Huey Lewis & The News
61	7	15	19	310	☐ **Will You Love Me Tomorrow** . . . The Shirelles
79	11	14	19	311	☐ **Babe** . . . Styx
84	9	14	19	312	☐ **Let's Go Crazy** . . . Prince & the Revolution
84	9	14	19	313	☐ **Let's Hear It For The Boy** . . . Deniece Williams
85	6	14	19	314	☐ **Heaven** . . . Bryan Adams
74	7	12	19	315	☐ **Billy, Don't Be A Hero** . . . Bo Donaldson & The Heywoods
60	8	16	18	316	☐ **Everybody's Somebody's Fool** . . . Connie Francis
73	8	15	18	317	☐ **Brother Louie** . . . Stories
60	10	14	18	318	☐ **Teen Angel** . . . Mark Dinning
74	6	14	18	319	☐ **TSOP (The Sound Of Philadelphia)** . . . MFSB featuring The Three Degrees
82	10	13	18	320	☐ **Truly** . . . Lionel Richie
76	9	13	18	321	☐ **Love Hangover** . . . Diana Ross
59	9	13	18	322	☐ **Sleep Walk** . . . Santo & Johnny
74	8	12	18	323	☐ **Kung Fu Fighting** . . . Carl Douglas
78	8	12	18	324	☐ **With A Little Luck** . . . Wings
62	7	12	18	325	☐ **He's A Rebel** . . . The Crystals
85	6	12	18	326	☐ **One More Night** . . . Phil Collins
74	6	12	18	327	☐ **I Can Help** . . . Billy Swan
69	11	15	17	328	☐ **I Can't Get Next To You** . . . The Temptations
78	10	15	17	329	☐ **You Don't Bring Me Flowers** . . . Barbra Streisand & Neil Diamond
60	10	14	17	330	☐ **My Heart Has A Mind Of Its Own** . . . Connie Francis
57	8	14	17	331	☐ **Butterfly** . . . Charlie Gracie
61	9	13	17	332	☐ **Calcutta** . . . Lawrence Welk
85	6	13	17	333	☐ **A View To A Kill** . . . Duran Duran
63	9	12	17	334	☐ **Go Away Little Girl** . . . Steve Lawrence
75	8	12	17	335	☐ **Jive Talkin'** . . . Bee Gees
72	6	12	17	336	☐ **My Ding-A-Ling** . . . Chuck Berry
61	9	11	17	337	☐ **Michael** . . . The Highwaymen
74	7	11	17	338	☐ **Annie's Song** . . . John Denver
74	5	10	17	339	☐ **Rock Your Baby** . . . George McCrae
69	11	15	16	340	☐ **Crimson And Clover** . . . Tommy James & The Shondells
68	11	15	16	341	☐ **Love Child** . . . Diana Ross & The Supremes
61	8	15	16	342	☐ **Travelin' Man** . . . Ricky Nelson

YR	WEEKS T 10	WEEKS T 40	WEEKS CHR	RNK	Title . . . Artist
					Peak Pos **1** Peak Wks **2**
70	10	14	16	**343**	☐ **The Tears Of A Clown** . . . Smokey Robinson & The Miracles
71	9	14	16	**344**	☐ **Gypsys, Tramps & Thieves** . . . Cher
58	6	14	16	**345**	☐ **Hard Headed Woman** . . . Elvis Presley
75	9	13	16	**346**	☐ **That's The Way (I Like It)** . . . KC & The Sunshine Band
65	9	13	16	**347**	☐ **You've Lost That Lovin' Feelin'** . . . The Righteous Brothers
68	8	13	16	**348**	☐ **Judy In Disguise (With Glasses)** . . . John Fred & His Playboy Band
69	8	13	16	**349**	☐ **Na Na Hey Hey Kiss Him Goodbye** . . . Steam
59	8	12	16	**350**	☐ **Kansas City** . . . Wilbert Harrison
58	11	15	15	**351**	☐ **Poor Little Fool** . . . Ricky Nelson
64	11	14	15	**352**	☐ **She Loves You** . . . The Beatles
64	9	13	15	**353**	☐ **I Get Around** . . . The Beach Boys
68	9	13	15	**354**	☐ **Tighten Up** . . . Archie Bell & The Drells
65	9	13	15	**355**	☐ **Downtown** . . . Petula Clark
62	9	13	15	**356**	☐ **Johnny Angel** . . . Shelley Fabares
79	9	13	15	**357**	☐ **No More Tears (Enough Is Enough)** . . . Barbra Streisand/Donna Summer
71	9	13	15	**358**	☐ **Just My Imagination (Running Away With Me)** . . . The Temptations
70	9	13	15	**359**	☐ **Mama Told Me (Not To Come)** . . . Three Dog Night
64	9	13	15	**360**	☐ **My Guy** . . . Mary Wells
58	8	13	15	**361**	☐ **Get A Job** . . . The Silhouettes
70	6	13	15	**362**	☐ **Everything Is Beautiful** . . . Ray Stevens
61	8	12	15	**363**	☐ **Quarter To Three** . . . U.S. Bonds
71	8	12	15	**364**	☐ **Me And Bobby McGee** . . . Janis Joplin
73	7	12	15	**365**	☐ **Time In A Bottle** . . . Jim Croce
63	7	12	15	**366**	☐ **I'm Leaving It Up To You** . . . Dale & Grace
66	6	12	15	**367**	☐ **Reach Out I'll Be There** . . . Four Tops
73	6	11	15	**368**	☐ **The Morning After** . . . Maureen McGovern
70	11	13	14	**369**	☐ **Let It Be** . . . The Beatles
65	10	13	14	**370**	☐ **I Can't Help Myself** . . . Four Tops
64	9	13	14	**371**	☐ **Come See About Me** . . . The Supremes
64	9	13	14	**372**	☐ **Where Did Our Love Go** . . . The Supremes
61	9	12	14	**373**	☐ **Runaround Sue** . . . Dion
69	8	12	14	**374**	☐ **Love Theme From Romeo & Juliet** . . . Henry Mancini
62	7	12	14	**375**	☐ **Breaking Up Is Hard To Do** . . . Neil Sedaka
66	5	12	14	**376**	☐ **The Sounds Of Silence** . . . Simon & Garfunkel
65	7	11	14	**377**	☐ **Help Me, Rhonda** . . . The Beach Boys
62	6	11	14	**378**	☐ **Sheila** . . . Tommy Roe
63	6	11	14	**379**	☐ **If You Wanna Be Happy** . . . Jimmy Soul
59	7	10	14	**380**	☐ **A Big Hunk O' Love** . . . Elvis Presley

YR	WEEKS T 10	WEEKS T 40	WEEKS CHR	RNK	Title . . . Artist
					Peak Pos 1 · Peak Wks 2
75	6	10	14	381	☐ **Lucy In The Sky With Diamonds** . . . Elton John
71	9	12	13	382	☐ **Theme From Shaft** . . . Isaac Hayes
70	9	12	13	383	☐ **ABC** . . . The Jackson 5
70	9	12	13	384	☐ **The Love You Save** . . . The Jackson 5
64	9	12	13	385	☐ **Do Wah Diddy Diddy** . . . Manfred Mann
64	8	12	13	386	☐ **A Hard Day's Night** . . . The Beatles
70	7	12	13	387	☐ **Thank You (Falettinme Be Mice Elf Agin)** . . . Sly & The Family Stone
61	8	11	13	388	☐ **Hit The Road Jack** . . . Ray Charles
66	8	11	13	389	☐ **You Can't Hurry Love** . . . The Supremes
63	7	11	13	390	☐ **It's My Party** . . . Lesley Gore
63	7	11	13	391	☐ **Surf City** . . . Jan & Dean
62	7	11	13	392	☐ **Good Luck Charm** . . . Elvis Presley
63	7	11	13	393	☐ **Walk Right In** . . . The Rooftop Singers
67	7	10	13	394	☐ **Kind Of A Drag** . . . The Buckinghams
63	7	10	13	395	☐ **Easier Said Than Done** . . . The Essex
66	6	10	13	396	☐ **My Love** . . . Petula Clark
66	6	10	13	397	☐ **When A Man Loves A Woman** . . . Percy Sledge
71	8	12	12	398	☐ **Brown Sugar** . . . The Rolling Stones
68	9	11	12	399	☐ **Hello, I Love You** . . . The Doors
65	9	11	12	400	☐ **This Diamond Ring** . . . Gary Lewis & The Playboys
61	8	11	12	401	☐ **Surrender** . . . Elvis Presley
64	7	11	12	402	☐ **Rag Doll** . . . The 4 Seasons
67	7	11	12	403	☐ **Respect** . . . Aretha Franklin
65	6	11	12	404	☐ **Get Off Of My Cloud** . . . The Rolling Stones
65	8	10	12	405	☐ **Stop! In The Name Of Love** . . . The Supremes
68	7	10	12	406	☐ **Grazing In The Grass** . . . Hugh Masekela
66	6	10	12	407	☐ **Hanky Panky** . . . Tommy James & The Shondells
66	6	10	12	408	☐ **You Keep Me Hangin' On** . . . The Supremes
66	7	10	11	409	☐ **Paint It, Black** . . . The Rolling Stones
66	8	9	11	410	☐ **Wild Thing** . . . The Troggs
65	6	8	11	411	☐ **I'm Telling You Now** . . . Freddie & The Dreamers
70	6	10	10	412	☐ **The Long And Winding Road** . . . The Beatles
65	6	10	10	413	☐ **I Hear A Symphony** . . . The Supremes
66	5	10	10	414	☐ **Paperback Writer** . . . The Beatles
65	5	9	10	415	☐ **Eight Days A Week** . . . The Beatles
					Peak Pos 1 · Peak Wks 1
78	9	18	31	416	☐ **Hot Child In The City** . . . Nick Gilder
57	12	18	29	417	☐ **Diana** . . . Paul Anka
57	13	22	28	418	☐ **Chances Are** . . . Johnny Mathis
76	10	22	28	419	☐ **A Fifth Of Beethoven** . . . Walter Murphy & The Big Apple Band

YR	WEEKS T 10	WEEKS T 40	WEEKS CHR	RNK	Title . . . Artist
					Peak Pos 1 Peak Wks 1
81	9	20	28	420	☐ **Keep On Loving You** . . . REO Speedwagon
76	6	19	28	421	☐ **Love Machine (Part 1)** . . . The Miracles
82	9	15	28	422	☐ **Chariots Of Fire - Titles** . . . Vangelis
80	14	22	27	423	☐ **Do That To Me One More Time** . . . The Captain & Tennille
79	9	19	27	424	☐ **Sad Eyes** . . . Robert John
82	10	18	27	425	☐ **Mickey** . . . Toni Basil
82	9	17	27	426	☐ **Who Can It Be Now?** . . . Men At Work
80	11	18	26	427	☐ **Please Don't Go** . . . K.C. & The Sunshine Band
77	7	18	26	428	☐ **You Don't Have To Be A Star (To Be In My Show)** . . . Marilyn McCoo & Billy Davis, Jr.
81	10	17	26	429	☐ **The Tide Is High** . . . Blondie
83	9	17	26	430	☐ **Sweet Dreams (Are Made of This)** . . . Eurythmics
78	8	17	26	431	☐ **You Needed Me** . . . Anne Murray
77	7	17	25	432	☐ **Undercover Angel** . . . Alan O'Day
76	10	16	25	433	☐ **Disco Duck (Part 1)** . . . Rick Dees & His Cast Of Idiots
79	9	20	24	434	☐ **Pop Muzik** . . . M
56	13	19	24	435	☐ **I Want You, I Need You, I Love You** . . . Elvis Presley
77	8	17	24	436	☐ **Don't Leave Me This Way** . . . Thelma Houston
78	9	16	24	437	☐ **You're The One That I Want** . . . John Travolta & Olivia Newton-John
84	9	16	24	438	☐ **Missing You** . . . John Waite
76	6	12	24	439	☐ **Theme From S.W.A.T.** . . . Rhythm Heritage
56	14	20	23	440	☐ **Hot Diggity (Dog Ziggity Boom)** . . . Perry Como
58	12	16	23	441	☐ **Catch A Falling Star** . . . Perry Como
77	6	16	23	442	☐ **I'm Your Boogie Man** . . . KC & The Sunshine Band
57	10	15	23	443	☐ **Party Doll** . . . Buddy Knox with The Rhythm Orchids
85	8	15	23	444	☐ **Everytime You Go Away** . . . Paul Young
61	7	15	23	445	☐ **Please Mr. Postman** . . . The Marvelettes
77	8	14	23	446	☐ **Car Wash** . . . Rose Royce
75	8	14	23	447	☐ **My Eyes Adored You** . . . Frankie Valli
83	6	14	23	448	☐ **Come On Eileen** . . . Dexys Midnight Runners
64	13	19	22	449	☐ **Hello, Dolly!** . . . Louis Armstrong & The All Stars
57	11	19	22	450	☐ **Don't Forbid Me** . . . Pat Boone
78	10	16	22	451	☐ **If I Can't Have You** . . . Yvonne Elliman
57	9	16	22	452	☐ **That'll Be The Day** . . . The Crickets
74	7	16	22	453	☐ **Love's Theme** . . . Love Unlimited Orchestra
74	7	16	22	454	☐ **Show And Tell** . . . Al Wilson
71	9	15	22	455	☐ **Indian Reservation (The Lament Of The Cherokee Reservation Indian)** . . . Raiders
77	8	15	22	456	☐ **Dancing Queen** . . . Abba
72	8	14	22	457	☐ **I Am Woman** . . . Helen Reddy

YR	WEEKS T 10	WEEKS T 40	WEEKS CHR	RNK	Title . . . Artist
					Peak Pos 1 / Peak Wks 1
85	8	14	22	458	☐ **Don't You (Forget About Me)** . . . Simple Minds
77	7	12	22	459	☐ **Da Doo Ron Ron** . . . Shaun Cassidy
58	12	18	21	460	☐ **Tom Dooley** . . . The Kingston Trio
58	15	17	21	461	☐ **Patricia** . . . Perez Prado
57	13	17	21	462	☐ **Young Love** . . . Sonny James
82	12	17	21	463	☐ **I Can't Go For That (No Can Do)** . . . Daryl Hall & John Oates
77	7	17	21	464	☐ **You Make Me Feel Like Dancing** . . . Leo Sayer
76	11	16	21	465	☐ **(Shake, Shake, Shake) Shake Your Booty** . . . KC & The Sunshine Band
73	8	16	21	466	☐ **Touch Me In The Morning** . . . Diana Ross
83	6	16	21	467	☐ **Africa** . . . Toto
62	8	15	21	468	☐ **Stranger On The Shore** . . . Mr. Acker Bilk
77	8	15	21	469	☐ **Southern Nights** . . . Glen Campbell
75	8	15	21	470	☐ **Before The Next Teardrop Falls** . . . Freddy Fender
76	7	15	21	471	☐ **Boogie Fever** . . . Sylvers
85	9	14	21	472	☐ **Crazy For You** . . . Madonna
81	8	14	21	473	☐ **Stars on 45 (Medley)** . . . Stars on 45
79	7	14	21	474	☐ **Heart Of Glass** . . . Blondie
80	7	13	21	475	☐ **Sailing** . . . Christopher Cross
79	6	12	21	476	☐ **Don't Stop 'Til You Get Enough** . . . Michael Jackson
76	10	16	20	477	☐ **I Write The Songs** . . . Barry Manilow
78	9	16	20	478	☐ **Miss You** . . . The Rolling Stones
74	8	16	20	479	☐ **The Joker** . . . Steve Miller Band
79	13	15	20	480	☐ **Still** . . . Commodores
77	8	15	20	481	☐ **Blinded By The Light** . . . Manfred Mann's Earth Band
75	7	15	20	482	☐ **Laughter In The Rain** . . . Neil Sedaka
83	10	14	20	483	☐ **Let's Dance** . . . David Bowie
79	9	14	20	484	☐ **What A Fool Believes** . . . Doobie Brothers
73	8	14	20	485	☐ **Delta Dawn** . . . Helen Reddy
77	7	14	20	486	☐ **When I Need You** . . . Leo Sayer
73	7	14	20	487	☐ **Frankenstein** . . . The Edgar Winter Group
79	6	14	20	488	☐ **Knock On Wood** . . . Amii Stewart
75	5	14	20	489	☐ **Shining Star** . . . Earth, Wind & Fire
77	8	13	20	490	☐ **Gonna Fly Now (Theme From "Rocky")** . . . Bill Conti
59	11	12	20	491	☐ **Mr. Blue** . . . The Fleetwoods
76	7	12	20	492	☐ **You Should Be Dancing** . . . Bee Gees
58	11	16	19	493	☐ **Little Star** . . . The Elegants
70	9	16	19	494	☐ **I Want You Back** . . . The Jackson 5
77	8	15	19	495	☐ **Hotel California** . . . Eagles
74	8	15	19	496	☐ **Then Came You** . . . Dionne Warwicke & Spinners
75	5	15	19	497	☐ **Thank God I'm A Country Boy** . . . John Denver

YR	WEEKS T 10	WEEKS T 40	WEEKS CHR	RNK	Title . . . Artist
					Peak Pos **1** Peak Wks **1**
79	9	14	19	**498**	☐ **Good Times** . . . Chic
81	8	14	19	**499**	☐ **The One That You Love** . . . Air Supply
74	7	14	19	**500**	☐ **You Haven't Done Nothin** . . . Stevie Wonder
75	6	14	19	**501**	☐ **Best Of My Love** . . . The Eagles
77	7	13	19	**502**	☐ **Dreams** . . . Fleetwood Mac
77	7	13	19	**503**	☐ **Don't Give Up On Us** . . . David Soul
79	5	13	19	**504**	☐ **Love You Inside Out** . . . Bee Gees
77	5	13	19	**505**	☐ **Looks Like We Made It** . . . Barry Manilow
76	7	12	19	**506**	☐ **Let Your Love Flow** . . . Bellamy Brothers
75	7	12	19	**507**	☐ **The Hustle** . . . Van McCoy & The Soul City Symphony
74	6	12	19	**508**	☐ **Cat's In The Cradle** . . . Harry Chapin
74	9	16	18	**509**	☐ **Bennie And The Jets** . . . Elton John
58	11	15	18	**510**	☐ **Bird Dog** . . . The Everly Brothers
77	9	15	18	**511**	☐ **Got To Give It Up - Pt. 1** . . . Marvin Gaye
83	7	15	18	**512**	☐ **Tell Her About It** . . . Billy Joel
74	7	14	18	**513**	☐ **Nothing From Nothing** . . . Billy Preston
75	7	14	18	**514**	☐ **(Hey Won't You Play) Another Somebody Done Somebody Wrong Song** . . . B.J. Thomas
76	5	14	18	**515**	☐ **Rock'n Me** . . . Steve Miller
60	5	14	18	**516**	☐ **Stay** . . . Maurice Williams & The Zodiacs
75	9	13	18	**517**	☐ **I'm Sorry** . . . John Denver
75	8	13	18	**518**	☐ **Lovin' You** . . . Minnie Riperton
74	7	13	18	**519**	☐ **Sunshine On My Shoulders** . . . John Denver
75	7	13	18	**520**	☐ **Lady Marmalade** . . . LaBelle
74	7	13	18	**521**	☐ **Band On The Run** . . . Paul McCartney & Wings
74	6	13	18	**522**	☐ **Rock Me Gently** . . . Andy Kim
78	8	11	18	**523**	☐ **Too Much, Too Little, Too Late** . . . Johnny Mathis/Deniece Williams
74	7	11	18	**524**	☐ **Sundown** . . . Gordon Lightfoot
74	5	10	18	**525**	☐ **Rock The Boat** . . . The Hues Corporation
69	10	15	17	**526**	☐ **Leaving On A Jet Plane** . . . Peter, Paul & Mary
77	7	15	17	**527**	☐ **I Wish** . . . Stevie Wonder
61	4	15	17	**528**	☐ **Running Scared** . . . Roy Orbison
58	12	14	17	**529**	☐ **Twilight Time** . . . The Platters
75	10	14	17	**530**	☐ **One Of These Nights** . . . Eagles
74	7	14	17	**531**	☐ **Hooked On A Feeling** . . . Blue Swede
59	7	14	17	**532**	☐ **The Happy Organ** . . . Dave "Baby" Cortez
85	6	14	17	**533**	☐ **Sussudio** . . . Phil Collins
70	10	13	17	**534**	☐ **Make It With You** . . . Bread
62	9	13	17	**535**	☐ **The Stripper** . . . David Rose
75	7	13	17	**536**	☐ **Pick Up The Pieces** . . . AWB (Average White Band)

YR	WEEKS T 10	WEEKS T 40	WEEKS CHR	RNK	Title . . . Artist
					Peak Pos 1 Peak Wks 1
76	7	13	17	537	☐ **Theme From Mahogany (Do You Know Where You're Going To)** . . . Diana Ross
73	7	13	17	538	☐ **You Are The Sunshine Of My Life** . . . Stevie Wonder
73	6	13	17	539	☐ **We're An American Band** . . . Grand Funk
74	6	13	17	540	☐ **Angie Baby** . . . Helen Reddy
75	7	12	17	541	☐ **Black Water** . . . The Doobie Brothers
76	6	12	17	542	☐ **Saturday Night** . . . Bay City Rollers
75	6	12	17	543	☐ **Fallin' In Love** . . . Hamilton, Joe Frank & Reynolds
75	5	12	17	544	☐ **Please Mr. Postman** . . . Carpenters
75	4	12	17	545	☐ **Fire** . . . Ohio Players
74	3	12	17	546	☐ **You Ain't Seen Nothing Yet** . . . Bachman-Turner Overdrive
74	6	11	17	547	☐ **The Night Chicago Died** . . . Paper Lace
69	9	16	16	548	☐ **Come Together/Something** . . . The Beatles
58	9	15	16	549	☐ **Yakety Yak** . . . The Coasters
72	9	15	16	550	☐ **Let's Stay Together** . . . Al Green
69	9	15	16	551	☐ **Someday We'll Be Together** . . . Diana Ross & The Supremes
72	10	14	16	552	☐ **Brandy (You're A Fine Girl)** . . . Looking Glass
76	10	14	16	553	☐ **Love Rollercoaster** . . . Ohio Players
67	9	14	16	554	☐ **Incense And Peppermints** . . . Strawberry Alarm Clock
73	7	13	16	555	☐ **Angie** . . . The Rolling Stones
74	6	13	16	556	☐ **Feel Like Makin' Love** . . . Roberta Flack
71	6	13	16	557	☐ **Want Ads** . . . The Honey Cone
73	6	13	16	558	☐ **Superstition** . . . Stevie Wonder
59	9	12	16	559	☐ **Why** . . . Frankie Avalon
61	7	12	16	560	☐ **Wooden Heart** . . . Joe Dowell
62	7	12	16	561	☐ **The Loco-Motion** . . . Little Eva
74	6	12	16	562	☐ **Dark Lady** . . . Cher
73	6	12	16	563	☐ **Photograph** . . . Ringo Starr
72	6	12	16	564	☐ **Papa Was A Rollin' Stone** . . . The Temptations
75	5	12	16	565	☐ **Mandy** . . . Barry Manilow
75	4	12	16	566	☐ **Sister Golden Hair** . . . America
72	7	11	16	567	☐ **Ben** . . . Michael Jackson
76	7	11	16	568	☐ **Convoy** . . . C.W. McCall
75	7	11	16	569	☐ **Have You Never Been Mellow** . . . Olivia Newton-John
75	5	10	16	570	☐ **You're No Good** . . . Linda Ronstadt
64	9	14	15	571	☐ **Mr. Lonely** . . . Bobby Vinton
72	8	14	15	572	☐ **I'll Take You There** . . . The Staple Singers
72	7	14	15	573	☐ **Oh Girl** . . . Chi-Lites
70	7	14	15	574	☐ **Cracklin' Rosie** . . . Neil Diamond
79	9	13	15	575	☐ **Heartache Tonight** . . . Eagles

YR	WEEKS T 10	WEEKS T 40	WEEKS CHR	RNK	Title . . . Artist
					Peak Pos 1 Peak Wks 1
60	8	13	15	576	☐ **Itsy Bitsy Teenie Weenie Yellow Polkadot Bikini** . . . Brian Hyland
64	8	13	15	577	☐ **Everybody Loves Somebody** . . . Dean Martin
77	7	13	15	578	☐ **New Kid In Town** . . . Eagles
60	6	13	15	579	☐ **I Want To Be Wanted** . . . Brenda Lee
69	6	13	15	580	☐ **Suspicious Minds** . . . Elvis Presley
66	9	12	15	581	☐ **Last Train To Clarksville** . . . The Monkees
66	9	12	15	582	☐ **96 Tears** . . . ? (Question Mark) & The Mysterians
66	7	12	15	583	☐ **Poor Side Of Town** . . . Johnny Rivers
75	7	12	15	584	☐ **Let's Do It Again** . . . The Staple Singers
74	7	12	15	585	☐ **You're Sixteen** . . . Ringo Starr
63	7	12	15	586	☐ **Deep Purple** . . . Nino Tempo & April Stevens
63	7	12	15	587	☐ **So Much In Love** . . . The Tymes
61	6	12	15	588	☐ **Moody River** . . . Pat Boone
60	8	11	15	589	☐ **Alley-Oop** . . . Hollywood Argyles
66	7	11	15	590	☐ **Strangers In The Night** . . . Frank Sinatra
74	3	11	15	591	☐ **Whatever Gets You Thru The Night** . . . John Lennon with The Plastic Ono Nuclear Band
66	6	10	15	592	☐ **Lightnin' Strikes** . . . Lou Christie
75	4	9	15	593	☐ **Get Down Tonight** . . . K.C. & The Sunshine Band
70	9	13	14	594	☐ **Venus** . . . The Shocking Blue
72	8	13	14	595	☐ **Heart Of Gold** . . . Neil Young
73	6	13	14	596	☐ **Love Train** . . . O'Jays
61	8	12	14	597	☐ **Mother-In-Law** . . . Ernie K-Doe
71	8	12	14	598	☐ **You've Got A Friend** . . . James Taylor
66	7	12	14	599	☐ **Good Vibrations** . . . The Beach Boys
66	7	12	14	600	☐ **Good Lovin'** . . . The Young Rascals
66	7	12	14	601	☐ **These Boots Are Made For Walkin'** . . . Nancy Sinatra
75	9	11	14	602	☐ **Listen To What The Man Said** . . . Wings
73	7	11	14	603	☐ **Give Me Love (Give Me Peace On Earth)** . . . George Harrison
65	7	11	14	604	☐ **Hang On Sloopy** . . . The McCoys
76	7	11	14	605	☐ **Welcome Back** . . . John Sebastian
64	6	11	14	606	☐ **Love Me Do** . . . The Beatles
74	5	10	14	607	☐ **I Shot The Sheriff** . . . Eric Clapton
68	9	12	13	608	☐ **Harper Valley P.T.A.** . . . Jeannie C. Riley
68	7	12	13	609	☐ **Green Tambourine** . . . The Lemon Pipers
71	7	12	13	610	☐ **Uncle Albert/Admiral Halsey** . . . Paul & Linda McCartney
72	6	12	13	611	☐ **Song Sung Blue** . . . Neil Diamond
65	8	11	13	612	☐ **My Girl** . . . The Temptations

YR	WEEKS T 10	WEEKS T 40	WEEKS CHR	RNK	Title . . . Artist
					Peak Pos 1 / Peak Wks 1
62	8	10	13	613	☐ **Don't Break The Heart That Loves You** . . . Connie Francis
65	7	10	13	614	☐ **Mr. Tambourine Man** . . . The Byrds
66	7	10	13	615	☐ **Sunshine Superman** . . . Donovan
60	7	10	13	616	☐ **Mr. Custer** . . . Larry Verne
63	6	10	13	617	☐ **Our Day Will Come** . . . Ruby & The Romantics
60	5	10	13	618	☐ **Georgia On My Mind** . . . Ray Charles
64	8	11	12	619	☐ **A World Without Love** . . . Peter & Gordon
65	6	11	12	620	☐ **Over And Over** . . . The Dave Clark Five
64	7	10	12	621	☐ **Ringo** . . . Lorne Greene
64	5	10	12	622	☐ **Leader Of The Pack** . . . The Shangri-Las
67	7	9	12	623	☐ **Ruby Tuesday** . . . The Rolling Stones
74	4	9	12	624	☐ **Can't Get Enough Of Your Love, Babe** . . . Barry White
65	7	10	11	625	☐ **Eve Of Destruction** . . . Barry McGuire
67	7	10	11	626	☐ **Love Is Here And Now You're Gone** . . . The Supremes
67	6	10	11	627	☐ **The Happening** . . . The Supremes
65	5	10	11	628	☐ **Game Of Love** . . . Wayne Fontana & The Mindbenders
65	5	10	11	629	☐ **Back In My Arms Again** . . . The Supremes
67	7	9	11	630	☐ **All You Need Is Love** . . . The Beatles
65	6	9	11	631	☐ **Ticket To Ride** . . . The Beatles
72	5	9	11	632	☐ **Black & White** . . . Three Dog Night
67	5	9	10	633	☐ **Penny Lane** . . . The Beatles
65	6	8	10	634	☐ **I'm Henry VIII, I Am** . . . Herman's Hermits
					Peak Pos 2 / Peak Wks 10
81	15	19	23	635	☐ **Waiting For A Girl Like You** . . . Foreigner
					Peak Pos 2 / Peak Wks 8
57	10	21	26	636	☐ **Little Darlin'** . . . The Diamonds
					Peak Pos 2 / Peak Wks 6
55	19	25	25	637	☐ **Moments To Remember** . . . The Four Lads
78	9	15	20	638	☐ **Baker Street** . . . Gerry Rafferty
82	10	14	18	639	☐ **Open Arms** . . . Journey
63	9	13	18	640	☐ **Louie Louie** . . . The Kingsmen
					Peak Pos 2 / Peak Wks 5
82	11	18	23	641	☐ **Rosanna** . . . Toto
80	9	15	23	642	☐ **More Than I Can Say** . . . Leo Sayer
83	8	15	22	643	☐ **Electric Avenue** . . . Eddy Grant
62	10	14	16	644	☐ **Return To Sender** . . . Elvis Presley

YR	WEEKS			RNK	Title . . . Artist
	T 10	T 40	CHR		
					Peak Pos 2 / Peak Wks 4
57	18	26	38	645	☐ **So Rare** . . . Jimmy Dorsey
82	16	22	28	646	☐ **Hurts So Good** . . . John Cougar
57	15	22	27	647	☐ **Bye Bye Love** . . . The Everly Brothers
80	10	17	27	648	☐ **All Out Of Love** . . . Air Supply
56	12	19	24	649	☐ **No, Not Much!** . . . The Four Lads
83	8	19	21	650	☐ **Shame On The Moon** . . . Bob Seger & The Silver Bullet Band
56	11	17	21	651	☐ **Blue Suede Shoes** . . . Carl Perkins
80	9	17	21	652	☐ **Ride Like The Wind** . . . Christopher Cross
82	11	16	21	653	☐ **Don't Talk To Strangers** . . . Rick Springfield
84	9	15	21	654	☐ **Dancing In The Dark** . . . Bruce Springsteen
58	9	13	21	655	☐ **Great Balls Of Fire** . . . Jerry Lee Lewis
60	10	15	20	656	☐ **Last Date** . . . Floyd Cramer
60	9	15	20	657	☐ **Greenfields** . . . The Brothers Four
83	10	15	18	658	☐ **Say It Isn't So** . . . Daryl Hall & John Oates
84	8	14	18	659	☐ **The Wild Boys** . . . Duran Duran
70	9	14	17	660	☐ **We've Only Just Begun** . . . Carpenters
63	7	12	15	661	☐ **Can't Get Used To Losing You** . . . Andy Williams
73	6	11	14	662	☐ **Dueling Banjos** . . . Eric Weissberg & Steve Mandell (from "Deliverance")
68	7	11	13	663	☐ **(Theme From) Valley Of The Dolls** . . . Dionne Warwick
66	8	11	12	664	☐ **Snoopy Vs. The Red Baron** . . . The Royal Guardsmen
64	7	9	11	665	☐ **Twist And Shout** . . . The Beatles
					Peak Pos 2 / Peak Wks 3
56	16	22	39	666	☐ **Honky Tonk (Parts 1 & 2)** . . . Bill Doggett
82	10	22	36	667	☐ **Gloria** . . . Laura Branigan
56	15	22	27	668	☐ **Whatever Will Be, Will Be (Que Sera, Sera)** . . . Doris Day
57	16	21	27	669	☐ **Blueberry Hill** . . . Fats Domino
79	13	20	26	670	☐ **Y.M.C.A.** . . . Village People
77	10	18	26	671	☐ **Don't It Make My Brown Eyes Blue** . . . Crystal Gayle
83	9	18	25	672	☐ **Do You Really Want To Hurt Me** . . . Culture Club
83	9	17	25	673	☐ **Making Love Out Of Nothing At All** . . . Air Supply
81	10	16	25	674	☐ **Being With You** . . . Smokey Robinson
77	8	15	25	675	☐ **Nobody Does It Better** . . . Carly Simon
81	11	19	24	676	☐ **Start Me Up** . . . The Rolling Stones
81	11	16	24	677	☐ **Slow Hand** . . . Pointer Sisters
81	11	16	24	678	☐ **Just The Two Of Us** . . . Grover Washington, Jr./Bill Withers
60	12	20	23	679	☐ **He'll Have To Go** . . . Jim Reeves
76	8	17	21	680	☐ **The Rubberband Man** . . . Spinners

YR	WEEKS T 10	WEEKS T 40	WEEKS CHR	RNK	Title . . . Artist
					Peak Pos **2** Peak Wks **3**
76	9	15	21	681	☐ **Get Up And Boogie (That's Right)** . . . Silver Convention
81	12	17	20	682	☐ **Woman** . . . John Lennon
81	10	17	20	683	☐ **Love On The Rocks** . . . Neil Diamond
58	8	14	20	684	☐ **26 Miles (Santa Catalina)** . . . The Four Preps
76	8	14	20	685	☐ **Dream Weaver** . . . Gary Wright
77	7	14	20	686	☐ **Keep It Comin' Love** . . . KC & The Sunshine Band
77	6	13	20	687	☐ **I'm In You** . . . Peter Frampton
78	5	13	20	688	☐ **Short People** . . . Randy Newman
82	9	15	19	689	☐ **We Got The Beat** . . . Go-Go's
59	10	14	19	690	☐ **Personality** . . . Lloyd Price
84	8	14	19	691	☐ **Somebody's Watching Me** . . . Rockwell
76	6	14	19	692	☐ **All By Myself** . . . Eric Carmen
55	14	17	18	693	☐ **I Hear You Knocking** . . . Gale Storm
59	11	14	18	694	☐ **Put Your Head On My Shoulder** . . . Paul Anka
83	10	14	18	695	☐ **The Girl Is Mine** . . . Michael Jackson/Paul McCartney
58	8	14	18	696	☐ **Stood Up** . . . Ricky Nelson
67	9	14	17	697	☐ **I Heard It Through The Grapevine** . . . Gladys Knight & The Pips
73	7	14	17	698	☐ **Goodbye Yellow Brick Road** . . . Elton John
75	5	11	17	699	☐ **I'm Not In Love** . . . 10cc
61	7	10	17	700	☐ **I Like It Like That, Part 1** . . . Chris Kenner
61	8	12	16	701	☐ **The Boll Weevil Song** . . . Brook Benton
58	7	11	16	702	☐ **Sweet Little Sixteen** . . . Chuck Berry
81	6	11	16	703	☐ **All Those Years Ago** . . . George Harrison
71	8	13	15	704	☐ **What's Going On** . . . Marvin Gaye
68	8	13	15	705	☐ **Young Girl** . . . The Union Gap featuring Gary Puckett
69	9	12	15	706	☐ **Crystal Blue Persuasion** . . . Tommy James & The Shondells
59	8	12	15	707	☐ **Charlie Brown** . . . The Coasters
67	8	11	15	708	☐ **Soul Man** . . . Sam & Dave
65	6	11	15	709	☐ **A Lover's Concerto** . . . The Toys
69	7	12	14	710	☐ **Proud Mary** . . . Creedence Clearwater Revival
68	7	12	14	711	☐ **Those Were The Days** . . . Mary Hopkin
73	7	12	14	712	☐ **Live And Let Die** . . . Wings
68	6	12	14	713	☐ **The Horse** . . . Cliff Nobles & Co.
69	7	12	13	714	☐ **Spinning Wheel** . . . Blood, Sweat & Tears
68	6	12	13	715	☐ **Born To Be Wild** . . . Steppenwolf
69	6	11	13	716	☐ **You've Made Me So Very Happy** . . . Blood, Sweat & Tears
63	6	11	13	717	☐ **Ruby Baby** . . . Dion
63	6	10	13	718	☐ **Be My Baby** . . . The Ronettes
64	5	10	13	719	☐ **You Don't Own Me** . . . Lesley Gore

YR	WEEKS T 10	WEEKS T 40	WEEKS CHR	RNK	Title . . . Artist
					Peak Pos 2 / Peak Wks 3
69	7	11	12	720	☐ **A Boy Named Sue** . . . Johnny Cash
71	7	11	12	721	☐ **Never Can Say Goodbye** . . . The Jackson 5
66	8	10	12	722	☐ **Mellow Yellow** . . . Donovan
67	6	9	10	723	☐ **Dedicated To The One I Love** . . . The Mamas & The Papas
66	6	9	10	724	☐ **19th Nervous Breakdown** . . . The Rolling Stones
63	6	8	10	725	☐ **Hello Mudduh, Hello Fadduh! (A Letter From Camp)** . . . Allan Sherman
					Peak Pos 2 / Peak Wks 2
56	14	23	31	726	☐ **Canadian Sunset** . . . Hugo Winterhalter/Eddie Heywood
56	12	22	27	727	☐ **Allegheny Moon** . . . Patti Page
81	9	19	27	728	☐ **Queen Of Hearts** . . . Juice Newton
76	7	18	27	729	☐ **Love Is Alive** . . . Gary Wright
77	9	17	27	730	☐ **Boogie Nights** . . . Heatwave
81	10	18	26	731	☐ **Theme From "Greatest American Hero" (Believe It or Not)** . . . Joey Scarbury
80	8	16	25	732	☐ **Working My Way Back To You/Forgive Me, Girl** . . . Spinners
84	8	14	25	733	☐ **Girls Just Want To Have Fun** . . . Cyndi Lauper
74	8	14	25	734	☐ **You Make Me Feel Brand New** . . . The Stylistics
76	10	17	24	735	☐ **I'd Really Love To See You Tonight** . . . England Dan & John Ford Coley
59	10	18	23	736	☐ **Donna** . . . Ritchie Valens
62	11	17	23	737	☐ **Limbo Rock** . . . Chubby Checker
79	8	16	23	738	☐ **Fire** . . . Pointer Sisters
85	7	16	23	739	☐ **Easy Lover** . . . Philip Bailey with Phil Collins
80	7	16	23	740	☐ **Yes, I'm Ready** . . . Teri DeSario with K.C.
73	8	15	23	741	☐ **Playground In My Mind** . . . Clint Holmes
74	9	16	22	742	☐ **Dancing Machine** . . . The Jackson 5
80	7	13	22	743	☐ **Longer** . . . Dan Fogelberg
85	6	12	22	744	☐ **All I Need** . . . Jack Wagner
58	10	19	21	745	☐ **Rock-in Robin** . . . Bobby Day
72	10	16	21	746	☐ **I Gotcha** . . . Joe Tex
79	9	14	21	747	☐ **Dim All The Lights** . . . Donna Summer
59	8	14	21	748	☐ **16 Candles** . . . The Crests
76	8	13	21	749	☐ **You'll Never Find Another Love Like Mine** . . . Lou Rawls
76	6	13	21	750	☐ **The Wreck Of The Edmund Fitzgerald** . . . Gordon Lightfoot
76	8	15	20	751	☐ **Right Back Where We Started From** . . . Maxine Nightingale
77	6	15	20	752	☐ **Fly Like An Eagle** . . . Steve Miller

YR	WEEKS T 10	WEEKS T 40	WEEKS CHR	RNK	Title . . . Artist
					Peak Pos 2 / Peak Wks 2
78	8	14	20	753	☐ **The Closer I Get To You** . . . Roberta Flack with Donny Hathaway
78	6	12	20	754	☐ **Double Vision** . . . Foreigner
70	10	15	19	755	☐ **One Less Bell To Answer** . . . The 5th Dimension
57	10	14	19	756	☐ **Love Me** . . . Elvis Presley
79	7	11	19	757	☐ **We Are Family** . . . Sister Sledge
62	9	15	18	758	☐ **Mashed Potato Time** . . . Dee Dee Sharp
65	9	14	18	759	☐ **Wooly Bully** . . . Sam The Sham & The Pharaohs
74	7	14	18	760	☐ **Do It ('Til You're Satisfied)** . . . B.T. Express
59	7	14	18	761	☐ **My Happiness** . . . Connie Francis
72	7	14	18	762	☐ **Nights In White Satin** . . . The Moody Blues
76	7	14	18	763	☐ **Love To Love You Baby** . . . Donna Summer
59	6	14	18	764	☐ **Sea Of Love** . . . Phil Phillips
83	9	13	18	765	☐ **Time (Clock Of The Heart)** . . . Culture Club
74	6	13	18	766	☐ **Boogie Down** . . . Eddie Kendricks
59	7	11	18	767	☐ **Sorry (I Ran All the Way Home)** . . . Impalas
79	9	13	17	768	☐ **After The Love Has Gone** . . . Earth, Wind & Fire
61	5	13	17	769	☐ **Apache** . . . Jorgen Ingmann & His Guitar
70	5	13	17	770	☐ **Which Way You Goin' Billy?** . . . The Poppy Family featuring Susan Jacks
85	6	12	17	771	☐ **Material Girl** . . . Madonna
57	6	12	17	772	☐ **Teen-Age Crush** . . . Tommy Sands
61	9	14	16	773	☐ **Bristol Stomp** . . . The Dovells
72	7	14	16	774	☐ **Clair** . . . Gilbert O'Sullivan
67	9	13	16	775	☐ **Little Bit O'Soul** . . . The Music Explosion
62	8	13	16	776	☐ **Ramblin' Rose** . . . Nat King Cole
60	8	13	16	777	☐ **Chain Gang** . . . Sam Cooke
71	8	13	16	778	☐ **Mr. Big Stuff** . . . Jean Knight
69	7	13	16	779	☐ **Hot Fun In The Summertime** . . . Sly & The Family Stone
67	8	12	16	780	☐ **The Rain, The Park & Other Things** . . . The Cowsills
67	8	12	16	781	☐ **Georgy Girl** . . . The Seekers
73	6	12	16	782	☐ **Neither One Of Us (Wants To Be The First To Say Goodbye)** . . . Gladys Knight & The Pips
84	7	11	16	783	☐ **Purple Rain** . . . Prince & the Revolution
77	5	11	16	784	☐ **Float On** . . . The Floaters
69	8	13	15	785	☐ **Hair** . . . The Cowsills
72	8	13	15	786	☐ **Long Cool Woman (In A Black Dress)** . . . The Hollies
75	7	13	15	787	☐ **When Will I Be Loved** . . . Linda Ronstadt
58	7	12	15	788	☐ **Lollipop** . . . The Chordettes
75	7	12	15	789	☐ **You're The First, The Last, My Everything** . . . Barry White
67	7	12	15	790	☐ **I Was Made To Love Her** . . . Stevie Wonder

YR	WEEKS T 10	WEEKS T 40	WEEKS CHR	RNK	Title . . . Artist
					Peak Pos 2 / Peak Wks 2
68	6	12	15	791	☐ **Cry Like A Baby** . . . The Box Tops
73	6	12	15	792	☐ **The Cisco Kid** . . . War
66	6	11	15	793	☐ **Sunny** . . . Bobby Hebb
65	6	11	15	794	☐ **Can't You Hear My Heartbeat** . . . Herman's Hermits
61	3	10	15	795	☐ **The Mountain's High** . . . Dick & DeeDee
74	5	9	15	796	☐ **Don't Let The Sun Go Down On Me** . . . Elton John
68	8	13	14	797	☐ **For Once In My Life** . . . Stevie Wonder
69	7	12	14	798	☐ **Jean** . . . Oliver
67	8	11	14	799	☐ **Never My Love** . . . The Association
72	8	11	14	800	☐ **Too Late To Turn Back Now** . . . Cornelius Brothers & Sister Rose
60	7	11	14	801	☐ **Puppy Love** . . . Paul Anka
64	7	11	14	802	☐ **Dancing In The Street** . . . Martha & The Vandellas
66	7	11	14	803	☐ **Lil' Red Riding Hood** . . . Sam The Sham & The Pharaohs
73	7	11	14	804	☐ **Kodachrome** . . . Paul Simon
75	6	11	14	805	☐ **Lyin' Eyes** . . . The Eagles
62	6	11	14	806	☐ **The Wah Watusi** . . . The Orlons
68	6	11	14	807	☐ **Classical Gas** . . . Mason Williams
72	5	10	14	808	☐ **I'd Love You To Want Me** . . . Lobo
71	8	12	13	809	☐ **Superstar** . . . Carpenters
69	8	12	13	810	☐ **I'm Gonna Make You Love Me** . . . Diana Ross & The Supremes & The Temptations
72	8	11	13	811	☐ **Rockin' Robin** . . . Michael Jackson
68	6	11	13	812	☐ **Lady Willpower** . . . Gary Puckett & The Union Gap
69	6	10	13	813	☐ **Love (Can Make You Happy)** . . . Mercy
66	5	10	13	814	☐ **A Groovy Kind Of Love** . . . The Mindbenders
71	7	11	12	815	☐ **Rainy Days And Mondays** . . . Carpenters
68	7	11	12	816	☐ **Chain Of Fools** . . . Aretha Franklin
64	7	11	12	817	☐ **Bread And Butter** . . . The Newbeats
72	6	11	12	818	☐ **Hurting Each Other** . . . Carpenters
71	6	11	12	819	☐ **Spanish Harlem** . . . Aretha Franklin
66	7	10	12	820	☐ **Daydream** . . . The Lovin' Spoonful
63	6	10	12	821	☐ **Sally, Go 'Round The Roses** . . . The Jaynetts
64	6	10	12	822	☐ **Memphis** . . . Johnny Rivers
72	5	10	12	823	☐ **Use Me** . . . Bill Withers
65	5	9	12	824	☐ **Like A Rolling Stone** . . . Bob Dylan
67	7	10	11	825	☐ **Reflections** . . . Diana Ross & The Supremes
66	6	9	11	826	☐ **Did You Ever Have To Make Up Your Mind?** . . . The Lovin' Spoonful
65	5	9	11	827	☐ **Treat Her Right** . . . Roy Head & The Traits
65	5	9	11	828	☐ **Count Me In** . . . Gary Lewis & The Playboys
66	4	9	11	829	☐ **Barbara Ann** . . . The Beach Boys

YR	WEEKS T 10	WEEKS T 40	WEEKS CHR	RNK	Title . . . Artist
					Peak Pos 2 / Peak Wks 2
70	5	9	10	830	☐ **Travelin' Band** . . . Creedence Clearwater Revival
71	5	9	10	831	☐ **Mama's Pearl** . . . The Jackson 5
					Peak Pos 2 / Peak Wks 1
63	7	20	30	832	☐ **Wipe Out** . . . The Surfaris
58	11	17	30	833	☐ **All The Way** . . . Frank Sinatra
56	18	23	28	834	☐ **Just Walking In The Rain** . . . Johnnie Ray
77	7	17	27	835	☐ **(Your Love Has Lifted Me) Higher And Higher** . . . Rita Coolidge
57	10	21	26	836	☐ **A White Sport Coat (And A Pink Carnation)** . . . Marty Robbins
56	12	18	24	837	☐ **Ivory Tower** . . . Cathy Carr
84	6	16	24	838	☐ **Joanna** . . . Kool & The Gang
85	6	13	24	839	☐ **The Heat Is On** . . . Glenn Frey
71	8	14	23	840	☐ **Take Me Home, Country Roads** . . . John Denver with Fat City
84	6	13	23	841	☐ **99 Luftballons** . . . Nena
83	7	14	22	842	☐ **Jeopardy** . . . Greg Kihn Band
68	7	14	22	843	☐ **The Good, The Bad And The Ugly** . . . Hugo Montenegro
61	11	18	21	844	☐ **Exodus** . . . Ferrante & Teicher
60	8	15	21	845	☐ **Only The Lonely (Know How I Feel)** . . . Roy Orbison
85	6	15	21	846	☐ **Loverboy** . . . Billy Ocean
55	12	20	20	847	☐ **A Blossom Fell** . . . Nat "King" Cole
57	9	14	20	848	☐ **Raunchy** . . . Bill Justis
64	8	12	20	849	☐ **Last Kiss** . . . J. Frank Wilson & The Cavaliers
57	8	15	19	850	☐ **A Teenager's Romance** . . . Ricky Nelson
59	6	14	19	851	☐ **There Goes My Baby** . . . The Drifters
60	9	15	18	852	☐ **Handy Man** . . . Jimmy Jones
59	8	15	18	853	☐ **Don't You Know** . . . Della Reese
60	9	14	18	854	☐ **Walk--Don't Run** . . . The Ventures
62	7	13	18	855	☐ **The Wanderer** . . . Dion
74	6	13	18	856	☐ **When Will I See You Again** . . . The Three Degrees
72	6	14	17	857	☐ **Outa-Space** . . . Billy Preston
85	6	14	17	858	☐ **Raspberry Beret** . . . Prince & the Revolution
59	10	13	17	859	☐ **Dream Lover** . . . Bobby Darin
63	6	13	17	860	☐ **The End Of The World** . . . Skeeter Davis
68	8	12	17	861	☐ **Little Green Apples** . . . O.C. Smith
67	8	14	16	862	☐ **Can't Take My Eyes Off You** . . . Frankie Valli
73	7	14	16	863	☐ **Loves Me Like A Rock** . . . Paul Simon with The Dixie Hummingbirds
61	5	14	16	864	☐ **Crying** . . . Roy Orbison
60	8	13	16	865	☐ **Wild One** . . . Bobby Rydell

YR	WEEKS T 10	WEEKS T 40	WEEKS CHR	RNK	Title . . . Artist
					Peak Pos 2 Peak Wks 1
73	6	13	16	**866**	☐ **Ramblin Man** . . . The Allman Brothers Band
61	6	13	16	**867**	☐ **Shop Around** . . . The Miracles
59	5	13	16	**868**	☐ **The All American Boy** . . . Bill Parsons
61	8	12	16	**869**	☐ **Raindrops** . . . Dee Clark
74	4	12	16	**870**	☐ **Jazzman** . . . Carole King
58	9	13	15	**871**	☐ **Wear My Ring Around Your Neck** . . . Elvis Presley
69	7	13	15	**872**	☐ **Take A Letter Maria** . . . R.B. Greaves
61	6	13	15	**873**	☐ **Run To Him** . . . Bobby Vee
64	8	12	15	**874**	☐ **She's Not There** . . . The Zombies
73	7	12	15	**875**	☐ **Daniel** . . . Elton John
63	7	12	15	**876**	☐ **Blowin' In The Wind** . . . Peter, Paul & Mary
60	7	12	15	**877**	☐ **Poetry In Motion** . . . Johnny Tillotson
72	6	12	15	**878**	☐ **Burning Love** . . . Elvis Presley
67	7	11	15	**879**	☐ **Sweet Soul Music** . . . Arthur Conley
58	7	11	15	**880**	☐ **Problems** . . . The Everly Brothers
59	5	11	15	**881**	☐ **(Now and Then There's) A Fool Such As I** . . . Elvis Presley
65	7	10	15	**882**	☐ **1-2-3** . . . Len Barry
71	8	12	14	**883**	☐ **She's A Lady** . . . Tom Jones
62	8	12	14	**884**	☐ **Can't Help Falling In Love** . . . Elvis Presley
62	7	12	14	**885**	☐ **Midnight In Moscow** . . . Kenny Ball & his Jazzmen
69	7	12	14	**886**	☐ **It's Your Thing** . . . The Isley Brothers
71	7	12	14	**887**	☐ **Put Your Hand In The Hand** . . . Ocean
63	7	12	14	**888**	☐ **Washington Square** . . . The Village Stompers
73	6	12	14	**889**	☐ **Yesterday Once More** . . . Carpenters
69	6	12	14	**890**	☐ **Bad Moon Rising** . . . Creedence Clearwater Revival
70	6	12	14	**891**	☐ **Hey There Lonely Girl** . . . Eddie Holman
67	8	11	14	**892**	☐ **Tell It Like It Is** . . . Aaron Neville
63	6	11	14	**893**	☐ **Puff The Magic Dragon** . . . Peter, Paul & Mary
62	4	11	14	**894**	☐ **Only Love Can Break A Heart** . . . Gene Pitney
61	4	11	14	**895**	☐ **Daddy's Home** . . . Shep & The Limelites
69	7	12	13	**896**	☐ **And When I Die** . . . Blood, Sweat & Tears
70	7	12	13	**897**	☐ **Lookin' Out My Back Door** . . . Creedence Clearwater Revival
69	8	11	13	**898**	☐ **Green River** . . . Creedence Clearwater Revival
68	7	11	13	**899**	☐ **Fire** . . . The Crazy World Of Arthur Brown
66	6	11	13	**900**	☐ **Red Rubber Ball** . . . The Cyrkle
70	6	11	13	**901**	☐ **The Rapper** . . . The Jaggerz
68	5	10	13	**902**	☐ **MacArthur Park** . . . Richard Harris
73	6	10	12	**903**	☐ **Also Sprach Zarathustra (2001)** . . . Deodato
70	5	10	12	**904**	☐ **Vehicle** . . . The Ides Of March
69	4	10	12	**905**	☐ **Traces** . . . Classics IV featuring Dennis Yost

YR	WEEKS T 10	WEEKS T 40	WEEKS CHR	RNK	Title . . . Artist
					Peak Pos 2 · Peak Wks 1
64	5	9	12	906	☐ **My Boy Lollipop** . . . Millie Small
66	6	9	11	907	☐ **Bang Bang (My Baby Shot Me Down)** . . . Cher
64	5	9	11	908	☐ **Do You Want To Know A Secret** . . . The Beatles
62	5	9	11	909	☐ **You Don't Know Me** . . . Ray Charles
65	5	9	11	910	☐ **Save Your Heart For Me** . . . Gary Lewis & The Playboys
67	6	10	10	911	☐ **A Little Bit Me, A Little Bit You** . . . The Monkees
66	5	9	10	912	☐ **Rainy Day Women #12 & 35** . . . Bob Dylan
66	6	8	9	913	☐ **Yellow Submarine** . . . The Beatles
					Peak Pos 3 · Peak Wks 6
81	10	15	21	914	☐ **Stop Draggin' My Heart Around** . . . Stevie Nicks with Tom Petty & The Heartbreakers
					Peak Pos 3 · Peak Wks 5
81	9	16	24	915	☐ **Let's Groove** . . . Earth, Wind & Fire
83	10	16	22	916	☐ **Uptown Girl** . . . Billy Joel
					Peak Pos 3 · Peak Wks 4
83	7	16	24	917	☐ **The Safety Dance** . . . Men Without Hats
57	9	18	23	918	☐ **I'm Gonna Sit Right Down And Write Myself A Letter** . . . Billy Williams
80	6	17	23	919	☐ **Lost In Love** . . . Air Supply
76	8	16	23	920	☐ **Love So Right** . . . Bee Gees
77	8	16	23	921	☐ **Blue Bayou** . . . Linda Ronstadt
76	8	16	22	922	☐ **Misty Blue** . . . Dorthy Moore
80	11	17	21	923	☐ **Little Jeannie** . . . Elton John
82	7	13	21	924	☐ **Heart Attack** . . . Olivia Newton-John
81	10	15	19	925	☐ **The Best Of Times** . . . Styx
80	8	15	19	926	☐ **Coward Of The County** . . . Kenny Rogers
79	7	13	17	927	☐ **The Main Event/Fight** . . . Barbra Streisand
62	8	13	16	928	☐ **Bobby's Girl** . . . Marcie Blane
76	7	11	16	929	☐ **Let 'Em In** . . . Wings
66	5	11	12	930	☐ **She's Just My Style** . . . Gary Lewis & The Playboys
					Peak Pos 3 · Peak Wks 3
82	6	14	27	931	☐ **I've Never Been To Me** . . . Charlene
84	9	17	26	932	☐ **I Feel For You** . . . Chaka Khan
80	5	17	26	933	☐ **He's So Shy** . . . Pointer Sisters
57	9	15	26	934	☐ **School Day** . . . Chuck Berry
84	7	15	26	935	☐ **Talking In Your Sleep** . . . The Romantics
82	8	17	25	936	☐ **Eye In The Sky** . . . The Alan Parsons Project
80	8	16	25	937	☐ **The Rose** . . . Bette Midler
81	8	16	24	938	☐ **Sukiyaki** . . . A Taste Of Honey
59	7	16	24	939	☐ **My Heart Is An Open Book** . . . Carl Dobkins, Jr.

YR	WEEKS T 10	WEEKS T 40	WEEKS CHR	RNK	Title . . . Artist
					Peak Pos **3** Peak Wks **3**
78	11	17	23	**940**	☐ **Lay Down Sally** . . . Eric Clapton
83	9	16	23	**941**	☐ **Hungry Like The Wolf** . . . Duran Duran
73	7	15	23	**942**	☐ **Little Willy** . . . The Sweet
57	9	16	22	**943**	☐ **Peggy Sue** . . . Buddy Holly
83	8	17	21	**944**	☐ **She Works Hard For The Money** . . . Donna Summer
83	10	15	21	**945**	☐ **Sexual Healing** . . . Marvin Gaye
76	8	15	21	**946**	☐ **You Sexy Thing** . . . Hot Chocolate
58	8	14	21	**947**	☐ **Topsy II** . . . Cozy Cole
78	7	14	21	**948**	☐ **How Much I Feel** . . . Ambrosia
56	11	18	20	**949**	☐ **Standing On The Corner** . . . The Four Lads
80	6	13	20	**950**	☐ **The Wanderer** . . . Donna Summer
79	11	16	19	**951**	☐ **My Life** . . . Billy Joel
78	10	16	19	**952**	☐ **Can't Smile Without You** . . . Barry Manilow
83	10	14	19	**953**	☐ **Dirty Laundry** . . . Don Henley
80	8	14	19	**954**	☐ **Biggest Part Of Me** . . . Ambrosia
84	7	14	19	**955**	☐ **Drive** . . . The Cars
83	5	14	19	**956**	☐ **Stray Cat Strut** . . . Stray Cats
76	8	13	19	**957**	☐ **Lonely Night (Angel Face)** . . . Captain & Tennille
85	5	12	19	**958**	☐ **Axel F** . . . Harold Faltermeyer
84	8	14	18	**959**	☐ **She Bop** . . . Cyndi Lauper
62	5	11	18	**960**	☐ **Do You Love Me** . . . The Contours
58	8	15	17	**961**	☐ **Secretly** . . . Jimmie Rodgers
72	8	13	17	**962**	☐ **The Lion Sleeps Tonight** . . . Robert John
75	6	13	17	**963**	☐ **Miracles** . . . Jefferson Starship
76	7	12	17	**964**	☐ **I'll Be Good To You** . . . The Brothers Johnson
83	6	12	17	**965**	☐ **Union Of The Snake** . . . Duran Duran
74	6	12	17	**966**	☐ **Tell Me Something Good** . . . Rufus
70	8	14	16	**967**	☐ **Fire And Rain** . . . James Taylor
67	7	13	16	**968**	☐ **Come Back When You Grow Up** . . . Bobby Vee
68	7	12	16	**969**	☐ **Stoned Soul Picnic** . . . The 5th Dimension
70	8	14	15	**970**	☐ **Spirit In The Sky** . . . Norman Greenbaum
70	9	13	15	**971**	☐ **Ball Of Confusion (That's What The World Is Today)** . . . The Temptations
69	8	13	15	**972**	☐ **Build Me Up Buttercup** . . . The Foundations
68	7	12	15	**973**	☐ **Spooky** . . . Classics IV
84	6	11	15	**974**	☐ **State Of Shock** . . . Jacksons
60	7	10	15	**975**	☐ **Good Timin'** . . . Jimmy Jones
63	5	11	14	**976**	☐ **If I Had A Hammer** . . . Trini Lopez
70	8	12	13	**977**	☐ **Instant Karma (We All Shine On)** . . . John Ono Lennon
71	8	12	13	**978**	☐ **Yo-Yo** . . . The Osmonds
64	6	11	13	**979**	☐ **Dawn (Go Away)** . . . The Four Seasons

YR	WEEKS T 10	WEEKS T 40	WEEKS CHR	RNK	Title . . . Artist
					Peak Pos **3** Peak Wks **3**
67	5	9	13	**980**	☐ **I Got Rhythm** . . . The Happenings
68	6	11	12	**981**	☐ **Light My Fire** . . . Jose Feliciano
68	6	11	12	**982**	☐ **Jumpin' Jack Flash** . . . The Rolling Stones
65	7	10	12	**983**	☐ **I Got You (I Feel Good)** . . . James Brown & The Famous Flames
					Peak Pos **3** Peak Wks **2**
57	9	20	29	**984**	☐ **Whole Lot Of Shakin' Going On** . . . Jerry Lee Lewis
78	8	18	27	**985**	☐ **Just The Way You Are** . . . Billy Joel
78	10	17	27	**986**	☐ **Emotion** . . . Samantha Sang
84	6	15	25	**987**	☐ **Hard Habit To Break** . . . Chicago
82	12	19	24	**988**	☐ **Harden My Heart** . . . Quarterflash
84	8	15	24	**989**	☐ **Jump (For My Love)** . . . Pointer Sisters
77	7	15	24	**990**	☐ **That's Rock 'N' Roll** . . . Shaun Cassidy
56	10	18	23	**991**	☐ **I'm In Love Again** . . . Fats Domino
78	8	15	22	**992**	☐ **Sometimes When We Touch** . . . Dan Hill
76	8	15	22	**993**	☐ **Lowdown** . . . Boz Scaggs
81	7	15	22	**994**	☐ **Guilty** . . . Barbra Streisand & Barry Gibb
85	7	14	22	**995**	☐ **Rhythm Of The Night** . . . DeBarge
85	6	14	22	**996**	☐ **You're The Inspiration** . . . Chicago
76	4	14	22	**997**	☐ **Moonlight Feels Right** . . . Starbuck
77	7	15	21	**998**	☐ **Dazz** . . . Brick
84	7	15	21	**999**	☐ **Hold Me Now** . . . Thompson Twins
78	6	15	21	**1000**	☐ **It's A Heartache** . . . Bonnie Tyler
80	7	14	21	**1001**	☐ **Take Your Time (Do It Right) Part 1** . . . The S.O.S. Band
78	7	14	21	**1002**	☐ **Last Dance** . . . Donna Summer
75	5	14	21	**1003**	☐ **Sky High** . . . Jigsaw
73	7	13	21	**1004**	☐ **Pillow Talk** . . . Sylvia
75	4	12	21	**1005**	☐ **Jackie Blue** . . . Ozark Mountain Daredevils
79	10	17	20	**1006**	☐ **A Little More Love** . . . Olivia Newton-John
57	9	17	20	**1007**	☐ **Silhouettes** . . . The Rays
61	9	14	20	**1008**	☐ **Dedicated To The One I Love** . . . The Shirelles
78	7	14	20	**1009**	☐ **Reminiscing** . . . Little River Band
85	6	14	20	**1010**	☐ **Never Surrender** . . . Corey Hart
75	6	14	20	**1011**	☐ **At Seventeen** . . . Janis Ian
70	8	13	20	**1012**	☐ **Gypsy Woman** . . . Brian Hyland
75	7	12	20	**1013**	☐ **Who Loves You** . . . Four Seasons
78	8	15	19	**1014**	☐ **Hopelessly Devoted To You** . . . Olivia Newton-John
81	4	15	19	**1015**	☐ **Every Little Thing She Does Is Magic** . . . The Police
80	8	14	19	**1016**	☐ **Emotional Rescue** . . . The Rolling Stones
59	8	14	19	**1017**	☐ **Pink Shoe Laces** . . . Dodie Stevens
84	7	14	19	**1018**	☐ **Stuck On You** . . . Lionel Richie

YR	WEEKS T 10	WEEKS T 40	WEEKS CHR	RNK	Title . . . Artist
					Peak Pos **3** Peak Wks **2**
78	6	13	19	**1019**	☐ **Here You Come Again** . . . Dolly Parton
75	4	13	19	**1020**	☐ **Wildfire** . . . Michael Murphey
61	4	12	19	**1021**	☐ **My True Story** . . . The Jive Five
83	8	16	18	**1022**	☐ **Mr. Roboto** . . . Styx
78	8	14	18	**1023**	☐ **Take A Chance On Me** . . . Abba
81	8	14	18	**1024**	☐ **I Don't Need You** . . . Kenny Rogers
77	6	14	18	**1025**	☐ **Don't Stop** . . . Fleetwood Mac
85	6	14	18	**1026**	☐ **If You Love Somebody Set Them Free** . . . Sting
70	8	13	18	**1027**	☐ **Candida** . . . Dawn
71	7	13	18	**1028**	☐ **Treat Her Like A Lady** . . . Cornelius Brothers & Sister Rose
71	6	13	18	**1029**	☐ **Smiling Faces Sometimes** . . . The Undisputed Truth
79	6	13	18	**1030**	☐ **In The Navy** . . . Village People
79	7	12	18	**1031**	☐ **The Devil Went Down To Georgia** . . . The Charlie Daniels Band
73	6	12	18	**1032**	☐ **Last Song** . . . Edward Bear
59	8	14	17	**1033**	☐ **The Big Hurt** . . . Miss Toni Fisher
78	8	14	17	**1034**	☐ **Hot Blooded** . . . Foreigner
75	8	14	17	**1035**	☐ **Boogie On Reggae Woman** . . . Stevie Wonder
71	6	14	17	**1036**	☐ **Rose Garden** . . . Lynn Anderson
70	8	12	17	**1037**	☐ **Green-Eyed Lady** . . . Sugarloaf
61	7	12	17	**1038**	☐ **Goodbye Cruel World** . . . James Darren
76	6	12	17	**1039**	☐ **Fooled Around And Fell In Love** . . . Elvin Bishop
60	6	12	17	**1040**	☐ **Burning Bridges** . . . Jack Scott
72	5	11	17	**1041**	☐ **If You Don't Know Me By Now** . . . Harold Melvin & The Bluenotes
74	5	11	17	**1042**	☐ **My Melody Of Love** . . . Bobby Vinton
74	4	10	17	**1043**	☐ **Rock And Roll Heaven** . . . The Righteous Brothers
55	10	16	16	**1044**	☐ **The Shifting, Whispering Sands** . . . Rusty Draper
72	8	13	16	**1045**	☐ **(If Loving You Is Wrong) I Don't Want To Be Right** . . . Luther Ingram
61	6	13	16	**1046**	☐ **Wheels** . . . The String-A-Longs
83	5	13	16	**1047**	☐ **King Of Pain** . . . The Police
73	5	13	16	**1048**	☐ **Leave Me Alone (Ruby Red Dress)** . . . Helen Reddy
74	7	12	16	**1049**	☐ **The Entertainer** . . . Marvin Hamlisch (from "The Sting")
71	6	12	16	**1050**	☐ **Ain't No Sunshine** . . . Bill Withers
58	5	12	16	**1051**	☐ **Short Shorts** . . . Royal Teens
75	4	11	16	**1052**	☐ **How Long** . . . Ace
70	5	14	15	**1053**	☐ **Love On A Two-Way Street** . . . The Moments
61	8	12	15	**1054**	☐ **A Hundred Pounds Of Clay** . . . Gene McDaniels
75	8	12	15	**1055**	☐ **Please Mr. Please** . . . Olivia Newton-John
62	7	12	15	**1056**	☐ **Palisades Park** . . . Freddy Cannon

YR	WEEKS			RNK	Title . . . Artist
	T 10	T 40	CHR		
					Peak Pos **3** Peak Wks **2**
72	7	12	15	**1057**	☐ **Precious And Few** . . . Climax
72	7	12	15	**1058**	☐ **You Ought To Be With Me** . . . Al Green
62	7	12	15	**1059**	☐ **All Alone Am I** . . . Brenda Lee
67	6	11	15	**1060**	☐ **It Must Be Him** . . . Vikki Carr
72	5	11	15	**1061**	☐ **I'll Be Around** . . . The Spinners
64	4	11	15	**1062**	☐ **Come A Little Bit Closer** . . . Jay & The Americans
64	7	10	15	**1063**	☐ **Suspicion** . . . Terry Stafford
59	6	9	15	**1064**	☐ **Alvin's Harmonica** . . . David Seville & The Chipmunks
58	9	14	14	**1065**	☐ **Big Man** . . . The Four Preps
71	8	13	14	**1066**	☐ **Have You Seen Her** . . . Chi-Lites
70	6	13	14	**1067**	☐ **Signed, Sealed, Delivered I'm Yours** . . . Stevie Wonder
63	7	12	14	**1068**	☐ **You're The Reason I'm Living** . . . Bobby Darin
65	6	12	14	**1069**	☐ **The Birds And The Bees** . . . Jewel Akens
59	6	12	14	**1070**	☐ **I'm Gonna Get Married** . . . Lloyd Price
61	5	12	14	**1071**	☐ **Fool #1** . . . Brenda Lee
61	5	12	14	**1072**	☐ **Last Night** . . . Mar-Keys
73	6	11	14	**1073**	☐ **Sing** . . . Carpenters
62	6	11	14	**1074**	☐ **Sealed With A Kiss** . . . Brian Hyland
64	6	11	14	**1075**	☐ **Popsicles And Icicles** . . . The Murmaids
63	6	11	14	**1076**	☐ **Everybody** . . . Tommy Roe
65	6	11	14	**1077**	☐ **Love Potion Number Nine** . . . The Searchers
63	6	11	14	**1078**	☐ **The Night Has A Thousand Eyes** . . . Bobby Vee
66	5	11	14	**1079**	☐ **See You In September** . . . The Happenings
64	5	11	14	**1080**	☐ **Out Of Limits** . . . The Marketts
65	5	10	14	**1081**	☐ **The Name Game** . . . Shirley Ellis
63	5	10	14	**1082**	☐ **Hello Stranger** . . . Barbara Lewis
75	5	10	14	**1083**	☐ **No No Song** . . . Ringo Starr
66	4	9	14	**1084**	☐ **Uptight (Everything's Alright)** . . . Stevie Wonder
71	7	12	13	**1085**	☐ **For All We Know** . . . Carpenters
68	7	11	13	**1086**	☐ **A Beautiful Morning** . . . The Rascals
69	7	11	13	**1087**	☐ **Little Woman** . . . Bobby Sherman
69	6	11	13	**1088**	☐ **Good Morning Starshine** . . . Oliver
69	6	11	13	**1089**	☐ **Time Of The Season** . . . The Zombies
64	7	10	13	**1090**	☐ **Please Please Me** . . . The Beatles
59	6	10	13	**1091**	☐ **Tiger** . . . Fabian
72	6	11	12	**1092**	☐ **I'm Still In Love With You** . . . Al Green
69	7	10	12	**1093**	☐ **Worst That Could Happen** . . . Brooklyn Bridge
71	5	10	12	**1094**	☐ **Baby I'm-A Want You** . . . Bread
65	5	10	12	**1095**	☐ **What's New Pussycat?** . . . Tom Jones
72	4	10	12	**1096**	☐ **Saturday In The Park** . . . Chicago
66	6	10	11	**1097**	☐ **I Am A Rock** . . . Simon & Garfunkel

YR	WEEKS T 10	WEEKS T 40	WEEKS CHR	RNK	Title ... Artist
					Peak Pos 3 / Peak Wks 2
65	5	9	11	1098	☐ **California Girls** ... The Beach Boys
63	6	8	11	1099	☐ **(You're the) Devil In Disguise** ... Elvis Presley
67	5	8	11	1100	☐ **Baby I Need Your Lovin'** ... Johnny Rivers
67	4	8	11	1101	☐ **She'd Rather Be With Me** ... The Turtles
67	5	9	10	1102	☐ **Pleasant Valley Sunday** ... The Monkees
68	5	7	10	1103	☐ **Valleri** ... The Monkees
71	6	9	9	1104	☐ **Imagine** ... John Lennon/Plastic Ono Band
					Peak Pos 3 / Peak Wks 1
56	12	22	31	1105	☐ **True Love** ... Bing Crosby & Grace Kelly
77	7	20	27	1106	☐ **I Like Dreamin'** ... Kenny Nolan
57	14	22	26	1107	☐ **Searchin'** ... The Coasters
63	6	14	25	1108	☐ **Surfin' U.S.A.** ... Beach Boys
60	7	17	24	1109	☐ **Sixteen Reasons** ... Connie Stevens
57	12	17	23	1110	☐ **Old Cape Cod** ... Patti Page
74	7	15	23	1111	☐ **Spiders & Snakes** ... Jim Stafford
57	11	18	22	1112	☐ **Moonlight Gambler** ... Frankie Laine
77	6	14	22	1113	☐ **Couldn't Get It Right** ... Climax Blues Band
85	6	13	22	1114	☐ **Nightshift** ... Commodores
74	6	17	21	1115	☐ **Until You Come Back To Me (That's What I'm Gonna Do)** ... Aretha Franklin
57	10	14	21	1116	☐ **Kisses Sweeter Than Wine** ... Jimmie Rodgers
70	7	13	21	1117	☐ **Spill The Wine** ... Eric Burdon & War
85	6	13	21	1118	☐ **You Give Good Love** ... Whitney Houston
57	8	18	20	1119	☐ **Be-Bop Baby** ... Ricky Nelson
70	8	15	20	1120	☐ **Band Of Gold** ... Freda Payne
85	6	14	20	1121	☐ **Sea Of Love** ... The Honeydrippers
84	7	13	20	1122	☐ **Oh Sherrie** ... Steve Perry
85	6	13	20	1123	☐ **One Night In Bangkok** ... Murray Head
79	5	12	20	1124	☐ **Music Box Dancer** ... Frank Mills
57	10	17	19	1125	☐ **Hey! Jealous Lover** ... Frank Sinatra
58	8	15	19	1126	☐ **My True Love** ... Jack Scott
85	6	13	19	1127	☐ **Freeway Of Love** ... Aretha Franklin
74	5	13	19	1128	☐ **Smokin' In The Boy's Room** ... Brownsville Station
62	6	11	19	1129	☐ **I Know (You Don't Love Me No More)** ... Barbara George
59	7	14	18	1130	☐ **It's Just A Matter Of Time** ... Brook Benton
59	6	14	18	1131	☐ **Lavender-Blue** ... Sammy Turner
60	7	13	18	1132	☐ **Sink The Bismarck** ... Johnny Horton
73	6	12	18	1133	☐ **I'm Gonna Love You Just A Little More Baby** ... Barry White
71	5	12	18	1134	☐ **Signs** ... Five Man Electrical Band
72	6	10	18	1135	☐ **Everybody Plays The Fool** ... The Main Ingredient

YR	WEEKS T 10	WEEKS T 40	WEEKS CHR	RNK	Title . . . Artist
					Peak Pos **3** Peak Wks **1**
60	8	15	17	**1136**	☐ **A Thousand Stars** . . . Kathy Young with The Innocents
73	7	14	17	**1137**	☐ **Heartbeat - It's A Lovebeat** . . . DeFranco Family featuring Tony DeFranco
58	7	14	17	**1138**	☐ **Are You Sincere** . . . Andy Williams
68	5	13	17	**1139**	☐ **Mony Mony** . . . Tommy James & The Shondells
74	5	13	17	**1140**	☐ **Best Thing That Ever Happened To Me** . . . Gladys Knight & The Pips
55	10	16	16	**1141**	☐ **The Yellow Rose Of Texas** . . . Johnny Desmond
72	6	14	16	**1142**	☐ **Betcha By Golly, Wow** . . . The Stylistics featuring Russell Thompkins, Jr.
63	9	13	16	**1143**	☐ **Rhythm Of The Rain** . . . The Cascades
57	9	13	16	**1144**	☐ **Marianne** . . . The Hilltoppers
83	8	13	16	**1145**	☐ **Overkill** . . . Men At Work
68	7	13	16	**1146**	☐ **Magic Carpet Ride** . . . Steppenwolf
73	6	13	16	**1147**	☐ **Say, Has Anybody Seen My Sweet Gypsy Rose** . . . Dawn featuring Tony Orlando
73	6	13	16	**1148**	☐ **Shambala** . . . Three Dog Night
69	5	13	16	**1149**	☐ **Grazing In The Grass** . . . The Friends Of Distinction
65	8	12	16	**1150**	☐ **Let's Hang On!** . . . The 4 Seasons
62	6	12	16	**1151**	☐ **Green Onions** . . . Booker T. & The MG's
62	7	11	16	**1152**	☐ **Norman** . . . Sue Thompson
63	6	11	16	**1153**	☐ **I Love You Because** . . . Al Martino
60	5	11	16	**1154**	☐ **Where Or When** . . . Dion & The Belmonts
85	5	11	16	**1155**	☐ **California Girls** . . . David Lee Roth
55	11	15	15	**1156**	☐ **Seventeen** . . . The Fontane Sisters
69	9	13	15	**1157**	☐ **Wichita Lineman** . . . Glen Campbell
71	8	13	15	**1158**	☐ **The Night They Drove Old Dixie Down** . . . Joan Baez
69	8	13	15	**1159**	☐ **Down On The Corner** . . . Creedence Clearwater Revival
58	7	13	15	**1160**	☐ **Splish Splash** . . . Bobby Darin
65	6	13	15	**1161**	☐ **You Were On My Mind** . . . We Five
72	7	12	15	**1162**	☐ **Back Stabbers** . . . O'Jays
61	7	12	15	**1163**	☐ **Don't Worry** . . . Marty Robbins
64	6	12	15	**1164**	☐ **Love Me With All Your Heart** . . . The Ray Charles Singers
73	5	12	15	**1165**	☐ **Oh, Babe, What Would You Say?** . . . Hurricane Smith
70	4	12	15	**1166**	☐ **Give Me Just A Little More Time** . . . Chairmen Of The Board
60	7	11	15	**1167**	☐ **Way Down Yonder In New Orleans** . . . Freddy Cannon
73	5	11	15	**1168**	☐ **Why Can't We Live Together** . . . Timmy Thomas
62	7	12	14	**1169**	☐ **Slow Twistin'** . . . Chubby Checker
62	6	12	14	**1170**	☐ **It Keeps Right On A-Hurtin'** . . . Johnny Tillotson

YR	WEEKS T 10	WEEKS T 40	WEEKS CHR	RNK	Title . . . Artist
					Peak Pos **3** / Peak Wks **1**
65	7	11	14	**1171**	☐ **Crying In The Chapel** . . . Elvis Presley
63	5	11	14	**1172**	☐ **You Can't Sit Down** . . . The Dovells
71	7	10	14	**1173**	☐ **Lonely Days** . . . Bee Gees
61	5	10	14	**1174**	☐ **I've Told Every Little Star** . . . Linda Scott
61	4	10	14	**1175**	☐ **There's A Moon Out Tonight** . . . The Capris
69	8	12	13	**1176**	☐ **Touch Me** . . . The Doors
75	5	12	13	**1177**	☐ **Some Kind Of Wonderful** . . . Grand Funk
69	5	12	13	**1178**	☐ **Soulful Strut** . . . Young-Holt Unlimited
70	6	11	13	**1179**	☐ **Turn Back The Hands Of Time** . . . Tyrone Davis
70	6	11	13	**1180**	☐ **In The Summertime** . . . Mungo Jerry
66	6	11	13	**1181**	☐ **No Matter What Shape (Your Stomach's In)** . . . The T-Bones
69	5	11	13	**1182**	☐ **In The Ghetto** . . . Elvis Presley
56	7	10	13	**1183**	☐ **The Flying Saucer (Parts 1 & 2)** . . . Buchanan & Goodman
63	5	10	13	**1184**	☐ **Candy Girl** . . . Four Seasons
63	5	10	13	**1185**	☐ **South Street** . . . The Orlons
63	5	10	13	**1186**	☐ **Blue On Blue** . . . Bobby Vinton
63	4	10	13	**1187**	☐ **You Don't Have To Be A Baby To Cry** . . . The Caravelles
63	4	10	13	**1188**	☐ **Da Doo Ron Ron (When He Walked Me Home)** . . . The Crystals
60	4	9	13	**1189**	☐ **You Talk Too Much** . . . Joe Jones
75	6	10	12	**1190**	☐ **Junior's Farm** . . . Paul McCartney & Wings
72	5	10	12	**1191**	☐ **Puppy Love** . . . Donny Osmond
63	4	10	12	**1192**	☐ **Hotel Happiness** . . . Brook Benton
65	6	9	12	**1193**	☐ **I Know A Place** . . . Petula Clark
67	5	9	12	**1194**	☐ **This Is My Song** . . . Petula Clark
62	5	9	12	**1195**	☐ **Things** . . . Bobby Darin
62	4	9	12	**1196**	☐ **Lovers Who Wander** . . . Dion
66	3	9	12	**1197**	☐ **Beauty Is Only Skin Deep** . . . The Temptations
66	6	10	11	**1198**	☐ **Sloop John B** . . . The Beach Boys
64	5	10	11	**1199**	☐ **The Little Old Lady (From Pasadena)** . . . Jan & Dean
66	5	10	11	**1200**	☐ **Secret Agent Man** . . . Johnny Rivers
63	5	9	11	**1201**	☐ **Tie Me Kangaroo Down, Sport** . . . Rolf Harris
64	5	9	10	**1202**	☐ **Because** . . . The Dave Clark Five
66	3	5	10	**1203**	☐ **They're Coming To Take Me Away, Ha-Haaa!** . . . Napoleon XIV
66	5	9	9	**1204**	☐ **Nowhere Man** . . . The Beatles
66	4	7	9	**1205**	☐ **Listen People** . . . Herman's Hermits
					Peak Pos **4** / Peak Wks **7**
82	10	15	17	**1206**	☐ **Hold Me** . . . Fleetwood Mac

YR	WEEKS T 10	WEEKS T 40	WEEKS CHR	RNK	Title . . . Artist
					Peak Pos **4** / Peak Wks **6**
58	10	15	19	**1207**	☐ **A Wonderful Time Up There** . . . Pat Boone
					Peak Pos **4** / Peak Wks **5**
76	8	15	20	**1208**	☐ **Muskrat Love** . . . Captain & Tennille
					Peak Pos **4** / Peak Wks **4**
80	6	15	29	**1209**	☐ **With You I'm Born Again** . . . Billy Preston & Syreeta
57	10	19	27	**1210**	☐ **Gone** . . . Ferlin Husky
80	7	17	25	**1211**	☐ **Cruisin'** . . . Smokey Robinson
56	10	16	25	**1212**	☐ **On The Street Where You Live** . . . Vic Damone
81	5	14	25	**1213**	☐ **For Your Eyes Only** . . . Sheena Easton
81	8	17	23	**1214**	☐ **Urgent** . . . Foreigner
83	8	16	23	**1215**	☐ **Never Gonna Let You Go** . . . Sergio Mendes
81	6	16	22	**1216**	☐ **Angel Of The Morning** . . . Juice Newton
79	9	14	18	**1217**	☐ **Send One Your Love** . . . Stevie Wonder
83	6	13	18	**1218**	☐ **True** . . . Spandau Ballet
66	7	14	16	**1219**	☐ **Devil With A Blue Dress On & Good Golly Miss Molly** . . . Mitch Ryder & The Detroit Wheels
82	8	12	16	**1220**	☐ **Freeze-Frame** . . . The J. Geils Band
80	8	12	15	**1221**	☐ **Desire** . . . Andy Gibb
68	6	11	14	**1222**	☐ **Simon Says** . . . 1910 Fruitgum Co.
67	5	10	14	**1223**	☐ **Release Me (And Let Me Love Again)** . . . Engelbert Humperdinck
67	5	10	12	**1224**	☐ **San Francisco (Be Sure To Wear Flowers In Your Hair)** . . . Scott McKenzie
					Peak Pos **4** / Peak Wks **3**
78	7	17	27	**1225**	☐ **We Are The Champions** . . . Queen
82	8	16	27	**1226**	☐ **867-5309/Jenny** . . . Tommy Tutone
82	7	17	22	**1227**	☐ **Shake It Up** . . . The Cars
78	5	15	22	**1228**	☐ **You're In My Heart (The Final Acclaim)** . . . Rod Stewart
58	11	18	21	**1229**	☐ **Return To Me** . . . Dean Martin
56	8	16	20	**1230**	☐ **(You've Got) The Magic Touch** . . . The Platters
81	4	15	20	**1231**	☐ **Oh No** . . . Commodores
80	7	14	19	**1232**	☐ **Cupid/I've Loved You For A Long Time** . . . Spinners
80	5	14	19	**1233**	☐ **Don't Fall In Love With A Dreamer** . . . Kenny Rogers with Kim Carnes
79	5	14	19	**1234**	☐ **Heaven Knows** . . . Donna Summer with Brooklyn Dreams
82	7	13	19	**1235**	☐ **I Keep Forgettin' (Every Time You're Near)** . . . Michael McDonald
77	8	12	19	**1236**	☐ **(Every Time I Turn Around) Back In Love Again** . . . L.T.D.

YR	WEEKS T 10	WEEKS T 40	WEEKS CHR	RNK	Title . . . Artist
					Peak Pos 4 / Peak Wks 3
58	9	15	18	1237	☐ **Just A Dream** . . . Jimmy Clanton
82	9	13	18	1238	☐ **That Girl** . . . Stevie Wonder
82	6	12	18	1239	☐ **Heat Of The Moment** . . . Asia
74	4	11	18	1240	☐ **Tin Man** . . . America
68	8	15	17	1241	☐ **Woman, Woman** . . . The Union Gap featuring Gary Puckett
64	6	13	17	1242	☐ **We'll Sing In The Sunshine** . . . Gale Garnett
59	7	13	16	1243	☐ **('Til) I Kissed You** . . . The Everly Brothers
72	6	12	16	1244	☐ **Sunshine** . . . Jonathan Edwards
59	6	12	16	1245	☐ **Waterloo** . . . Stonewall Jackson
67	7	12	15	1246	☐ **I Second That Emotion** . . . Smokey Robinson & The Miracles
75	5	11	15	1247	☐ **Express** . . . B.T. Express
68	6	11	14	1248	☐ **I Wish It Would Rain** . . . The Temptations
68	5	11	14	1249	☐ **Yummy Yummy Yummy** . . . Ohio Express
63	6	11	12	1250	☐ **Busted** . . . Ray Charles
61	6	10	12	1251	☐ **Dum Dum** . . . Brenda Lee
66	5	8	12	1252	☐ **The Pied Piper** . . . Crispian St. Peters
68	7	10	11	1253	☐ **Lady Madonna** . . . The Beatles
64	5	10	11	1254	☐ **Bits And Pieces** . . . The Dave Clark Five
71	5	10	11	1255	☐ **An Old Fashioned Love Song** . . . Three Dog Night
					Peak Pos 4 / Peak Wks 2
76	7	17	28	1256	☐ **Sara Smile** . . . Daryl Hall & John Oates
81	6	15	27	1257	☐ **A Woman Needs Love (Just Like You Do)** . . . Ray Parker Jr. & Raydio
80	6	12	26	1258	☐ **Fame** . . . Irene Cara
84	6	15	25	1259	☐ **Self Control** . . . Laura Branigan
80	7	14	23	1260	☐ **Give Me The Night** . . . George Benson
58	7	15	22	1261	☐ **Who's Sorry Now** . . . Connie Francis
79	7	15	22	1262	☐ **Stumblin' In** . . . Suzi Quatro & Chris Norman
84	6	14	22	1263	☐ **Eyes Without A Face** . . . Billy Idol
76	5	14	22	1264	☐ **Take It To The Limit** . . . Eagles
77	6	13	22	1265	☐ **Easy** . . . Commodores
77	5	13	22	1266	☐ **Feels Like The First Time** . . . Foreigner
85	4	13	22	1267	☐ **Suddenly** . . . Billy Ocean
77	5	12	22	1268	☐ **It's Ecstasy When You Lay Down Next To Me** . . . Barry White
81	8	14	21	1269	☐ **Who's Crying Now** . . . Journey
82	7	14	21	1270	☐ **The Other Woman** . . . Ray Parker Jr.
83	6	14	21	1271	☐ **Puttin' On The Ritz** . . . Taco
78	8	13	21	1272	☐ **I Just Wanna Stop** . . . Gino Vannelli
77	6	13	21	1273	☐ **Night Moves** . . . Bob Seger

YR	WEEKS T 10	WEEKS T 40	WEEKS CHR	RNK	Title . . . Artist
					Peak Pos **4** · Peak Wks **2**
70	5	17	20	**1274**	☐ **Get Ready** . . . Rare Earth
84	7	14	20	**1275**	☐ **Here Comes The Rain Again** . . . Eurythmics
79	6	14	20	**1276**	☐ **Just When I Needed You Most** . . . Randy Vanwarmer
72	8	13	20	**1277**	☐ **Daddy Don't You Walk So Fast** . . . Wayne Newton
77	4	13	20	**1278**	☐ **Handy Man** . . . James Taylor
73	6	14	19	**1279**	☐ **Just You 'N' Me** . . . Chicago
78	7	11	19	**1280**	☐ **Use Ta Be My Girl** . . . The O'Jays
83	4	16	18	**1281**	☐ **You Are** . . . Lionel Richie
73	6	13	18	**1282**	☐ **Space Race** . . . Billy Preston
62	4	12	18	**1283**	☐ **Let Me In** . . . The Sensations
58	8	14	17	**1284**	☐ **One Night** . . . Elvis Presley
77	6	14	17	**1285**	☐ **My Heart Belongs To Me** . . . Barbra Streisand
75	5	14	17	**1286**	☐ **I'm Not Lisa** . . . Jessi Colter
79	7	12	17	**1287**	☐ **Sail On** . . . Commodores
60	6	12	17	**1288**	☐ **Night** . . . Jackie Wilson
74	3	11	17	**1289**	☐ **Beach Baby** . . . First Class
59	7	13	16	**1290**	☐ **Quiet Village** . . . The Exotic Sounds of Martin Denny
74	6	13	16	**1291**	☐ **I've Got To Use My Imagination** . . . Gladys Knight & The Pips
59	8	12	16	**1292**	☐ **Teen Beat** . . . Sandy Nelson
73	5	12	16	**1293**	☐ **Smoke On The Water** . . . Deep Purple
63	5	12	16	**1294**	☐ **Since I Fell For You** . . . Lenny Welch
63	5	11	16	**1295**	☐ **Pipeline** . . . Chantay's
72	4	11	16	**1296**	☐ **Freddie's Dead (Theme From "Superfly")** . . . Curtis Mayfield
79	7	12	15	**1297**	☐ **Sultans Of Swing** . . . Dire Straits
58	7	12	15	**1298**	☐ **Beep Beep** . . . The Playmates
73	6	12	15	**1299**	☐ **Ain't No Woman (Like The One I've Got)** . . . Four Tops
79	6	12	15	**1300**	☐ **Chuck E.'s In Love** . . . Rickie Lee Jones
73	6	12	15	**1301**	☐ **Could It Be I'm Falling In Love** . . . Spinners
70	5	12	15	**1302**	☐ **Rainy Night In Georgia** . . . Brook Benton
60	4	12	15	**1303**	☐ **Because They're Young** . . . Duane Eddy & The Rebels
75	4	12	15	**1304**	☐ **Bad Time** . . . Grand Funk
79	6	11	15	**1305**	☐ **Don't Bring Me Down** . . . Electric Light Orchestra
68	7	12	14	**1306**	☐ **Abraham, Martin And John** . . . Dion
70	6	12	14	**1307**	☐ **Patches** . . . Clarence Carter
69	6	12	14	**1308**	☐ **Sweet Caroline (Good Times Never Seemed So Good)** . . . Neil Diamond
72	6	12	14	**1309**	☐ **Down By The Lazy River** . . . The Osmonds
66	6	12	14	**1310**	☐ **Five O'Clock World** . . . The Vogues

YR	WEEKS T 10	WEEKS T 40	WEEKS CHR	RNK	Title . . . Artist
					Peak Pos 4 · Peak Wks 2
71	6	11	14	1311	☐ **Don't Pull Your Love** . . . Hamilton, Joe Frank & Reynolds
63	6	11	14	1312	☐ **Heat Wave** . . . Martha & The Vandellas
64	6	11	14	1313	☐ **Hey Little Cobra** . . . The Rip Chords
69	5	11	14	1314	☐ **My Cherie Amour** . . . Stevie Wonder
61	4	11	14	1315	☐ **Stand By Me** . . . Ben E. King
65	6	10	14	1316	☐ **Shotgun** . . . Jr. Walker & The All Stars
84	5	9	14	1317	☐ **Thriller** . . . Michael Jackson
62	5	9	14	1318	☐ **Let's Dance** . . . Chris Montez
71	7	12	13	1319	☐ **Black Magic Woman** . . . Santana
69	7	12	13	1320	☐ **Easy To Be Hard** . . . Three Dog Night
59	6	11	13	1321	☐ **Kookie, Kookie (Lend Me Your Comb)** . . . Edward Byrnes & Connie Stevens
65	5	11	13	1322	☐ **Unchained Melody** . . . The Righteous Brothers
78	6	10	13	1323	☐ **Don't Look Back** . . . Boston
63	5	10	13	1324	☐ **Tell Him** . . . The Exciters
64	5	10	13	1325	☐ **Surfin' Bird** . . . The Trashmen
75	5	9	13	1326	☐ **Only Yesterday** . . . Carpenters
71	7	11	12	1327	☐ **It Don't Come Easy** . . . Ringo Starr
67	6	10	12	1328	☐ **Good Thing** . . . Paul Revere & The Raiders
71	4	10	12	1329	☐ **Mercy Mercy Me (The Ecology)** . . . Marvin Gaye
71	6	9	12	1330	☐ **I Hear You Knocking** . . . Dave Edmunds
64	5	9	12	1331	☐ **Don't Let The Sun Catch You Crying** . . . Gerry & The Pacemakers
67	4	9	12	1332	☐ **There's A Kind Of Hush** . . . Herman's Hermits
66	5	8	12	1333	☐ **Black Is Black** . . . Los Bravos
60	6	10	11	1334	☐ **He'll Have To Stay** . . . Jeanne Black
66	6	9	11	1335	☐ **That's Life** . . . Frank Sinatra
65	4	9	11	1336	☐ **Catch Us If You Can** . . . The Dave Clark Five
67	4	9	11	1337	☐ **How Can I Be Sure** . . . The Young Rascals
61	4	8	11	1338	☐ **Mama Said** . . . The Shirelles
69	4	9	10	1339	☐ **Oh Happy Day** . . . The Edwin Hawkins' Singers
68	3	9	10	1340	☐ **Hush** . . . Deep Purple
67	5	8	10	1341	☐ **Bernadette** . . . Four Tops
64	2	8	9	1342	☐ **She's A Woman** . . . The Beatles
					Peak Pos 4 · Peak Wks 1
57	9	22	31	1343	☐ **Come Go With Me** . . . The Dell-Vikings
56	11	17	25	1344	☐ **Tonight You Belong To Me** . . . Patience & Prudence
76	6	16	25	1345	☐ **More, More, More (Pt. I)** . . . Andrea True Connection
78	5	16	25	1346	☐ **Feels So Good** . . . Chuck Mangione
57	7	14	25	1347	☐ **I'm Walkin'** . . . Fats Domino
85	6	14	25	1348	☐ **Cool It Now** . . . New Edition

YR	WEEKS T 10	WEEKS T 40	WEEKS CHR	RNK	Title . . . Artist
					Peak Pos **4** Peak Wks **1**
60	7	15	24	**1349**	☐ **Sweet Nothin's** . . . Brenda Lee
85	5	13	24	**1350**	☐ **Lovergirl** . . . Teena Marie
57	10	18	23	**1351**	☐ **Dark Moon** . . . Gale Storm
60	8	18	23	**1352**	☐ **North To Alaska** . . . Johnny Horton
57	7	17	23	**1353**	☐ **Rainbow** . . . Russ Hamilton
84	6	15	23	**1354**	☐ **I Guess That's Why They Call It The Blues** . . . Elton John
55	11	22	22	**1355**	☐ **He** . . . Al Hibbler
56	10	19	22	**1356**	☐ **Moonglow and Theme From "Picnic"** . . . George Cates
56	13	18	22	**1357**	☐ **I'll Be Home** . . . Pat Boone
56	11	18	22	**1358**	☐ **Band Of Gold** . . . Don Cherry
74	7	16	22	**1359**	☐ **Jungle Boogie** . . . Kool & The Gang
72	5	13	22	**1360**	☐ **Nice To Be With You** . . . Gallery
58	7	14	21	**1361**	☐ **The Stroll** . . . The Diamonds
85	5	14	21	**1362**	☐ **The Search Is Over** . . . Survivor
59	7	15	20	**1363**	☐ **Gotta Travel On** . . . Billy Grammer
55	12	19	19	**1364**	☐ **Hard To Get** . . . Gisele MacKenzie
57	11	16	19	**1365**	☐ **The Banana Boat Song** . . . The Tarriers
58	8	14	19	**1366**	☐ **Tears On My Pillow** . . . Little Anthony & The Imperials
57	7	14	19	**1367**	☐ **Marianne** . . . Terry Gilkyson & The Easy Riders
59	4	14	19	**1368**	☐ **In The Mood** . . . Ernie Field's Orch.
83	7	13	19	**1369**	☐ **One Thing Leads To Another** . . . The Fixx
74	4	12	19	**1370**	☐ **The Show Must Go On** . . . Three Dog Night
74	3	11	19	**1371**	☐ **Rikki Don't Lose That Number** . . . Steely Dan
56	8	14	18	**1372**	☐ **More** . . . Perry Como
75	5	13	18	**1373**	☐ **Fight The Power - Part 1** . . . The Isley Brothers
57	7	12	18	**1374**	☐ **Raunchy** . . . Ernie Freeman
78	7	11	18	**1375**	☐ **Still The Same** . . . Bob Seger & The Silver Bullet Band
74	3	10	18	**1376**	☐ **Be Thankful For What You Got** . . . William DeVaughn
75	5	14	17	**1377**	☐ **The Way I Want To Touch You** . . . Captain & Tennille
77	6	13	17	**1378**	☐ **Baby, What A Big Surprise** . . . Chicago
66	6	13	17	**1379**	☐ **California Dreamin'** . . . The Mama's & The Papa's
83	6	12	17	**1380**	☐ **Is There Something I Should Know** . . . Duran Duran
67	5	12	17	**1381**	☐ **I Think We're Alone Now** . . . Tommy James & The Shondells
70	6	13	16	**1382**	☐ **All Right Now** . . . Free
64	6	13	16	**1383**	☐ **Java** . . . Al Hirt
73	6	13	16	**1384**	☐ **Your Mama Don't Dance** . . . Kenny Loggins & Jim Messina
58	8	12	16	**1385**	☐ **Magic Moments** . . . Perry Como
76	7	12	16	**1386**	☐ **Shop Around** . . . Captain & Tennille

YR	WEEKS			RNK	Title . . . Artist
	T 10	T 40	CHR		
					Peak Pos **4** Peak Wks **1**
84	5	12	16	**1387**	☐ **Lucky Star** . . . Madonna
64	5	12	16	**1388**	☐ **Forget Him** . . . Bobby Rydell
69	6	11	16	**1389**	☐ **What Does It Take (To Win Your Love)** . . . Jr. Walker & The All Stars
61	4	11	16	**1390**	☐ **But I Do** . . . Clarence Henry
70	7	13	15	**1391**	☐ **Whole Lotta Love** . . . Led Zeppelin
69	5	13	15	**1392**	☐ **Too Busy Thinking About My Baby** . . . Marvin Gaye
68	6	12	15	**1393**	☐ **La - La - Means I Love You** . . . The Delfonics
67	6	12	15	**1394**	☐ **Expressway To Your Heart** . . . Soul Survivors
59	5	12	15	**1395**	☐ **It's Time To Cry** . . . Paul Anka
70	5	12	15	**1396**	☐ **Ride Captain Ride** . . . Blues Image
61	5	12	15	**1397**	☐ **Where The Boys Are** . . . Connie Francis
61	5	12	15	**1398**	☐ **Calendar Girl** . . . Neil Sedaka
62	6	11	15	**1399**	☐ **Don't Hang Up** . . . The Orlons
60	5	11	15	**1400**	☐ **Volare** . . . Bobby Rydell
74	5	10	15	**1401**	☐ **I'm Leaving It (All) Up To You** . . . Donny & Marie Osmond
71	8	13	14	**1402**	☐ **Got To Be There** . . . Michael Jackson
66	6	12	14	**1403**	☐ **Kicks** . . . Paul Revere & The Raiders
73	6	12	14	**1404**	☐ **Higher Ground** . . . Stevie Wonder
72	5	12	14	**1405**	☐ **Day After Day** . . . Badfinger
64	5	12	14	**1406**	☐ **Under The Boardwalk** . . . The Drifters
63	6	11	14	**1407**	☐ **Cry Baby** . . . Garnet Mimms & The Enchanters
68	5	11	14	**1408**	☐ **The Look Of Love** . . . Sergio Mendes & Brasil '66
63	4	11	14	**1409**	☐ **It's All Right** . . . The Impressions
69	6	10	14	**1410**	☐ **Put A Little Love In Your Heart** . . . Jackie DeShannon
74	5	9	14	**1411**	☐ **The Bitch Is Back** . . . Elton John
63	3	9	14	**1412**	☐ **Foolish Little Girl** . . . The Shirelles
69	3	9	14	**1413**	☐ **Hawaii Five-O** . . . The Ventures
62	7	12	13	**1414**	☐ **Break It To Me Gently** . . . Brenda Lee
65	7	12	13	**1415**	☐ **King Of The Road** . . . Roger Miller
69	6	12	13	**1416**	☐ **Only The Strong Survive** . . . Jerry Butler
70	5	12	13	**1417**	☐ **Cecilia** . . . Simon & Garfunkel
61	6	11	13	**1418**	☐ **On The Rebound** . . . Floyd Cramer
71	6	11	13	**1419**	☐ **Draggin' The Line** . . . Tommy James
65	5	11	13	**1420**	☐ **Cara, Mia** . . . Jay & The Americans
71	5	11	13	**1421**	☐ **Proud Mary** . . . Ike & Tina Turner
65	4	11	13	**1422**	☐ **Keep On Dancing** . . . The Gentrys
74	4	11	13	**1423**	☐ **The Lord's Prayer** . . . Sister Janet Mead
72	4	11	13	**1424**	☐ **Mother And Child Reunion** . . . Paul Simon
65	6	10	13	**1425**	☐ **Rescue Me** . . . Fontella Bass
75	6	10	13	**1426**	☐ **Someone Saved My Life Tonight** . . . Elton John

YR	WEEKS T 10	WEEKS T 40	WEEKS CHR	RNK	Title . . . Artist
					Peak Pos 4 / Peak Wks 1
64	6	10	13	1427	☐ **G.T.O.** . . . Ronny & The Daytonas
65	6	10	13	1428	☐ **I'll Never Find Another You** . . . The Seekers
67	6	10	13	1429	☐ **I Say A Little Prayer** . . . Dionne Warwick
59	5	10	13	1430	☐ **I Need Your Love Tonight** . . . Elvis Presley
66	5	10	13	1431	☐ **You Don't Have To Say You Love Me** . . . Dusty Springfield
75	4	9	13	1432	☐ **Run Joey Run** . . . David Geddes
66	2	9	13	1433	☐ **Flowers On The Wall** . . . The Statler Brothers
62	4	8	13	1434	☐ **(The Man Who Shot) Liberty Valance** . . . Gene Pitney
72	6	11	12	1435	☐ **Look What You Done For Me** . . . Al Green
71	5	11	12	1436	☐ **If** . . . Bread
70	5	11	12	1437	☐ **25 Or 6 To 4** . . . Chicago
69	6	10	12	1438	☐ **Galveston** . . . Glen Campbell
61	5	10	12	1439	☐ **Yellow Bird** . . . Arthur Lyman Group
58	3	10	12	1440	☐ **Believe What You Say** . . . Ricky Nelson
61	3	10	12	1441	☐ **Hurt** . . . Timi Yuro
65	5	9	12	1442	☐ **The Jolly Green Giant** . . . The Kingsmen
65	5	9	12	1443	☐ **You're The One** . . . The Vogues
61	4	9	12	1444	☐ **You Don't Know What You've Got (Until You Lose It)** . . . Ral Donner
74	4	9	12	1445	☐ **Americans** . . . Byron MacGregor
62	3	9	12	1446	☐ **Dream Baby (How Long Must I Dream)** . . . Roy Orbison
70	5	10	11	1447	☐ **Up Around The Bend** . . . Creedence Clearwater Revival
63	3	9	11	1448	☐ **Loop De Loop** . . . Johnny Thunder
67	5	8	11	1449	☐ **Baby I Love You** . . . Aretha Franklin
65	4	8	11	1450	☐ **Everybody Loves A Clown** . . . Gary Lewis & The Playboys
67	3	8	11	1451	☐ **Little Ole Man (Uptight-Everything's Alright)** . . . Bill Cosby
61	2	7	11	1452	☐ **(Marie's the Name) His Latest Flame** . . . Elvis Presley
64	4	9	10	1453	☐ **Can't You See That She's Mine** . . . The Dave Clark Five
65	5	8	10	1454	☐ **Wonderful World** . . . Herman's Hermits
71	4	8	10	1455	☐ **I Am...I Said** . . . Neil Diamond
75	2	7	10	1456	☐ **Mr. Jaws** . . . Dickie Goodman
					Peak Pos 5 / Peak Wks 6
57	9	17	20	1457	☐ **Banana Boat (Day-O)** . . . Harry Belafonte
					Peak Pos 5 / Peak Wks 5
81	8	15	20	1458	☐ **(There's) No Gettin' Over Me** . . . Ronnie Milsap
80	8	14	18	1459	☐ **Hungry Heart** . . . Bruce Springsteen

YR	WEEKS T 10	WEEKS T 40	WEEKS CHR	RNK	Title . . . Artist
					Peak Pos 5 / Peak Wks 5
68	7	12	12	**1460**	☐ **(Sweet Sweet Baby) Since You've Been Gone** . . . Aretha Franklin
					Peak Pos 5 / Peak Wks 4
83	8	15	22	**1461**	☐ **She Blinded Me With Science** . . . Thomas Dolby
81	8	14	22	**1462**	☐ **Elvira** . . . The Oak Ridge Boys
79	5	13	22	**1463**	☐ **Shake Your Groove Thing** . . . Peaches & Herb
81	6	15	19	**1464**	☐ **Young Turks** . . . Rod Stewart
59	6	13	19	**1465**	☐ **Tragedy** . . . Thomas Wayne
82	6	11	19	**1466**	☐ **Heartlight** . . . Neil Diamond
77	6	12	18	**1467**	☐ **It's So Easy** . . . Linda Ronstadt
60	7	12	16	**1468**	☐ **What In The World's Come Over You** . . . Jack Scott
55	8	15	15	**1469**	☐ **The Shifting Whispering Sands (Parts 1 & 2)** . . . Billy Vaughn
68	5	11	14	**1470**	☐ **Girl Watcher** . . . The O'Kaysions
					Peak Pos 5 / Peak Wks 3
78	7	19	31	**1471**	☐ **I Love The Nightlife (Disco 'Round)** . . . Alicia Bridges
84	7	14	29	**1472**	☐ **Break My Stride** . . . Matthew Wilder
58	10	18	26	**1473**	☐ **Sail Along Silvery Moon** . . . Billy Vaughn
82	5	15	25	**1474**	☐ **You Should Hear How She Talks About You** . . . Melissa Manchester
80	5	14	25	**1475**	☐ **Shining Star** . . . Manhattans
57	10	16	24	**1476**	☐ **Tammy** . . . The Ames Brothers
83	5	14	24	**1477**	☐ **Back On The Chain Gang** . . . Pretenders
80	8	16	23	**1478**	☐ **Master Blaster (Jammin')** . . . Stevie Wonder
82	6	15	23	**1479**	☐ **Always On My Mind** . . . Willie Nelson
80	6	14	23	**1480**	☐ **I'm Coming Out** . . . Diana Ross
55	12	20	22	**1481**	☐ **Only You (And You Alone)** . . . The Platters
81	5	14	21	**1482**	☐ **You Make My Dreams** . . . Daryl Hall & John Oates
81	6	15	20	**1483**	☐ **Here I Am (Just When I Thought I Was Over You)** . . . Air Supply
57	8	14	20	**1484**	☐ **Melodie D'Amour** . . . The Ames Brothers
81	6	15	18	**1485**	☐ **Crying** . . . Don McLean
58	6	14	18	**1486**	☐ **Oh Julie** . . . The Crescendos
75	5	14	18	**1487**	☐ **Love Won't Let Me Wait** . . . Major Harris
55	12	15	17	**1488**	☐ **Love And Marriage** . . . Frank Sinatra
59	6	12	17	**1489**	☐ **Lipstick On Your Collar** . . . Connie Francis
80	6	11	17	**1490**	☐ **Against The Wind** . . . Bob Seger
72	6	13	16	**1491**	☐ **It Never Rains In Southern California** . . . Albert Hammond
79	6	13	16	**1492**	☐ **Goodnight Tonight** . . . Wings
61	8	12	16	**1493**	☐ **Walk On By** . . . Leroy Van Dyke

YR	WEEKS T 10	WEEKS T 40	WEEKS CHR	RNK	Title . . . Artist
					Peak Pos 5 / Peak Wks 3
69	7	12	16	1494	☐ **One** . . . Three Dog Night
70	6	13	15	1495	☐ **Julie, Do Ya Love Me** . . . Bobby Sherman
71	5	11	15	1496	☐ **If You Could Read My Mind** . . . Gordon Lightfoot
69	4	11	15	1497	☐ **Baby It's You** . . . Smith
82	5	10	14	1498	☐ **Make A Move On Me** . . . Olivia Newton-John
66	4	9	14	1499	☐ **Bus Stop** . . . The Hollies
70	7	12	13	1500	☐ **Love Grows (Where My Rosemary Goes)** . . . Edison Lighthouse
72	6	11	13	1501	☐ **Everything I Own** . . . Bread
66	6	9	13	1502	☐ **Sugar Town** . . . Nancy Sinatra
63	5	9	12	1503	☐ **Baby Workout** . . . Jackie Wilson
64	6	9	11	1504	☐ **Remember (Walkin' In The Sand)** . . . The Shangri-Las
					Peak Pos 5 / Peak Wks 2
80	6	15	25	1505	☐ **Drivin' My Life Away** . . . Eddie Rabbitt
69	5	12	25	1506	☐ **Get Together** . . . The Youngbloods
79	9	17	24	1507	☐ **I'll Never Love This Way Again** . . . Dionne Warwick
77	4	17	24	1508	☐ **Hot Line** . . . The Sylvers
79	6	16	24	1509	☐ **Makin' It** . . . David Naughton
84	4	12	24	1510	☐ **Sister Christian** . . . Night Ranger
74	4	18	23	1511	☐ **Come And Get Your Love** . . . Redbone
56	11	17	23	1512	☐ **A Tear Fell** . . . Teresa Brewer
82	6	16	23	1513	☐ **Let It Whip** . . . Dazz Band
79	5	14	23	1514	☐ **Lead Me On** . . . Maxine Nightingale
76	4	14	23	1515	☐ **Sweet Love** . . . Commodores
82	6	16	22	1516	☐ **Turn Your Love Around** . . . George Benson
77	6	16	22	1517	☐ **Do You Wanna Make Love** . . . Peter McCann
81	8	15	22	1518	☐ **Step By Step** . . . Eddie Rabbitt
70	4	14	22	1519	☐ **Hitchin' A Ride** . . . Vanity Fare
80	6	15	21	1520	☐ **Sexy Eyes** . . . Dr. Hook
79	6	14	21	1521	☐ **Hold The Line** . . . Toto
83	5	14	21	1522	☐ **Der Kommissar** . . . After The Fire
83	5	14	21	1523	☐ **Cum On Feel The Noize** . . . Quiet Riot
80	5	13	21	1524	☐ **Lookin' For Love** . . . Johnny Lee
84	5	13	21	1525	☐ **Better Be Good To Me** . . . Tina Turner
56	9	17	20	1526	☐ **Born To Be With You** . . . The Chordettes
81	6	17	20	1527	☐ **Passion** . . . Rod Stewart
82	7	15	20	1528	☐ **Sweet Dreams** . . . Air Supply
78	7	15	20	1529	☐ **Whenever I Call You "Friend"** . . . Kenny Loggins
81	6	15	20	1530	☐ **Take It On The Run** . . . REO Speedwagon
85	7	14	20	1531	☐ **We Belong** . . . Pat Benatar
73	4	14	20	1532	☐ **Funny Face** . . . Donna Fargo
85	5	13	20	1533	☐ **Smooth Operator** . . . Sade

YR	WEEKS T 10	WEEKS T 40	WEEKS CHR	RNK	Title ... Artist
					Peak Pos **5** / Peak Wks **2**
74	4	12	20	1534	☐ **If You Love Me (Let Me Know)** ... Olivia Newton-John
58	7	16	19	1535	☐ **Looking Back** ... Nat "King" Cole
76	6	14	19	1536	☐ **More Than A Feeling** ... Boston
77	5	14	19	1537	☐ **The Things We Do For Love** ... 10cc
77	6	13	19	1538	☐ **Strawberry Letter 23** ... The Brothers Johnson
77	6	13	19	1539	☐ **Lucille** ... Kenny Rogers
81	5	12	19	1540	☐ **Tryin' To Live My Life Without You** ... Bob Seger
64	5	12	19	1541	☐ **People** ... Barbra Streisand
84	7	14	18	1542	☐ **Twist Of Fate** ... Olivia Newton-John
80	4	14	18	1543	☐ **Special Lady** ... Ray, Goodman & Brown
82	8	13	18	1544	☐ **Even The Nights Are Better** ... Air Supply
80	5	13	18	1545	☐ **Too Hot** ... Kool & The Gang
79	5	13	18	1546	☐ **Gold** ... John Stewart
75	4	13	18	1547	☐ **They Just Can't Stop It the (Games People Play)** ... Spinners
72	5	11	18	1548	☐ **Go All The Way** ... Raspberries
74	4	10	18	1549	☐ **Please Come To Boston** ... Dave Loggins
76	6	14	17	1550	☐ **I Love Music (Part I)** ... O'Jays
58	6	14	17	1551	☐ **Endless Sleep** ... Jody Reynolds
80	6	12	17	1552	☐ **On The Radio** ... Donna Summer
85	4	12	17	1553	☐ **Summer Of '69** ... Bryan Adams
76	4	12	17	1554	☐ **Sing A Song** ... Earth, Wind & Fire
74	3	11	17	1555	☐ **On And On** ... Gladys Knight & The Pips
75	3	10	17	1556	☐ **You Are So Beautiful** ... Joe Cocker
79	7	13	16	1557	☐ **She Believes In Me** ... Kenny Rogers
78	7	12	16	1558	☐ **Summer Nights** ... John Travolta, Olivia Newton-John & Cast
84	6	12	16	1559	☐ **Miss Me Blind** ... Culture Club
73	6	12	16	1560	☐ **Paper Roses** ... Marie Osmond
59	6	12	16	1561	☐ **Guitar Boogie Shuffle** ... The Virtues
84	5	12	16	1562	☐ **Love Somebody** ... Rick Springfield
69	5	12	16	1563	☐ **Hooked On A Feeling** ... B.J. Thomas
80	5	11	16	1564	☐ **Real Love** ... The Doobie Brothers
74	3	10	16	1565	☐ **Back Home Again** ... John Denver
58	7	13	15	1566	☐ **When** ... Kalin Twins
70	6	13	15	1567	☐ **Indiana Wants Me** ... R. Dean Taylor
68	5	12	15	1568	☐ **Hold Me Tight** ... Johnny Nash
83	4	12	15	1569	☐ **(She's) Sexy + 17** ... Stray Cats
83	6	11	15	1570	☐ **Wanna Be Startin' Somethin'** ... Michael Jackson
60	5	11	15	1571	☐ **A Million To One** ... Jimmy Charles
72	3	11	15	1572	☐ **Hold Your Head Up** ... Argent

YR	WEEKS T 10	WEEKS T 40	WEEKS CHR	RNK	Title . . . Artist
					Peak Pos **5** Peak Wks **2**
75	5	10	15	**1573**	☐ **How Sweet It Is (To Be Loved By You)** . . . James Taylor
72	4	10	15	**1574**	☐ **Sylvia's Mother** . . . Dr. Hook & The Medicine Show
74	3	10	15	**1575**	☐ **Longfellow Serenade** . . . Neil Diamond
66	3	10	15	**1576**	☐ **Time Won't Let Me** . . . The Outsiders
68	8	13	14	**1577**	☐ **Who's Making Love** . . . Johnnie Taylor
68	7	12	14	**1578**	☐ **Bend Me, Shape Me** . . . The American Breed
67	5	10	14	**1579**	☐ **(We Ain't Got) Nothin' Yet** . . . Blues Magoos
76	5	10	14	**1580**	☐ **Happy Days** . . . Pratt & McClain with Brother Love
68	5	11	13	**1581**	☐ **1, 2, 3, Red Light** . . . 1910 Fruitgum Company
61	5	11	13	**1582**	☐ **Hats Off To Larry** . . . Del Shannon
67	5	10	13	**1583**	☐ **Your Precious Love** . . . Marvin Gaye & Tammi Terrell
71	5	10	13	**1584**	☐ **Me And You And A Dog Named Boo** . . . Lobo
63	5	10	13	**1585**	☐ **Mean Woman Blues** . . . Roy Orbison
66	4	9	13	**1586**	☐ **Elusive Butterfly** . . . Bob Lind
71	5	11	12	**1587**	☐ **Another Day** . . . Paul McCartney
67	7	10	12	**1588**	☐ **A Whiter Shade Of Pale** . . . Procol Harum
64	5	10	12	**1589**	☐ **C'mon And Swim** . . . Bobby Freeman
64	4	10	12	**1590**	☐ **The Girl From Ipanema** . . . Stan Getz/Astrud Gilberto
66	4	10	12	**1591**	☐ **Homeward Bound** . . . Simon & Garfunkel
72	4	10	12	**1592**	☐ **Never Been To Spain** . . . Three Dog Night
67	5	9	12	**1593**	☐ **Words Of Love** . . . The Mamas & The Papas
66	3	9	12	**1594**	☐ **Psychotic Reaction** . . . Count Five
64	6	10	11	**1595**	☐ **Um, Um, Um, Um, Um, Um** . . . Major Lance
70	3	10	11	**1596**	☐ **Without Love (There Is Nothing)** . . . Tom Jones
63	5	9	11	**1597**	☐ **Judy's Turn To Cry** . . . Lesley Gore
62	5	9	11	**1598**	☐ **Ahab, The Arab** . . . Ray Stevens
61	5	9	11	**1599**	☐ **The Writing On The Wall** . . . Adam Wade
62	4	9	11	**1600**	☐ **Next Door To An Angel** . . . Neil Sedaka
66	4	8	11	**1601**	☐ **Dandy** . . . Herman's Hermits
62	4	8	11	**1602**	☐ **I Remember You** . . . Frank Ifield
66	4	8	11	**1603**	☐ **My World Is Empty Without You** . . . The Supremes
65	3	8	11	**1604**	☐ **Hold What You've Got** . . . Joe Tex
75	4	7	11	**1605**	☐ **Old Days** . . . Chicago
68	4	8	10	**1606**	☐ **Just Dropped In (To See What Condition My Condition Was In)** . . . The First Edition
67	3	7	10	**1607**	☐ **Don't Sleep In The Subway** . . . Petula Clark
65	4	8	9	**1608**	☐ **It's The Same Old Song** . . . Four Tops
66	4	8	9	**1609**	☐ **Ebb Tide** . . . The Righteous Brothers
					Peak Pos **5** Peak Wks **1**
57	11	23	34	**1610**	☐ **It's Not For Me To Say** . . . Johnny Mathis
68	5	12	26	**1611**	☐ **Sunshine Of Your Love** . . . The Cream

YR	WEEKS T 10	WEEKS T 40	WEEKS CHR	RNK	Title . . . Artist
					Peak Pos **5** Peak Wks **1**
71	3	11	26	**1612**	☐ **I've Found Someone Of My Own** . . . The Free Movement
74	5	14	25	**1613**	☐ **Rock On** . . . David Essex
75	5	14	25	**1614**	☐ **Ballroom Blitz** . . . Sweet
56	11	17	24	**1615**	☐ **Friendly Persuasion (Thee I Love)** . . . Pat Boone
85	6	14	23	**1616**	☐ **Things Can Only Get Better** . . . Howard Jones
81	7	17	22	**1617**	☐ **Every Woman In The World** . . . Air Supply
83	7	14	22	**1618**	☐ **Love Is A Battlefield** . . . Pat Benatar
85	4	14	22	**1619**	☐ **The Boys Of Summer** . . . Don Henley
57	5	17	21	**1620**	☐ **Short Fat Fannie** . . . Larry Williams
73	6	15	21	**1621**	☐ **Drift Away** . . . Dobie Gray
77	6	14	21	**1622**	☐ **I've Got Love On My Mind** . . . Natalie Cole
57	6	13	21	**1623**	☐ **Why Baby Why** . . . Pat Boone
84	6	12	21	**1624**	☐ **To All The Girls I've Loved Before** . . . Julio Iglesias & Willie Nelson
76	5	12	21	**1625**	☐ **Sweet Thing** . . . Rufus featuring Chaka Khan
84	6	14	20	**1626**	☐ **Automatic** . . . Pointer Sisters
78	5	14	20	**1627**	☐ **Slip Slidin' Away** . . . Paul Simon
57	5	12	20	**1628**	☐ **Party Doll** . . . Steve Lawrence
75	4	12	20	**1629**	☐ **Magic** . . . Pilot
73	4	12	20	**1630**	☐ **Hello It's Me** . . . Todd Rundgren
63	3	11	20	**1631**	☐ **Up On The Roof** . . . The Drifters
84	6	14	19	**1632**	☐ **All Through The Night** . . . Cyndi Lauper
83	6	14	19	**1633**	☐ **Stand Back** . . . Stevie Nicks
57	4	14	19	**1634**	☐ **Happy, Happy Birthday Baby** . . . The Tune Weavers
84	5	13	19	**1635**	☐ **Sad Songs (Say So Much)** . . . Elton John
85	3	13	19	**1636**	☐ **Would I Lie To You?** . . . Eurythmics
83	4	12	19	**1637**	☐ **Too Shy** . . . Kajagoogoo
85	4	11	19	**1638**	☐ **Method Of Modern Love** . . . Daryl Hall & John Oates
60	4	14	18	**1639**	☐ **Sailor (Your Home Is The Sea)** . . . Lolita
60	5	13	18	**1640**	☐ **Mule Skinner Blues** . . . The Fendermen
85	5	13	18	**1641**	☐ **Glory Days** . . . Bruce Springsteen
58	7	12	18	**1642**	☐ **Book Of Love** . . . The Monotones
57	6	12	18	**1643**	☐ **Blue Monday** . . . Fats Domino
76	4	12	18	**1644**	☐ **Still The One** . . . Orleans
75	4	11	18	**1645**	☐ **Poetry Man** . . . Phoebe Snow
55	5	17	17	**1646**	☐ **Seventeen** . . . Boyd Bennett & his Rockets
58	7	15	17	**1647**	☐ **Susie Darlin'** . . . Robin Luke
59	6	13	17	**1648**	☐ **Red River Rock** . . . Johnny & The Hurricanes
76	5	13	17	**1649**	☐ **Rock And Roll Music** . . . The Beach Boys
60	6	12	17	**1650**	☐ **Paper Roses** . . . Anita Bryant
58	5	12	17	**1651**	☐ **Do You Want To Dance** . . . Bobby Freeman

YR	WEEKS T 10	WEEKS T 40	WEEKS CHR	RNK	Title . . . Artist
					Peak Pos 5 Peak Wks 1
85	5	12	17	1652	☐ **Too Late For Goodbyes** . . . Julian Lennon
75	4	12	17	1653	☐ **Chevy Van** . . . Sammy Johns
85	4	12	17	1654	☐ **Angel** . . . Madonna
78	8	13	16	1655	☐ **An Everlasting Love** . . . Andy Gibb
74	6	13	16	1656	☐ **Mockingbird** . . . Carly Simon & James Taylor
65	6	12	16	1657	☐ **The "In" Crowd** . . . Ramsey Lewis Trio
83	5	12	16	1658	☐ **My Love** . . . Lionel Richie
76	6	11	16	1659	☐ **Fox On The Run** . . . Sweet
77	5	11	16	1660	☐ **Brick House** . . . Commodores
59	5	11	16	1661	☐ **Lonely Street** . . . Andy Williams
60	4	11	16	1662	☐ **Go, Jimmy, Go** . . . Jimmy Clanton
56	2	9	16	1663	☐ **Memories Are Made Of This** . . . Gale Storm
59	7	13	15	1664	☐ **A Teenager In Love** . . . Dion & The Belmonts
60	6	12	15	1665	☐ **Baby (You've Got What It Takes)** . . . Dinah Washington & Brook Benton
68	5	12	15	1666	☐ **Stormy** . . . Classics IV featuring Dennis Yost
68	5	12	15	1667	☐ **Midnight Confessions** . . . The Grass Roots
60	3	12	15	1668	☐ **The Old Lamplighter** . . . The Browns
74	4	11	15	1669	☐ **Can't Get Enough** . . . Bad Company
63	4	11	15	1670	☐ **She's A Fool** . . . Lesley Gore
61	3	11	15	1671	☐ **I Love How You Love Me** . . . The Paris Sisters
59	3	10	15	1672	☐ **Petite Fleur (Little Flower)** . . . Chris Barber's Jazz Band
62	3	10	15	1673	☐ **Party Lights** . . . Claudine Clark
75	3	10	15	1674	☐ **Heat Wave** . . . Linda Ronstadt
67	4	9	15	1675	☐ **Somebody To Love** . . . Jefferson Airplane
55	10	14	14	1676	☐ **Tina Marie** . . . Perry Como
55	8	14	14	1677	☐ **Something's Gotta Give** . . . The McGuire Sisters
58	7	12	14	1678	☐ **Sugar Moon** . . . Pat Boone
69	4	12	14	1679	☐ **Smile A Little Smile For Me** . . . The Flying Machine
61	5	11	14	1680	☐ **Sad Movies (Make Me Cry)** . . . Sue Thompson
84	4	11	14	1681	☐ **Nobody Told Me** . . . John Lennon
62	3	11	14	1682	☐ **She Cried** . . . Jay & The Americans
62	3	11	14	1683	☐ **Love Letters** . . . Ketty Lester
74	3	11	14	1684	☐ **Oh My My** . . . Ringo Starr
75	6	10	14	1685	☐ **Lonely People** . . . America
65	6	10	14	1686	☐ **Yes, I'm Ready** . . . Barbara Mason
70	4	10	14	1687	☐ **No Time** . . . The Guess Who
73	4	9	14	1688	☐ **Break Up To Make Up** . . . The Stylistics
75	2	9	14	1689	☐ **Supernatural Thing - Part I** . . . Ben E. King
61	7	12	13	1690	☐ **Angel Baby** . . . Rosie & The Originals

YR	WEEKS T 10	WEEKS T 40	WEEKS CHR	RNK	Title . . . Artist
					Peak Pos **5** Peak Wks **1**
72	6	11	13	**1691**	☐ **Where Is The Love** . . . Roberta Flack & Donny Hathaway
64	5	11	13	**1692**	☐ **Let It Be Me** . . . Betty Everett & Jerry Butler
72	4	11	13	**1693**	☐ **In The Rain** . . . Dramatics
69	4	11	13	**1694**	☐ **Indian Giver** . . . 1910 Fruitgum Co.
69	3	11	13	**1695**	☐ **Can I Change My Mind** . . . Tyrone Davis
63	5	10	13	**1696**	☐ **Memphis** . . . Lonnie Mack
61	5	10	13	**1697**	☐ **Tower Of Strength** . . . Gene McDaniels
65	4	10	13	**1698**	☐ **Silhouettes** . . . Herman's Hermits
66	4	10	13	**1699**	☐ **Walk Away Renee** . . . The Left Banke
62	4	10	13	**1700**	☐ **Young World** . . . Rick Nelson
61	3	10	13	**1701**	☐ **Little Sister** . . . Elvis Presley
64	5	9	13	**1702**	☐ **Have I The Right?** . . . The Honeycombs
62	4	9	13	**1703**	☐ **Ride!** . . . Dee Dee Sharp
55	7	12	12	**1704**	☐ **Wake The Town And Tell The People** . . . Les Baxter
72	5	11	12	**1705**	☐ **Day Dreaming** . . . Aretha Franklin
68	5	10	12	**1706**	☐ **Hurdy Gurdy Man** . . . Donovan
67	4	10	12	**1707**	☐ **Mercy, Mercy, Mercy** . . . The Buckinghams
70	3	10	12	**1708**	☐ **Ma Belle Amie** . . . The Tee Set
67	5	9	12	**1709**	☐ **Western Union** . . . The Five Americans
60	3	8	12	**1710**	☐ **Swingin' School** . . . Bobby Rydell
55	8	11	11	**1711**	☐ **Maybellene** . . . Chuck Berry
64	4	9	11	**1712**	☐ **Fun, Fun, Fun** . . . The Beach Boys
61	4	9	11	**1713**	☐ **School Is Out** . . . Gary (U.S.) Bonds
62	4	9	11	**1714**	☐ **Old Rivers** . . . Walter Brennan
61	4	9	11	**1715**	☐ **Does Your Chewing Gum Lose It's Flavor (On The Bedpost Over Night)** . . . Lonnie Donegan
61	3	9	11	**1716**	☐ **You Must Have Been A Beautiful Baby** . . . Bobby Darin
62	3	9	11	**1717**	☐ **Teen Age Idol** . . . Rick Nelson
63	4	9	10	**1718**	☐ **One Fine Day** . . . The Chiffons
62	4	9	10	**1719**	☐ **She's Not You** . . . Elvis Presley
64	4	9	10	**1720**	☐ **California Sun** . . . The Rivieras
63	3	9	10	**1721**	☐ **Pepino The Italian Mouse** . . . Lou Monte
66	3	8	10	**1722**	☐ **Day Tripper** . . . The Beatles
66	4	8	9	**1723**	☐ **I Saw Her Again** . . . The Mamas & The Papas
67	3	8	9	**1724**	☐ **Him Or Me - What's It Gonna Be?** . . . Paul Revere & The Raiders
67	3	7	9	**1725**	☐ **Creeque Alley** . . . The Mamas & The Papas
61	2	7	9	**1726**	☐ **I Feel So Bad** . . . Elvis Presley
					Peak Pos **6** Peak Wks **4**
82	8	15	27	**1727**	☐ **Steppin' Out** . . . Joe Jackson

YR	WEEKS T 10	WEEKS T 40	WEEKS CHR	RNK	Title . . . Artist
					Peak Pos 6 / Peak Wks 4
79	6	13	21	1728	☐ **The Logical Song** . . . Supertramp
84	7	14	20	1729	☐ **The Heart Of Rock & Roll** . . . Huey Lewis & The News
56	9	15	19	1730	☐ **See You Later, Alligator** . . . Bill Haley & His Comets
					Peak Pos 6 / Peak Wks 3
77	6	16	23	1731	☐ **Heaven On The 7th Floor** . . . Paul Nicholas
85	6	14	23	1732	☐ **Neutron Dance** . . . Pointer Sisters
76	5	12	22	1733	☐ **Devil Woman** . . . Cliff Richard
56	11	16	21	1734	☐ **Why Do Fools Fall In Love** . . . The Teenagers featuring Frankie Lymon
73	6	15	20	1735	☐ **That Lady (Part 1)** . . . Isley Brothers
81	7	14	20	1736	☐ **Living Inside Myself** . . . Gino Vannelli
56	6	14	20	1737	☐ **The Happy Whistler** . . . Don Robertson
76	6	13	20	1738	☐ **Shannon** . . . Henry Gross
82	8	15	19	1739	☐ **Leather And Lace** . . . Stevie Nicks with Don Henley
83	7	15	18	1740	☐ **We've Got Tonight** . . . Kenny Rogers & Sheena Easton
72	6	15	17	1741	☐ **Scorpio** . . . Dennis Coffey & The Detroit Guitar Band
57	5	13	17	1742	☐ **Little Bitty Pretty One** . . . Thurston Harris
71	5	12	17	1743	☐ **Do You Know What I Mean** . . . Lee Michaels
73	4	11	17	1744	☐ **Do It Again** . . . Steely Dan
80	7	12	16	1745	☐ **Late In The Evening** . . . Paul Simon
59	6	12	16	1746	☐ **Never Be Anyone Else But You** . . . Ricky Nelson
58	5	11	16	1747	☐ **Kewpie Doll** . . . Perry Como
59	5	11	15	1748	☐ **What'd I Say (Part 1)** . . . Ray Charles
64	5	12	14	1749	☐ **Goin' Out Of My Head** . . . Little Anthony & The Imperials
62	6	11	14	1750	☐ **Happy Birthday, Sweet Sixteen** . . . Neil Sedaka
76	3	11	14	1751	☐ **Sorry Seems To Be The Hardest Word** . . . Elton John
67	5	11	13	1752	☐ **Please Love Me Forever** . . . Bobby Vinton
62	5	10	13	1753	☐ **Speedy Gonzales** . . . Pat Boone
64	5	10	13	1754	☐ **Wishin' And Hopin'** . . . Dusty Springfield
64	6	9	13	1755	☐ **Time Is On My Side** . . . The Rolling Stones
72	4	10	12	1756	☐ **Troglodyte (Cave Man)** . . . The Jimmy Castor Bunch
63	4	9	12	1757	☐ **Then He Kissed Me** . . . The Crystals
68	5	9	11	1758	☐ **White Room** . . . Cream
					Peak Pos 6 / Peak Wks 2
78	5	17	28	1759	☐ **Dance, Dance, Dance (Yowsah, Yowsah, Yowsah)** . . . Chic
77	6	19	27	1760	☐ **Angel In Your Arms** . . . Hot
57	8	18	27	1761	☐ **Send For Me** . . . Nat "King" Cole
76	4	15	26	1762	☐ **Get Closer** . . . Seals & Crofts featuring Carolyn Willis
77	5	14	26	1763	☐ **Whatcha Gonna Do?** . . . Pablo Cruise

YR	WEEKS T 10	WEEKS T 40	WEEKS CHR	RNK	Title . . . Artist
					Peak Pos 6 / Peak Wks 2
58	5	22	25	1764	☐ **Chantilly Lace** . . . Big Bopper
80	5	16	25	1765	☐ **Never Knew Love Like This Before** . . . Stephanie Mills
79	4	16	25	1766	☐ **When You're In Love With A Beautiful Woman** . . . Dr. Hook
84	4	16	25	1767	☐ **I Can Dream About You** . . . Dan Hartman
57	6	14	24	1768	☐ **Mr. Lee** . . . The Bobbettes
80	7	15	23	1769	☐ **Steal Away** . . . Robbie Dupree
69	4	14	23	1770	☐ **I'll Never Fall In Love Again** . . . Tom Jones
79	7	16	22	1771	☐ **Sharing The Night Together** . . . Dr. Hook
83	6	15	22	1772	☐ **Little Red Corvette** . . . Prince
77	4	14	22	1773	☐ **Right Time Of The Night** . . . Jennifer Warnes
76	3	14	22	1774	☐ **Only Sixteen** . . . Dr. Hook
77	4	15	21	1775	☐ **Enjoy Yourself** . . . The Jacksons
59	3	15	21	1776	☐ **I Cried A Tear** . . . LaVern Baker
81	6	14	21	1777	☐ **The Night Owls** . . . Little River Band
78	7	15	20	1778	☐ **Dust In The Wind** . . . Kansas
84	4	14	20	1779	☐ **That's All!** . . . Genesis
82	7	13	20	1780	☐ **'65 Love Affair** . . . Paul Davis
85	4	12	20	1781	☐ **I'm On Fire** . . . Bruce Springsteen
73	3	11	20	1782	☐ **The Cover Of "Rolling Stone"** . . . Dr. Hook & The Medicine Show
84	5	13	19	1783	☐ **I Want A New Drug** . . . Huey Lewis & The News
60	5	13	19	1784	☐ **Devil Or Angel** . . . Bobby Vee
72	4	12	19	1785	☐ **Garden Party** . . . Rick Nelson & The Stone Canyon Band
79	6	14	18	1786	☐ **Lonesome Loser** . . . Little River Band
56	6	14	18	1787	☐ **Ivory Tower** . . . Gale Storm
76	5	14	18	1788	☐ **Show Me The Way** . . . Peter Frampton
84	5	14	18	1789	☐ **No More Lonely Nights** . . . Paul McCartney
79	4	13	18	1790	☐ **Every 1's A Winner** . . . Hot Chocolate
84	4	13	18	1791	☐ **Infatuation** . . . Rod Stewart
85	5	12	18	1792	☐ **Some Like It Hot** . . . The Power Station
75	4	12	18	1793	☐ **Could It Be Magic** . . . Barry Manilow
73	2	12	18	1794	☐ **Diamond Girl** . . . Seals & Crofts
60	5	11	18	1795	☐ **Image Of A Girl** . . . Safaris
72	4	11	18	1796	☐ **Summer Breeze** . . . Seals & Crofts
78	4	11	18	1797	☐ **You Belong To Me** . . . Carly Simon
59	5	14	17	1798	☐ **We Got Love** . . . Bobby Rydell
84	4	13	17	1799	☐ **If This Is It** . . . Huey Lewis & The News
80	5	12	17	1800	☐ **Him** . . . Rupert Holmes
75	4	12	17	1801	☐ **Walking In Rhythm** . . . Blackbyrds

YR	WEEKS T 10	WEEKS T 40	WEEKS CHR	RNK	Title . . . Artist
					Peak Pos 6 / Peak Wks 2
83	3	12	17	1802	☐ **Come Dancing** . . . The Kinks
67	5	11	17	1803	☐ **Apples, Peaches, Pumpkin Pie** . . . Jay & The Techniques
75	3	11	17	1804	☐ **Lady** . . . Styx
59	5	13	16	1805	☐ **So Many Ways** . . . Brook Benton
79	6	12	16	1806	☐ **Boogie Wonderland** . . . Earth, Wind & Fire with The Emotions
81	5	12	16	1807	☐ **Hello Again** . . . Neil Diamond
80	4	12	16	1808	☐ **Fire Lake** . . . Bob Seger
59	4	11	16	1809	☐ **I've Had It** . . . The Bell Notes
56	8	12	15	1810	☐ **Teen Age Prayer** . . . Gale Storm
67	4	12	15	1811	☐ **Come On Down To My Boat** . . . Every Mothers' Son
83	4	12	15	1812	☐ **It's A Mistake** . . . Men At Work
74	3	10	15	1813	☐ **Everlasting Love** . . . Carl Carlton
63	3	10	15	1814	☐ **Two Faces Have I** . . . Lou Christie
74	4	8	15	1815	☐ **Call On Me** . . . Chicago
58	7	12	14	1816	☐ **Rebel-'Rouser** . . . Duane Eddy
62	7	11	14	1817	☐ **Patches** . . . Dickey Lee
64	6	11	14	1818	☐ **Don't Let The Rain Come Down (Crooked Little Man)** . . . The Serendipity Singers
68	5	11	14	1819	☐ **Cowboys To Girls** . . . The Intruders
72	4	11	14	1820	☐ **Morning Has Broken** . . . Cat Stevens
66	4	10	14	1821	☐ **I'm Your Puppet** . . . James & Bobby Purify
64	5	11	13	1822	☐ **Walk On By** . . . Dionne Warwick
70	4	11	13	1823	☐ **Love Or Let Me Be Lonely** . . . The Friends Of Distinction
69	3	10	13	1824	☐ **Time Is Tight** . . . Booker T. & The M.G.'s
64	3	10	13	1825	☐ **The Shoop Shoop Song (It's In His Kiss)** . . . Betty Everett
62	5	9	13	1826	☐ **Crying In The Rain** . . . The Everly Brothers
69	3	9	13	1827	☐ **Ruby, Don't Take Your Love To Town** . . . Kenny Rogers & The First Edition
63	3	8	13	1828	☐ **From A Jack To A King** . . . Ned Miller
69	4	11	12	1829	☐ **Run Away Child, Running Wild** . . . The Temptations
69	3	11	12	1830	☐ **Cloud Nine** . . . The Temptations
61	4	10	12	1831	☐ **You Can Depend On Me** . . . Brenda Lee
68	3	10	12	1832	☐ **I Got The Feelin'** . . . James Brown & the Famous Flames
67	4	9	12	1833	☐ **(Your Love Keeps Lifting Me) Higher And Higher** . . . Jackie Wilson
64	5	8	12	1834	☐ **Navy Blue** . . . Diane Renay
65	4	9	11	1835	☐ **Ferry Across The Mersey** . . . Gerry & The Pacemakers
63	4	8	11	1836	☐ **Donna The Prima Donna** . . . Dion Di Muci

YR	WEEKS T 10	WEEKS T 40	WEEKS CHR	RNK	Title . . . Artist
					Peak Pos **6** Peak Wks **2**
65	4	8	11	**1837**	☐ **I Can Never Go Home Anymore** . . . The Shangri-Las
67	4	8	11	**1838**	☐ **The Beat Goes On** . . . Sonny & Cher
65	3	8	11	**1839**	☐ **Tired Of Waiting For You** . . . The Kinks
62	3	8	11	**1840**	☐ **Everybody Loves Me But You** . . . Brenda Lee
65	2	8	11	**1841**	☐ **Tell Her No** . . . The Zombies
67	5	9	10	**1842**	☐ **Standing In The Shadows Of Love** . . . Four Tops
68	3	8	9	**1843**	☐ **The House That Jack Built** . . . Aretha Franklin
71	2	8	9	**1844**	☐ **Sweet Hitch-Hiker** . . . Creedence Clearwater Revival
					Peak Pos **6** Peak Wks **1**
75	6	16	32	**1845**	☐ **Feelings** . . . Morris Albert
76	4	11	29	**1846**	☐ **Dream On** . . . Aerosmith
59	7	20	24	**1847**	☐ **A Lover's Question** . . . Clyde McPhatter
74	6	14	24	**1848**	☐ **Midnight At The Oasis** . . . Maria Muldaur
85	5	14	24	**1849**	☐ **Obsession** . . . Animotion
77	5	14	23	**1850**	☐ **I Feel Love** . . . Donna Summer
57	1	10	22	**1851**	☐ **Dark Moon** . . . Bonnie Guitar
77	5	15	21	**1852**	☐ **Cold As Ice** . . . Foreigner
57	4	14	21	**1853**	☐ **Remember You're Mine** . . . Pat Boone
74	4	11	21	**1854**	☐ **The Air That I Breathe** . . . The Hollies
57	2	6	21	**1855**	☐ **Jingle Bell Rock** . . . Bobby Helms
56	6	14	20	**1856**	☐ **A Rose And A Baby Ruth** . . . George Hamilton IV
71	6	13	20	**1857**	☐ **Groove Me** . . . King Floyd
75	4	13	20	**1858**	☐ **Why Can't We Be Friends?** . . . War
74	7	14	19	**1859**	☐ **Let Me Be There** . . . Olivia Newton-John
73	6	14	19	**1860**	☐ **Rockin' Pneumonia - Boogie Woogie Flu** . . . Johnny Rivers
85	4	12	19	**1861**	☐ **Run To You** . . . Bryan Adams
85	3	12	19	**1862**	☐ **Who's Holding Donna Now** . . . DeBarge
56	1	12	19	**1863**	☐ **Long Tall Sally** . . . Little Richard
74	3	11	19	**1864**	☐ **Hollywood Swinging** . . . Kool & The Gang
57	4	13	18	**1865**	☐ **Valley Of Tears** . . . Fats Domino
73	4	13	18	**1866**	☐ **Stuck In The Middle With You** . . . Stealers Wheel
78	5	12	18	**1867**	☐ **Love Will Find A Way** . . . Pablo Cruise
71	4	12	18	**1868**	☐ **Stoney End** . . . Barbra Streisand
57	2	12	18	**1869**	☐ **Freight Train** . . . Rusty Draper
75	3	11	18	**1870**	☐ **Dance With Me** . . . Orleans
70	6	14	17	**1871**	☐ **Lay Down (Candles In The Rain)** . . . Melanie with The Edwin Hawkins Singers
74	3	12	17	**1872**	☐ **Waterloo** . . . Abba
75	5	11	17	**1873**	☐ **This Will Be** . . . Natalie Cole
75	4	11	17	**1874**	☐ **Midnight Blue** . . . Melissa Manchester
68	1	8	17	**1875**	☐ **You Keep Me Hangin' On** . . . The Vanilla Fudge

YR	WEEKS T 10	WEEKS T 40	WEEKS CHR	RNK	Title . . . Artist
					Peak Pos **6** Peak Wks **1**
58	4	14	16	**1876**	☐ **Witchcraft** . . . Frank Sinatra
83	5	13	16	**1877**	☐ **Don't Let It End** . . . Styx
83	3	12	16	**1878**	☐ **Family Man** . . . Daryl Hall & John Oates
58	6	11	16	**1879**	☐ **Chanson D'Amour (Song Of Love)** . . . Art & Dotty Todd
60	5	11	16	**1880**	☐ **Let's Go, Let's Go, Let's Go** . . . Hank Ballard & The Midnighters
74	4	11	16	**1881**	☐ **Clap For The Wolfman** . . . The Guess Who
62	4	11	16	**1882**	☐ **Wolverton Mountain** . . . Claude King
68	3	11	16	**1883**	☐ **Slip Away** . . . Clarence Carter
63	4	10	16	**1884**	☐ **My Dad** . . . Paul Petersen
59	5	12	15	**1885**	☐ **Whole Lotta Loving** . . . Fats Domino
72	4	12	15	**1886**	☐ **Rocket Man** . . . Elton John
59	6	10	15	**1887**	☐ **Tallahassee Lassie** . . . Freddy Cannon
55	4	10	15	**1888**	☐ **You Are My Love** . . . Joni James
60	3	10	15	**1889**	☐ **Lonely Blue Boy** . . . Conway Twitty
66	2	9	15	**1890**	☐ **Crying Time** . . . Ray Charles
55	6	14	14	**1891**	☐ **The Longest Walk** . . . Jaye P. Morgan
69	3	12	14	**1892**	☐ **Holly Holy** . . . Neil Diamond
72	3	12	14	**1893**	☐ **Clean Up Woman** . . . Betty Wright
58	1	12	14	**1894**	☐ **Everybody Loves A Lover** . . . Doris Day
64	5	11	14	**1895**	☐ **Glad All Over** . . . The Dave Clark Five
69	5	11	14	**1896**	☐ **These Eyes** . . . The Guess Who?
61	5	11	14	**1897**	☐ **Rubber Ball** . . . Bobby Vee
60	4	11	14	**1898**	☐ **Beyond The Sea** . . . Bobby Darin
65	4	11	14	**1899**	☐ **How Sweet It Is To Be Loved By You** . . . Marvin Gaye
62	3	11	14	**1900**	☐ **The Lonely Bull** . . . The Tijuana Brass featuring Herb Alpert
60	3	11	14	**1901**	☐ **New Orleans** . . . By - U.S. Bonds
60	2	11	14	**1902**	☐ **Walking To New Orleans** . . . Fats Domino
72	4	10	14	**1903**	☐ **Joy** . . . Apollo 100 featuring Tom Parker
69	4	10	14	**1904**	☐ **This Magic Moment** . . . Jay & The Americans
63	4	10	14	**1905**	☐ **Maria Elena** . . . Los Indios Tabajaras
65	3	10	14	**1906**	☐ **Make The World Go Away** . . . Eddy Arnold
67	3	10	14	**1907**	☐ **Don't You Care** . . . The Buckinghams
61	3	10	14	**1908**	☐ **Baby Sittin' Boogie** . . . Buzz Clifford
62	3	10	14	**1909**	☐ **Al Di La'** . . . Emilio Pericoli
66	3	10	14	**1910**	☐ **Lady Godiva** . . . Peter & Gordon
60	5	9	14	**1911**	☐ **That's All You Gotta Do** . . . Brenda Lee
62	3	9	14	**1912**	☐ **Shout! Shout! (Knock Yourself Out)** . . . Ernie Maresca
69	3	9	14	**1913**	☐ **Twenty-Five Miles** . . . Edwin Starr

YR	WEEKS T 10	WEEKS T 40	WEEKS CHR	RNK	Title . . . Artist
					Peak Pos **6** Peak Wks **1**
74	3	9	14	**1914**	☐ **Another Saturday Night** . . . Cat Stevens
75	3	9	14	**1915**	☐ **Swearin' To God** . . . Frankie Valli
61	5	12	13	**1916**	☐ **This Time** . . . Troy Shondell
70	3	11	13	**1917**	☐ **Don't Cry Daddy** . . . Elvis Presley
66	2	11	13	**1918**	☐ **Hooray For Hazel** . . . Tommy Roe
61	6	10	13	**1919**	☐ **Every Beat Of My Heart** . . . Pips
67	4	10	13	**1920**	☐ **Then You Can Tell Me Goodbye** . . . The Casinos
63	4	10	13	**1921**	☐ **Losing You** . . . Brenda Lee
75	3	10	13	**1922**	☐ **Only You** . . . Ringo Starr
58	2	7	13	**1923**	☐ **Dinner With Drac - Part 1** . . . John Zacherle "The Cool Ghoul"
71	6	11	12	**1924**	☐ **Bridge Over Troubled Water** . . . Aretha Franklin
71	6	11	12	**1925**	☐ **Doesn't Somebody Want To Be Wanted** . . . The Partridge Family
68	2	10	12	**1926**	☐ **The Fool On The Hill** . . . Sergio Mendes & Brasil '66
62	5	9	12	**1927**	☐ **Gina** . . . Johnny Mathis
67	5	9	12	**1928**	☐ **You're My Everything** . . . The Temptations
63	4	9	12	**1929**	☐ **Those Lazy-Hazy-Crazy Days Of Summer** . . . Nat King Cole
62	4	9	12	**1930**	☐ **Shout - Part I** . . . Joey Dee & The Starliters
68	4	9	12	**1931**	☐ **Elenore** . . . The Turtles
66	3	9	12	**1932**	☐ **Cherry, Cherry** . . . Neil Diamond
64	3	9	12	**1933**	☐ **(Just Like) Romeo & Juliet** . . . The Reflections
69	3	9	12	**1934**	☐ **You Showed Me** . . . The Turtles
65	3	9	12	**1935**	☐ **For Your Love** . . . The Yardbirds
63	2	9	12	**1936**	☐ **It's Up To You** . . . Rick Nelson
69	2	9	12	**1937**	☐ **Everybody's Talkin'** . . . Nilsson
63	4	8	12	**1938**	☐ **Be True To Your School** . . . The Beach Boys
55	4	11	11	**1939**	☐ **Black Denim Trousers** . . . The Cheers
70	4	10	11	**1940**	☐ **I'll Never Fall In Love Again** . . . Dionne Warwick
61	4	9	11	**1941**	☐ **Together** . . . Connie Francis
67	4	9	11	**1942**	☐ **Sock It To Me-Baby!** . . . Mitch Ryder & The Detroit Wheels
69	3	9	11	**1943**	☐ **I Started A Joke** . . . The Bee Gees
63	3	9	11	**1944**	☐ **Drip Drop** . . . Dion Di Muci
64	3	9	11	**1945**	☐ **For You** . . . Rick Nelson
62	3	8	11	**1946**	☐ **Her Royal Majesty** . . . James Darren
64	3	8	11	**1947**	☐ **The Door Is Still Open To My Heart** . . . Dean Martin
66	3	8	11	**1948**	☐ **Land Of 1000 Dances** . . . Wilson Pickett
66	3	7	11	**1949**	☐ **Hungry** . . . Paul Revere & The Raiders
64	4	8	10	**1950**	☐ **Ronnie** . . . The 4 Seasons
63	4	8	10	**1951**	☐ **Young Lovers** . . . Paul & Paula

YR	WEEKS T 10	WEEKS T 40	WEEKS CHR	RNK	Title . . . Artist
					Peak Pos 6 / Peak Wks 1
66	4	7	9	1952	☐ **The Men In My Little Girl's Life** . . . Mike Douglas
66	3	6	9	1953	☐ **As Tears Go By** . . . The Rolling Stones
55	3	4	4	1954	☐ **Nuttin' For Christmas** . . . Barry Gordon with Art Mooney
					Peak Pos 7 / Peak Wks 4
83	6	21	29	1955	☐ **You And I** . . . Eddie Rabbitt with Crystal Gayle
57	5	21	29	1956	☐ **Fascination** . . . Jane Morgan & The Troubadors
77	6	13	20	1957	☐ **We're All Alone** . . . Rita Coolidge
					Peak Pos 7 / Peak Wks 3
78	5	25	40	1958	☐ **I Go Crazy** . . . Paul Davis
79	5	14	22	1959	☐ **Shake Your Body (Down To The Ground)** . . . The Jacksons
85	5	12	22	1960	☐ **In My House** . . . Mary Jane Girls
81	6	13	21	1961	☐ **Boy From New York City** . . . The Manhattan Transfer
77	5	13	21	1962	☐ **Lonely Boy** . . . Andrew Gold
79	4	13	21	1963	☐ **You're Only Lonely** . . . J.D. Souther
56	9	15	20	1964	☐ **Be-Bop-A-Lula** . . . Gene Vincent & His Blue Caps
81	6	14	20	1965	☐ **Why Do Fools Fall In Love** . . . Diana Ross
77	6	14	19	1966	☐ **So In To You** . . . Atlanta Rhythm Section
82	6	12	19	1967	☐ **Somebody's Baby** . . . Jackson Browne
58	8	16	18	1968	☐ **Lonesome Town** . . . Ricky Nelson
83	6	15	18	1969	☐ **One On One** . . . Daryl Hall & John Oates
82	4	13	17	1970	☐ **Do You Believe In Love** . . . Huey Lewis & The News
84	4	11	17	1971	☐ **You Might Think** . . . The Cars
82	6	13	16	1972	☐ **Keep The Fire Burnin'** . . . REO Speedwagon
68	4	12	16	1973	☐ **Angel Of The Morning** . . . Merrilee Rush & The Turnabouts
76	5	11	16	1974	☐ **Got To Get You Into My Life** . . . The Beatles
80	4	11	15	1975	☐ **You May Be Right** . . . Billy Joel
64	5	10	15	1976	☐ **You Really Got Me** . . . The Kinks
80	5	11	14	1977	☐ **Sara** . . . Fleetwood Mac
69	3	11	12	1978	☐ **This Girl's In Love With You** . . . Dionne Warwick
71	5	10	12	1979	☐ **Peace Train** . . . Cat Stevens
67	4	10	12	1980	☐ **Up-Up And Away** . . . The 5th Dimension
65	4	10	12	1981	☐ **All Day And All Of The Night** . . . The Kinks
70	4	9	12	1982	☐ **The Letter** . . . Joe Cocker with Leon Russell & The Shelter People
65	6	8	11	1983	☐ **Seventh Son** . . . Johnny Rivers
61	4	8	11	1984	☐ **Pretty Little Angel Eyes** . . . Curtis Lee
					Peak Pos 7 / Peak Wks 2
76	5	16	28	1985	☐ **She's Gone** . . . Daryl Hall & John Oates

YR	WEEKS T 10	WEEKS T 40	WEEKS CHR	RNK	Title . . . Artist
					Peak Pos **7** Peak Wks **2**
84	3	11	27	**1986**	☐ **On The Dark Side** . . . John Cafferty & The Beaver Brown Band
82	7	18	24	**1987**	☐ **The Sweetest Thing (I've Ever Known)** . . . Juice Newton
77	5	16	23	**1988**	☐ **Telephone Line** . . . Electric Light Orchestra
56	9	17	22	**1989**	☐ **Canadian Sunset** . . . Andy Williams
80	5	12	22	**1990**	☐ **I'm Alright (Theme From "Caddyshack")** . . . Kenny Loggins
59	5	16	21	**1991**	☐ **Lonely Teardrops** . . . Jackie Wilson
56	6	15	21	**1992**	☐ **The Fool** . . . Sanford Clark
84	5	15	21	**1993**	☐ **The Warrior** . . . Scandal featuring Patty Smyth
78	5	15	21	**1994**	☐ **Love Is In The Air** . . . John Paul Young
77	3	12	21	**1995**	☐ **Just A Song Before I Go** . . . Crosby, Stills & Nash
56	7	16	20	**1996**	☐ **A Sweet Old Fashioned Girl** . . . Teresa Brewer
58	6	14	20	**1997**	☐ **Tea For Two Cha Cha** . . . The Tommy Dorsey Orchestra starring Warren Covington
80	4	14	20	**1998**	☐ **We Don't Talk Anymore** . . . Cliff Richard
84	4	13	20	**1999**	☐ **Almost Paradise...Love Theme From Footloose** . . . Mike Reno & Ann Wilson
57	7	15	19	**2000**	☐ **White Silver Sands** . . . Don Rondo

THE ARTISTS

This section lists, alphabetically by artist name, every single listed in the Top 2000 ranking.

Each artist's hits are listed in rank order, showing their Top 2000 ranking, along with the original label and number.

RANK	Title . . . Label & No.	

A

ABBA
456 Dancing Queen .... Atlantic 3372
1023 Take A Chance On Me .... Atlantic 3457
1872 Waterloo .... Atlantic 3035

ACE
1052 How Long .... Anchor 21000

BRYAN ADAMS
314 Heaven .... A&M 2729
1553 Summer Of '69 .... A&M 2739
1861 Run To You.......................... A&M 2686

AEROSMITH
1846 Dream On .... Columbia 10278

AFTER THE FIRE
1522 Der Kommissar .... Epic 03559

AIR SUPPLY
499 The One That You Love........ Arista 0604
648 All Out Of Love .... Arista 0520
673 Making Love Out Of Nothing At All .... Arista 9056
919 Lost In Love .... Arista 0479
1483 Here I Am (Just When I Thought I Was Over You) .... Arista 0626
1528 Sweet Dreams .... Arista 0655
1544 Even The Nights Are Better... Arista 0692
1617 Every Woman In The World... Arista 0564

JEWEL AKENS
1069 The Birds And The Bees......... Era 3141

MORRIS ALBERT
1845 Feelings............................ RCA 10279

ALLMAN BROTHERS BAND
866 Ramblin Man .... Capricorn 0027

HERB ALPERT
143 This Guy's In Love With You ... A&M 929
264 Rise .... A&M 2151
1900 The Lonely Bull .... A&M 703

AMBROSIA
948 How Much I Feel ....Warner 8640
954 Biggest Part Of Me .... Warner 49225

AMERICA
230 A Horse With No Name ....Warner 7555
566 Sister Golden Hair ....Warner 8086
1240 Tin Man ....Warner 7839
1685 Lonely People....................Warner 8048

AMERICAN BREED
1578 Bend Me, Shape Me ....Acta 811

AMES BROTHERS
1476 Tammy .... RCA 6930
1484 Melodie D'Amour.................. RCA 7046

LYNN ANDERSON
1036 Rose Garden .... Columbia 45252

ANGELS
231 My Boyfriend's Back .... Smash 1834

ANIMALS
249 The House Of The Rising Sun .... MGM 13264

RANK	Title . . . Label & No.	

ANIMOTION
1849 Obsession..................... Mercury 880266

PAUL ANKA
135 Lonely Boy .... ABC-Para. 10022
226 (You're) Having My Baby .. United Art. 454
417 Diana .... ABC-Para. 9831
694 Put Your Head On My Shoulder......... .... ABC-Para. 10040
801 Puppy Love .... ABC-Para. 10082
1395 It's Time To Cry .... ABC-Para. 10064

APOLLO 100 featuring Tom Parker
1903 Joy .... Mega 0050

ARCHIES
112 Sugar, Sugar .... Calendar 1008

ARGENT
1572 Hold Your Head Up .... Epic 10852

LOUIS ARMSTRONG & The All Stars
449 Hello, Dolly!........................... Kapp 573

EDDY ARNOLD
1906 Make The World Go Away ..... RCA 8679

ASIA
1239 Heat Of The Moment.......... Geffen 50040

ASSOCIATION
141 Windy...............................Warner 7041
233 Cherish............................. Valiant 747
799 Never My Love ....Warner 7074

ATLANTA RHYTHM SECTION
1966 So In To You .... Polydor 14373

PATTI AUSTIN & JAMES INGRAM
254 Baby, Come To Me........... Qwest 50036

FRANKIE AVALON
74 Venus.......................... Chancellor 1031
559 Why .... Chancellor 1045

AWB (AVERAGE WHITE BAND)
536 Pick Up The Pieces .... Atlantic 3229

B

BACHMAN-TURNER OVERDRIVE
546 You Ain't Seen Nothing YetMercury 73622

BAD COMPANY
1669 Can't Get Enough......... Swan Song 70015

BADFINGER
1405 Day After Day .... Apple 1841

JOAN BAEZ
1158 The Night They Drove Old Dixie Down .... Vanguard 35138

PHILIP BAILEY with PHIL COLLINS
739 Easy Lover.................... Columbia 04679

LaVERN BAKER
1776 I Cried A Tear .... Atlantic 2007

KENNY BALL & His Jazzmen
885 Midnight In Moscow................Kapp 442

HANK BALLARD & The Midnighters
1880 Let's Go, Let's Go, Let's Go... King 5400

CHRIS BARBER'S Jazz Band
1672 Petite Fleur (Little Flower) .....Laurie 3022

RANK	Title . . . Label & No.	
LEN BARRY		
882	1-2-3	Decca 31827
TONI BASIL		
425	Mickey	Chrysalis 2638
FONTELLA BASS		
1425	Rescue Me	Checker 1120
LES BAXTER		
38	The Poor People Of Paris	Capitol 3336
1704	Wake The Town And Tell The People	Capitol 3120
BAY CITY ROLLERS		
542	Saturday Night	Arista 0149
BEACH BOYS		
353	I Get Around	Capitol 5174
377	Help Me, Rhonda	Capitol 5395
599	Good Vibrations	Capitol 5676
829	Barbara Ann	Capitol 5561
1098	California Girls	Capitol 5464
1108	Surfin' U.S.A.	Capitol 4932
1198	Sloop John B	Capitol 5602
1649	Rock And Roll Music	Brother 1354
1712	Fun, Fun, Fun	Capitol 5118
1938	Be True To Your School	Capitol 5069
BEATLES		
10	Hey Jude	Apple 2276
28	I Want To Hold Your Hand	Capitol 5112
87	Get Back	Apple 2490
88	Can't Buy Me Love	Capitol 5150
150	Yesterday	Capitol 5498
242	Help!	Capitol 5476
245	We Can Work It Out	Capitol 5555
247	I Feel Fine	Capitol 5327
250	Hello Goodbye	Capitol 2056
352	She Loves You	Swan 4152
369	Let It Be	Apple 2764
386	A Hard Day's Night	Capitol 5222
412	The Long And Winding Road	Apple 2832
414	Paperback Writer	Capitol 5651
415	Eight Days A Week	Capitol 5371
548	Come Together/Something	Apple 2654
606	Love Me Do	Tollie 9008
630	All You Need Is Love	Capitol 5964
631	Ticket To Ride	Capitol 5407
633	Penny Lane	Capitol 5810
665	Twist And Shout	Tollie 9001
908	Do You Want To Know A Secret	Vee-Jay 587
913	Yellow Submarine	Capitol 5715
1090	Please Please Me	Vee-Jay 581
1204	Nowhere Man	Capitol 5587
1253	Lady Madonna	Capitol 2138
1342	She's A Woman	Capitol 5327
1722	Day Tripper	Capitol 5555
1974	Got To Get You Into My Life	Capitol 4274

RANK	Title . . . Label & No.	
BEE GEES		
17	Night Fever	RSO 889
95	Stayin' Alive	RSO 885
136	How Can You Mend A Broken Heart	Atco 6824
152	How Deep Is Your Love	RSO 882
284	Too Much Heaven	RSO 913
304	Tragedy	RSO 918
335	Jive Talkin'	RSO 510
492	You Should Be Dancing	RSO 853
504	Love You Inside Out	RSO 925
920	Love So Right	RSO 859
1173	Lonely Days	Atco 6795
1943	I Started A Joke	Atco 6639
HARRY BELAFONTE		
1457	Banana Boat (Day-O)	RCA 6771
BELL NOTES		
1809	I've Had It	Time 1004
ARCHIE BELL & THE DRELLS		
354	Tighten Up	Atlantic 2478
BELLAMY BROTHERS		
506	Let Your Love Flow	Warner 8169
PAT BENATAR		
1531	We Belong	Chrysalis 42826
1618	Love Is A Battlefield	Chrysalis 42732
BOYD BENNETT & His Rockets		
1646	Seventeen	King 1470
GEORGE BENSON		
1260	Give Me The Night	Warner 49505
1516	Turn Your Love Around	Warner 49846
BROOK BENTON		
701	The Boll Weevil Song	Mercury 71820
1130	It's Just A Matter Of Time	Mercury 71394
1192	Hotel Happiness	Mercury 72055
1302	Rainy Night In Georgia	Cotillion 44057
1665	Baby (You've Got What It Takes) *BROOK BENTON & DINAH WASHINGTON*	Mercury 71565
1805	So Many Ways	Mercury 71512
CHUCK BERRY		
336	My Ding-A-Ling	Chess 2131
702	Sweet Little Sixteen	Chess 1683
934	School Day	Chess 1653
1711	Maybellene	Chess 1604
BIG BOPPER		
1764	Chantilly Lace	Mercury 71343
MR. ACKER BILK		
468	Stranger On The Shore	Atco 6217
ELVIN BISHOP		
1039	Fooled Around And Fell In Love	Capricorn 0252
BLACKBYRDS		
1801	Walking In Rhythm	Fantasy 736
JEANNE BLACK		
1334	He'll Have To Stay	Capitol 4368

RANK	**Title** . . . Label & No.
MARCIE BLANE	
928	Bobby's Girl .... Seville 120
BLONDIE	
36	Call Me .... Chrysalis 2414
297	Rapture .... Chrysalis 2485
429	The Tide Is High .... Chrysalis 2465
474	Heart Of Glass .... Chrysalis 2295
BLOOD, SWEAT & TEARS	
714	Spinning Wheel .... Columbia 44871
716	You've Made Me So Very Happy........ .... Columbia 44776
896	And When I Die............. Columbia 45008
BLUE SWEDE	
531	Hooked On A Feeling .... EMI 3627
BLUES IMAGE	
1396	Ride Captain Ride................ Atco 6746
BLUES MAGOOS	
1579	(We Ain't Got) Nothin' Yet . Mercury 72622
BOBBETTES	
1768	Mr. Lee.......................... Atlantic 1144
GARY 'U.S.' BONDS	
363	Quarter To Three..............Legrand 1008
1713	School Is Out...................Legrand 1009
1901	New Orleans....................Legrand 1003
BOOKER T. & THE MG's	
1151	Green Onions ....Stax 127
1824	Time Is Tight .... Stax 0028
DEBBY BOONE	
4	You Light Up My Life ....Warner 8455
PAT BOONE	
18	Love Letters In The Sand....... Dot 15570
30	April Love .... Dot 15660
102	I Almost Lost My Mind .... Dot 15472
292	Ain't That A Shame................ Dot 15377
450	Don't Forbid Me .... Dot 15521
588	Moody River....................... Dot 16209
1207	A Wonderful Time Up There ... Dot 15690
1357	I'll Be Home .... Dot 15443
1615	Friendly Persuasion (Thee I Love)....... .... Dot 15490
1623	Why Baby Why .... Dot 15545
1678	Sugar Moon .... Dot 15750
1753	Speedy Gonzales .... Dot 16368
1853	Remember You're Mine .... Dot 15602
BOSTON	
1323	Don't Look Back .... Epic 50590
1536	More Than A Feeling........... Epic 50266
DAVID BOWIE	
291	Fame.............................. RCA 10320
483	Let's Dance ....EMI America 8158
BOX TOPS	
132	The Letter .... Mala 565
791	Cry Like A Baby .... Mala 593
LAURA BRANIGAN	
667	Gloria .... Atlantic 4048
1259	Self Control .... Atlantic 89676

RANK	**Title** . . . Label & No.
BREAD	
534	Make It With You...............Elektra 45686
1094	Baby I'm-A Want You.........Elektra 45751
1436	If ....Elektra 45720
1501	Everything I Own ....Elektra 45765
WALTER BRENNAN	
1714	Old Rivers .... Liberty 55436
TERESA BREWER	
1512	A Tear Fell .... Coral 61590
1996	A Sweet Old Fashioned Girl . Coral 61636
BRICK	
998	Dazz .... Bang 727
ALICIA BRIDGES	
1471	I Love The Nightlife (Disco 'Round)..... .... Polydor 14483
BROOKLYN BRIDGE	
1093	Worst That Could Happen..... Buddah 75
BROTHERS FOUR	
657	Greenfields.................... Columbia 41571
BROTHERS JOHNSON	
964	I'll Be Good To You .... A&M 1806
1538	Strawberry Letter 23 .... A&M 1949
ARTHUR BROWN	
899	Fire .... Atlantic 2556
JAMES BROWN	
983	I Got You (I Feel Good) .... King 6015
1832	I Got The Feelin' .... King 6155
JACKSON BROWNE	
1967	Somebody's Baby .... Asylum 69982
BROWNS	
128	The Three Bells................... RCA 7555
1668	The Old Lamplighter .... RCA 7700
BROWNSVILLE STATION	
1128	Smokin' In The Boy's Room............. .... Big Tree 16011
ANITA BRYANT	
1650	Paper Roses.......................Carlton 528
B.T. EXPRESS	
760	Do It ('Til You're Satisfied) .... Roadshow 12395
1247	Express .... Roadshow 7001
BUCHANAN & GOODMAN	
1183	The Flying Saucer (Parts 1 & 2) .... Luniverse 101
BUCKINGHAMS	
394	Kind Of A Drag ....................U.S.A. 860
1707	Mercy, Mercy, Mercy....... Columbia 44182
1907	Don't You Care .... Columbia 44053
ERIC BURDON & WAR	
1117	Spill The Wine.................... MGM 14118
JERRY BUTLER	
1416	Only The Strong Survive ... Mercury 72898
1692	Let It Be Me .... Vee-Jay 613 *BETTY EVERETT & JERRY BUTLER*

RANK **Title** . . . Label & No.

BYRDS
235 Turn! Turn! Turn!............ Columbia 43424
614 Mr. Tambourine Man....... Columbia 43271

EDWARD BYRNES & CONNIE STEVENS
1321 Kookie, Kookie (Lend Me Your Comb). ....Warner 5047

C

JOHN CAFFERTY & THE BEAVER BROWN BAND
1986 On The Dark Side........... Scotti Br. 04594

GLEN CAMPBELL
269 Rhinestone Cowboy...........Capitol 4095
469 Southern Nights ....Capitol 4376
1157 Wichita Lineman................Capitol 2302
1438 Galveston..........................Capitol 2428

FREDDY CANNON
1056 Palisades Park .... Swan 4106
1167 Way Down Yonder In New Orleans..... .... Swan 4043
1887 Tallahassee Lassie .... Swan 4031

CAPRIS
1175 There's A Moon Out Tonight .... Old Town 1094

CAPTAIN & TENNILLE
108 Love Will Keep Us Together ... A&M 1672
423 Do That To Me One More Time .... Casablanca 2215
957 Lonely Night (Angel Face) ...... A&M 1782
1208 Muskrat Love........................ A&M 1870
1377 The Way I Want To Touch You A&M 1725
1386 Shop Around .... A&M 1817

IRENE CARA
32 Flashdance...What A Feeling............. .... Casablanca 811440
1258 Fame................................... RSO 1034

CARAVELLES
1187 You Don't Have To Be A Baby To Cry .... Smash 1852

CARL CARLTON
1813 Everlasting Love........... Back Beat 27001

ERIC CARMEN
692 All By Myself .... Arista 0165

KIM CARNES
8 Bette Davis Eyes .... EMI America 8077
1233 Don't Fall In Love With A Dreamer .... United Art. 1345
KENNY ROGERS with KIM CARNES

CARPENTERS
127 (They Long To Be) Close To You .... A&M 1183
295 Top Of The World................... A&M 1468
544 Please Mr. Postman................ A&M 1646
660 We've Only Just Begun .... A&M 1217
809 Superstar .... A&M 1289
815 Rainy Days And Mondays ...... A&M 1260
818 Hurting Each Other .... A&M 1322
889 Yesterday Once More............ A&M 1446
1073 Sing .... A&M 1413
1085 For All We Know .... A&M 1243
1326 Only Yesterday...................... A&M 1677

CATHY CARR
837 Ivory Tower .... Fraternity 734

VIKKI CARR
1060 It Must Be Him.................. Liberty 55986

CARS
955 Drive .... Elektra 69706
1227 Shake It Up .... Elektra 47250
1971 You Might Think................ Elektra 69744

CLARENCE CARTER
1307 Patches .... Atlantic 2748
1883 Slip Away......................... Atlantic 2508

CASCADES
1143 Rhythm Of The Rain .... Valiant 6026

JOHNNY CASH
720 A Boy Named Sue .... Columbia 44944

CASINOS
1920 Then You Can Tell Me Goodbye .... Fraternity 977

SHAUN CASSIDY
459 Da Doo Ron Ron................Warner 8365
990 That's Rock 'N' Roll............Warner 8423

JIMMY CASTOR Bunch
1756 Troglodyte (Cave Man) .... RCA 1029

GEORGE CATES
1356 Moonglow and Theme From 'Picnic' ... . Coral 61618

CHAIRMEN OF THE BOARD
1166 Give Me Just A Little More Time........ .... Invictus 9074

CHAMPS
67 Tequila .... Challenge 1016

GENE CHANDLER
224 Duke Of Earl...................... Vee-Jay 416

BRUCE CHANNEL
220 Hey! Baby .... Smash 1731

CHANTAY'S
1295 Pipeline................................ Dot 16440

HARRY CHAPIN
508 Cat's In The Cradle............Elektra 45203

CHARLENE
931 I've Never Been To Me.......Motown 1611

JIMMY CHARLES
1571 A Million To One .... Promo 1002

RAY CHARLES
70 I Can't Stop Loving You . ABC-Para. 10330
388 Hit The Road Jack......... ABC-Para. 10244
618 Georgia On My Mind...... ABC-Para. 10135
909 You Don't Know Me....... ABC-Para. 10345
1250 Busted........................... ABC-Para. 10481
1748 What'd I Say....................... Atlantic 2031
1890 Crying Time.................. ABC-Para. 10739

RANK	Title . . . Label & No.
RAY CHARLES Singers	
1164	Love Me With All Your Heart .... Command 4046
CHUBBY CHECKER	
151	The Twist .... Parkway 811
208	Pony Time .... Parkway 818
737	Limbo Rock .... Parkway 849
1169	Slow Twistin' .... Parkway 835
CHEERS	
1939	Black Denim Trousers .... Capitol 3219
CHER	
298	Half-Breed .... MCA 40102
344	Gypsys, Tramps & Thieves ..... Kapp 2146
562	Dark Lady .... MCA 40161
907	Bang Bang (My Baby Shot Me Down) .... Imperial 66160
DON CHERRY	
1358	Band Of Gold .... Columbia 40597
CHI-LITES	
573	Oh Girl .... Brunswick 55471
1066	Have You Seen Her .... Brunswick 55462
CHIC	
34	Le Freak .... Atlantic 3519
498	Good Times .... Atlantic 3584
1759	Dance, Dance, Dance (Yowsah, Yowsah, Yowsah) .... Atlantic 3435
CHICAGO	
266	Hard To Say I'm Sorry ... Full Moon 29979
285	If You Leave Me Now...... Columbia 10390
987	Hard Habit To Break ...... Full Moon 29214
996	You're The Inspiration .... Full Moon 29126
1096	Saturday In The Park ...... Columbia 45657
1279	Just You 'N' Me .... Columbia 45933
1378	Baby, What A Big Surprise .... Columbia 10620
1437	25 Or 6 To 4 .... Columbia 45194
1605	Old Days .... Columbia 10131
1815	Call On Me .... Columbia 46062
CHIFFONS	
139	He's So Fine .... Laurie 3152
1718	One Fine Day .... Laurie 3179
CHIPMUNKS	
94	The Chipmunk Song .... Liberty 55168
1064	Alvin's Harmonica .... Liberty 55179
CHORDETTES	
788	Lollipop .... Cadence 1345
1526	Born To Be With You .... Cadence 1291
LOU CHRISTIE	
592	Lightnin' Strikes .... MGM 13412
1814	Two Faces Have I .... Roulette 4481
JIMMY CLANTON	
1237	Just A Dream .... Ace 546
1662	Go, Jimmy, Go .... Ace 575
ERIC CLAPTON	
607	I Shot The Sheriff .... RSO 409
940	Lay Down Sally .... RSO 886

RANK	Title . . . Label & No.
CLAUDINE CLARK	
1673	Party Lights .... Chancellor 1113
DAVE CLARK FIVE	
620	Over And Over .... Epic 9863
1202	Because .... Epic 9704
1254	Bits And Pieces .... Epic 9671
1336	Catch Us If You Can .... Epic 9833
1453	Can't You See That She's Mine .... Epic 9692
1895	Glad All Over .... Epic 9656
DEE CLARK	
869	Raindrops .... Vee-Jay 383
PETULA CLARK	
355	Downtown .... Warner 5494
396	My Love .... Warner 5684
1193	I Know A Place .... Warner 5612
1194	This Is My Song .... Warner 7002
1607	Don't Sleep In The Subway .. Warner 7049
SANFORD CLARK	
1992	The Fool .... Dot 15481
CLASSICS IV	
905	Traces .... Imperial 66352
973	Spooky .... Imperial 66259
1666	Stormy .... Imperial 66328
BUZZ CLIFFORD	
1908	Baby Sittin' Boogie .... Columbia 41876
CLIMAX	
1057	Precious And Few .... Carousel 30055
CLIMAX BLUES BAND	
1113	Couldn't Get It Right .... Sire 736
COASTERS	
549	Yakety Yak .... Atco 6116
707	Charlie Brown .... Atco 6132
1107	Searchin' .... Atco 6087
JOE COCKER	
177	Up Where We Belong .... Island 99996 *JOE COCKER & JENNIFER WARNES*
1556	You Are So Beautiful .... A&M 1641
1982	The Letter .... A&M 1174
DENNIS COFFEY & The Detroit Guitar Band	
1741	Scorpio .... Sussex 226
COZY COLE	
947	Topsy II .... Love 5004
NAT KING COLE	
776	Ramblin' Rose .... Capitol 4804
847	A Blossom Fell .... Capitol 3095
1535	Looking Back .... Capitol 3939
1761	Send For Me .... Capitol 3737
1929	Those Lazy-Hazy-Crazy Days Of Summer .... Capitol 4965
NATALIE COLE	
1622	I've Got Love On My Mind ... Capitol 4360
1873	This Will Be .... Capitol 4109

RANK	Title . . . Label & No.
PHIL COLLINS	
169	Against All Odds (Take A Look At Me Now) .... Atlantic 89700
326	One More Night .... Atlantic 89588
533	Sussudio .... Atlantic 89560
739	Easy Lover .... Columbia 04679 *PHILIP BAILEY with PHIL COLLINS*
JESSI COLTER	
1286	I'm Not Lisa .... Capitol 4009
COMMODORES	
293	Three Times A Lady .... Motown 1443
480	Still .... Motown 1474
1114	Nightshift .... Motown 1773
1231	Oh No .... Motown 1527
1265	Easy .... Motown 1418
1287	Sail On .... Motown 1466
1515	Sweet Love .... Motown 1381
1660	Brick House .... Motown 1425
PERRY COMO	
257	Round And Round .... RCA 6815
440	Hot Diggity (Dog Ziggity Boom) .... RCA 6427
441	Catch A Falling Star .... RCA 7128
1372	More .... RCA 6554
1385	Magic Moments .... RCA 7128
1676	Tina Marie .... RCA 6192
1747	Kewpie Doll .... RCA 7202
ARTHUR CONLEY	
879	Sweet Soul Music .... Atco 6463
BILL CONTI	
490	Gonna Fly Now (Theme From 'Rocky') .... United Art. 940
CONTOURS	
960	Do You Love Me .... Gordy 7005
SAM COOKE	
162	You Send Me .... Keen 34013
777	Chain Gang .... RCA 7783
RITA COOLIDGE	
835	(Your Love Has Lifted Me) Higher And Higher .... A&M 1922
1957	We're All Alone .... A&M 1965
CORNELIUS BROTHERS & SISTER ROSE	
800	Too Late To Turn Back Now .... United Art. 50910
1028	Treat Her Like A Lady .... United Art. 50721
DAVE 'BABY' CORTEZ	
532	The Happy Organ .... Clock 1009
BILL COSBY	
1451	Little Ole Man (Uptight-Everything's Alright) .... Warner 7072
JOHN COUGAR	
114	Jack & Diane .... Riva 210
646	Hurts So Good .... Riva 209
COUNT FIVE	
1594	Psychotic Reaction .... Double Shot 104

RANK	Title . . . Label & No.
COWSILLS	
780	The Rain, The Park & Other Things .... MGM 13810
785	Hair .... MGM 14026
FLOYD CRAMER	
656	Last Date .... RCA 7775
1418	On The Rebound .... RCA 7840
CREAM	
1611	Sunshine Of Your Love .... Atco 6544
1758	White Room .... Atco 6617
CREEDENCE CLEARWATER REVIVAL	
710	Proud Mary .... Fantasy 619
830	Travelin' Band .... Fantasy 637
890	Bad Moon Rising .... Fantasy 622
897	Lookin' Out My Back Door .... Fantasy 645
898	Green River .... Fantasy 625
1159	Down On The Corner .... Fantasy 634
1447	Up Around The Bend .... Fantasy 641
1844	Sweet Hitch-Hiker .... Fantasy 665
CRESCENDOS	
1486	Oh Julie .... Nasco 6005
CRESTS	
748	16 Candles .... Coed 506
CRICKETS	
452	That'll Be The Day .... Brunswick 55009
JIM CROCE	
278	Bad, Bad Leroy Brown .... ABC 11359
365	Time In A Bottle .... ABC 11405
BING CROSBY & GRACE KELLY	
1105	True Love .... Capitol 3507
CROSBY, STILLS & NASH	
1995	Just A Song Before I Go .... Atlantic 3401
CHRISTOPHER CROSS	
168	Arthur's Theme (Best That You Can Do) .... Warner 49787
475	Sailing .... Warner 49507
652	Ride Like The Wind .... Warner 49184
CRYSTALS	
325	He's A Rebel .... Philles 106
1188	Da Doo Ron Ron (When He Walked Me Home) .... Philles 112
1757	Then He Kissed Me .... Philles 115
CULTURE CLUB	
179	Karma Chameleon .... Virgin 04221
672	Do You Really Want To Hurt Me .... Epic 03368
765	Time (Clock Of The Heart) .... Epic 03796
1559	Miss Me Blind .... Virgin 04388
CYRKLE	
900	Red Rubber Ball .... Columbia 43589

D

RANK	Title . . . Label & No.
DALE & GRACE	
366	I'm Leaving It Up To You .... Montel 921

RANK	Title . . . Label & No.
VIC DAMONE	
1212	On The Street Where You Live .... Columbia 40654
CHARLIE DANIELS Band	
1031	The Devil Went Down To Georgia....... .... Epic 50700
DANNY & THE JUNIORS	
24	At The Hop .... ABC-Para. 9871
BOBBY DARIN	
7	Mack The Knife..................... Atco 6147
859	Dream Lover........................ Atco 6140
1068	You're The Reason I'm Living........... .... Capitol 4897
1160	Splish Splash...................... Atco 6117
1195	Things .... Atco 6229
1716	You Must Have Been A Beautiful Baby .... Atco 6206
1898	Beyond The Sea.................. Atco 6158
JAMES DARREN	
1038	Goodbye Cruel World .... Colpix 609
1946	Her Royal Majesty .... Colpix 622
MAC DAVIS	
199	Baby Don't Get Hooked On Me.......... .... Columbia 45618
PAUL DAVIS	
1780	'65 Love Affair .... Arista 0661
1958	I Go Crazy .... Bang 733
SAMMY DAVIS, JR.	
184	The Candy Man.................. MGM 14320
SKEETER DAVIS	
860	The End Of The World .... RCA 8098
TYRONE DAVIS	
1179	Turn Back The Hands Of Time Dakar 616
1695	Can I Change My Mind.......... Dakar 602
DAWN	
106	Tie A Yellow Ribbon Round The Ole Oak Tree .... Bell 45318
194	Knock Three Times................ Bell 938
239	He Don't Love You (Like I Love You) .. .. Elektra 45240
1027	Candida .... Bell 903
1147	Say, Has Anybody Seen My Sweet Gypsy Rose .... Bell 45374
BOBBY DAY	
745	Rock-in Robin...................... Class 229
DORIS DAY	
668	Whatever Will Be, Will Be (Que Sera, Sera)......................... Columbia 40704
1894	Everybody Loves A Lover Columbia 41195
DAZZ BAND	
1513	Let It Whip .... Motown 1609
JIMMY DEAN	
78	Big Bad John................ Columbia 42175
DeBARGE	
995	Rhythm Of The Night .... Gordy 1770
1862	Who's Holding Donna Now ... Gordy 1793

RANK	Title . . . Label & No.
JOEY DEE & The Starliters	
195	Peppermint Twist .... Roulette 4401
1930	Shout .... Roulette 4416
KIKI DEE - see ELTON JOHN	
DEEP PURPLE	
1293	Smoke On The Water.......... Warner 7710
1340	Hush .... Tetragramm. 1503
RICK DEES	
433	Disco Duck........................... RSO 857
DeFRANCO FAMILY featuring Tony DeFranco	
1137	Heartbeat - It's A Lovebeat .... 20th Century 2030
DELFONICS	
1393	La - La - Means I Love You .... Philly Groove 150
DELL-VIKINGS	
1343	Come Go With Me .... Dot 15538
MARTIN DENNY	
1290	Quiet Village .... Liberty 55162
JOHN DENVER	
338	Annie's Song .... RCA 0295
497	Thank God I'm A Country Boy .... RCA 10239
517	I'm Sorry............................ RCA 10353
519	Sunshine On My Shoulders .... RCA 0213
840	Take Me Home, Country Roads .... RCA 0445
1565	Back Home Again................ RCA 10065
DEODATO	
903	Also Sprach Zarathustra (2001)... CTI 12
TERI DeSARIO with K.C.	
740	Yes, I'm Ready .... Casablanca 2227
JACKIE DeSHANNON	
1410	Put A Little Love In Your Heart .... Imperial 66385
JOHNNY DESMOND	
1141	The Yellow Rose Of Texas... Coral 61476
WILLIAM DeVAUGHN	
1376	Be Thankful For What You Got .... Roxbury 0236
DEXYS MIDNIGHT RUNNERS	
448	Come On Eileen .... Mercury 76189
NEIL DIAMOND	
329	You Don't Bring Me Flowers .... Columbia 10840 *BARBRA STREISAND & NEIL DIAMOND*
574	Cracklin' Rosie..................... Uni 55250
611	Song Sung Blue .... Uni 55326
683	Love On The Rocks .... Capitol 4939
1308	Sweet Caroline..................... Uni 55136
1455	I Am...I Said........................ Uni 55278
1466	Heartlight .... Columbia 03219
1575	Longfellow Serenade....... Columbia 10043
1807	Hello Again........................ Capitol 4960
1892	Holly Holy .... Uni 55175

RANK	Title . . . Label & No.
1932	Cherry, Cherry .... Bang 528

DIAMONDS

636	Little Darlin' .... Mercury 71060
1361	The Stroll .... Mercury 71242

DICK & DEEDEE

795	The Mountain's High .... Liberty 55350

MARK DINNING

318	Teen Angel .... MGM 12845

DION

373	Runaround Sue .... Laurie 3110
717	Ruby Baby .... Columbia 42662
855	The Wanderer .... Laurie 3115
1196	Lovers Who Wander .... Laurie 3123
1306	Abraham, Martin And John .... Laurie 3464
1836	Donna The Prima Donna .. Columbia 42852
1944	Drip Drop .... Columbia 42917

DION & THE BELMONTS

1154	Where Or When .... Laurie 3044
1664	A Teenager In Love .... Laurie 3027

DIRE STRAITS

1297	Sultans Of Swing .... Warner 8736

DIXIE CUPS

244	Chapel Of Love .... Red Bird 001

CARL DOBKINS, JR.

939	My Heart Is An Open Book . Decca 30803

DR. HOOK

1520	Sexy Eyes .... Capitol 4831
1574	Sylvia's Mother .... Columbia 45562
1766	When You're In Love With A Beautiful Woman .... Capitol 4705
1771	Sharing The Night Together . Capitol 4621
1774	Only Sixteen .... Capitol 4171
1782	The Cover Of 'Rolling Stone' .... Columbia 45732

BILL DOGGETT

666	Honky Tonk (Parts 1 & 2) .... King 4950

THOMAS DOLBY

1461	She Blinded Me With Science .... Capitol 5204

FATS DOMINO

669	Blueberry Hill .... Imperial 5407
991	I'm In Love Again .... Imperial 5386
1347	I'm Walkin' .... Imperial 5428
1643	Blue Monday .... Imperial 5417
1865	Valley Of Tears .... Imperial 5442
1885	Whole Lotta Loving .... Imperial 5553
1902	Walking To New Orleans .... Imperial 5675

BO DONALDSON & THE HEYWOODS

315	Billy, Don't Be A Hero .... ABC 11435

LONNIE DONEGAN

1715	Does Your Chewing Gum Lose It's Flavor (On The Bedpost Over Night). .... Dot 15911

RAL DONNER

1444	You Don't Know What You've Got (Until You Lose It) .... Gone 5108

RANK	Title . . . Label & No.

DONOVAN

615	Sunshine Superman .... Epic 10045
722	Mellow Yellow .... Epic 10098
1706	Hurdy Gurdy Man .... Epic 10345

DOOBIE BROTHERS

484	What A Fool Believes .... Warner 8725
541	Black Water .... Warner 8062
1564	Real Love .... Warner 49503

DOORS

178	Light My Fire .... Elektra 45615
399	Hello, I Love You .... Elektra 45635
1176	Touch Me .... Elektra 45646

JIMMY DORSEY

645	So Rare .... Fraternity 755

TOMMY DORSEY Orchestra

1997	Tea For Two Cha Cha .... Decca 30704

CARL DOUGLAS

323	Kung Fu Fighting .... 20th Century 2140

MIKE DOUGLAS

1952	The Men In My Little Girl's Life Epic 9876

DOVELLS

773	Bristol Stomp .... Parkway 827
1172	You Can't Sit Down .... Parkway 867

JOE DOWELL

560	Wooden Heart .... Smash 1708

DRAMATICS

1693	In The Rain .... Volt 4075

RUSTY DRAPER

1044	The Shifting, Whispering Sands .... Mercury 70696
1869	Freight Train .... Mercury 71102

DRIFTERS

197	Save The Last Dance For Me .... Atlantic 2071
851	There Goes My Baby .... Atlantic 2025
1406	Under The Boardwalk .... Atlantic 2237
1631	Up On The Roof .... Atlantic 2162

ROBBIE DUPREE

1769	Steal Away .... Elektra 46621

DURAN DURAN

289	The Reflex .... Capitol 5345
333	A View To A Kill .... Capitol 5475
659	The Wild Boys .... Capitol 5417
941	Hungry Like The Wolf .... Harvest 5195
965	Union Of The Snake .... Capitol 5290
1380	Is There Something I Should Know..... .... Capitol 5233

BOB DYLAN

824	Like A Rolling Stone .... Columbia 43346
912	Rainy Day Women #12 & 35 .... Columbia 43592

E

EAGLES

495	Hotel California .... Asylum 45386
501	Best Of My Love .... Asylum 45218

RANK	Title . . . Label & No.
530	One Of These Nights .... Asylum 45257
575	Heartache Tonight .... Asylum 46545
578	New Kid In Town.............. Asylum 45373
805	Lyin' Eyes .... Asylum 45279
1264	Take It To The Limit.......... Asylum 45293

EARTH, WIND & FIRE

489	Shining Star.................. Columbia 10090
768	After The Love Has Gone ..... ARC 11033
915	Let's Groove...................... ARC 02536
1554	Sing A Song .... Columbia 10251
1806	Boogie Wonderland .... ARC 10956 *EARTH, WIND & FIRE with THE EMOTIONS*

SHEENA EASTON

290	Morning Train (Nine To Five) .... EMI America 8071
1213	For Your Eyes Only .... Liberty 1418
1740	We've Got Tonight.............. Liberty 1492 *KENNY ROGERS & SHEENA EASTON*

DUANE EDDY

1303	Because They're Young........ Jamie 1156
1816	Rebel-'Rouser...................... Jamie 1104

EDISON LIGHTHOUSE

1500	Love Grows (Where My Rosemary Goes) .... Bell 858

DAVE EDMUNDS

1330	I Hear You Knocking .... MAM 3601

EDWARD BEAR

1032	Last Song .... Capitol 3452

JONATHAN EDWARDS

1244	Sunshine....................... Capricorn 8021

TOMMY EDWARDS

40	It's All In The Game .... MGM 12688

ELECTRIC LIGHT ORCHESTRA

1305	Don't Bring Me Down............. Jet 5060
1988	Telephone Line .... United Art. 1000

ELEGANTS

493	Little Star .... Apt 25005

YVONNE ELLIMAN

451	If I Can't Have You .... RSO 884

SHIRLEY ELLIS

1081	The Name Game .... Congress 230

EMOTIONS

59	Best Of My Love .... Columbia 10544
1806	Boogie Wonderland .... ARC 10956 *EARTH, WIND & FIRE with THE EMOTIONS*

ENGLAND DAN & JOHN FORD COLEY

735	I'd Really Love To See You Tonight.... .... Big Tree 16069

ESSEX

395	Easier Said Than Done...... Roulette 4494

DAVID ESSEX

1613	Rock On .... Columbia 45940

EURYTHMICS

430	Sweet Dreams (Are Made of This)...... .... RCA 13533
1275	Here Comes The Rain Again . RCA 13725
1636	Would I Lie To You? .... RCA 14078

BETTY EVERETT

1692	Let It Be Me .... Vee-Jay 613 *BETTY EVERETT & JERRY BUTLER*
1825	The Shoop Shoop Song (It's In His Kiss) .... Vee-Jay 585

EVERLY BROTHERS

66	All I Have To Do Is Dream . Cadence 1348
75	Cathy's Clown ....Warner 5151
97	Wake Up Little Susie......... Cadence 1337
510	Bird Dog .... Cadence 1350
647	Bye Bye Love .... Cadence 1315
880	Problems .... Cadence 1355
1243	('Til) I Kissed You .... Cadence 1369
1826	Crying In The Rain..............Warner 5250

EVERY MOTHERS' SON

1811	Come On Down To My Boat MGM 13733

EXCITERS

1324	Tell Him .... United Art. 544

EXILE

104	Kiss You All Over ....Warner 8589

F

SHELLEY FABARES

356	Johnny Angel.......................Colpix 621

FABIAN

1091	Tiger .... Chancellor 1037

PERCY FAITH

9	The Theme From 'A Summer Place ... . Columbia 41490

HAROLD FALTERMEYER

958	Axel F ....MCA 52536

DONNA FARGO

1532	Funny Face .... Dot 17429

JOSE FELICIANO

981	Light My Fire .... RCA 9550

FREDDY FENDER

470	Before The Next Teardrop Falls ....ABC/Dot 17540

FENDERMEN

1640	Mule Skinner Blues............. Soma 1137

FERRANTE & TEICHER

844	Exodus .... United Art. 274

ERNIE FIELD'S ORCH.

1368	In The Mood..................Rendezvous 110

5TH DIMENSION

50	Aquarius/Let The Sunshine In........... .... Soul City 772
211	Wedding Bell Blues............ Soul City 779
755	One Less Bell To Answer .... Bell 940
969	Stoned Soul Picnic .... Soul City 766
1980	Up-Up And Away............... Soul City 756

RANK **Title** . . . Label & No.

FIRST CLASS
1289 Beach Baby .... UK 49022
FIRST EDITION - see KENNY ROGERS
MISS TONI FISHER
1033 The Big Hurt .... Signet 275
FIVE AMERICANS
1709 Western Union .... Abnak 118
FIVE MAN ELECTRICAL BAND
1134 Signs .... Lionel 3213
FIXX
1369 One Thing Leads To Another. MCA 52264
ROBERTA FLACK
48 The First Time Ever I Saw Your Face.. .... Atlantic 2864
80 Killing Me Softly With His Song......... .... Atlantic 2940
556 Feel Like Makin' Love .... Atlantic 3025
ROBERTA FLACK & DONNY HATHAWAY
753 The Closer I Get To You..... Atlantic 3463
1691 Where Is The Love .... Atlantic 2879
FLEETWOOD MAC
502 Dreams .... Warner 8371
1025 Don't Stop .... Warner 8413
1206 Hold Me .... Warner 29966
1977 Sara .... Warner 49150
FLEETWOODS
133 Come Softly To Me .... Dolphin 1
491 Mr. Blue .... Dolton 5
FLOATERS
784 Float On .... ABC 12284
FLYING MACHINE
1679 Smile A Little Smile For Me Congress 6000
DAN FOGELBERG
743 Longer .... Full Moon 50824
FONTANE SISTERS
1156 Seventeen .... Dot 15386
TENNESSEE ERNIE FORD
16 Sixteen Tons .... Capitol 3262
FOREIGNER
287 I Want To Know What Love Is .... Atlantic 89596
635 Waiting For A Girl Like You . Atlantic 3868
754 Double Vision .... Atlantic 3514
1034 Hot Blooded .... Atlantic 3488
1214 Urgent .... Atlantic 3831
1266 Feels Like The First Time.... Atlantic 3394
1852 Cold As Ice .... Atlantic 3410
FOUNDATIONS
972 Build Me Up Buttercup .... Uni 55101
FOUR ACES
43 Love Is A Many-Splendored Thing...... .... Decca 29625
FOUR LADS
637 Moments To Remember .. Columbia 40539
649 No, Not Much! .... Columbia 40629
949 Standing On The Corner .. Columbia 40674

FOUR PREPS
684 26 Miles (Santa Catalina) ..... Capitol 3845
1065 Big Man .... Capitol 3960
FOUR SEASONS
77 Big Girls Don't Cry .... Vee-Jay 465
85 Sherry .... Vee-Jay 456
159 December, 1963 (Oh, What a Night).... .... Warner 8168
240 Walk Like A Man .... Vee-Jay 485
402 Rag Doll .... Philips 40211
979 Dawn (Go Away) .... Philips 40166
1013 Who Loves You .... Warner 8122
1150 Let's Hang On! .... Philips 40317
1184 Candy Girl .... Vee-Jay 539
1950 Ronnie .... Philips 40185
FOUR TOPS
367 Reach Out I'll Be There ...... Motown 1098
370 I Can't Help Myself .... Motown 1076
1299 Ain't No Woman (Like The One I've Got) .... Dunhill 4339
1341 Bernadette .... Motown 1104
1608 It's The Same Old Song...... Motown 1081
1842 Standing In The Shadows Of Love .... Motown 1102
PETER FRAMPTON
687 I'm In You .... A&M 1941
1788 Show Me The Way .... A&M 1795
CONNIE FRANCIS
316 Everybody's Somebody's Fool .... MGM 12899
330 My Heart Has A Mind Of Its Own .... MGM 12923
613 Don't Break The Heart That Loves You .... MGM 13059
761 My Happiness .... MGM 12738
1261 Who's Sorry Now .... MGM 12588
1397 Where The Boys Are .... MGM 12971
1489 Lipstick On Your Collar .... MGM 12793
1941 Together .... MGM 13019
ARETHA FRANKLIN
403 Respect .... Atlantic 2403
816 Chain Of Fools .... Atlantic 2464
819 Spanish Harlem .... Atlantic 2817
1115 Until You Come Back To Me (That's What I'm Gonna Do) .... Atlantic 2995
1127 Freeway Of Love .... Arista 9354
1449 Baby I Love You .... Atlantic 2427
1460 (Sweet Sweet Baby) Since You've Been Gone .... Atlantic 2486
1705 Day Dreaming .... Atlantic 2866
1843 The House That Jack Built .. Atlantic 2546
1924 Bridge Over Troubled Water Atlantic 2796
JOHN FRED & His Playboy Band
348 Judy In Disguise (With Glasses) .... Paula 282

RANK **Title** . . . Label & No.

FREDDIE & THE DREAMERS
411 I'm Telling You Now .... Tower 125
FREE
1382 All Right Now .... A&M 1206
FREE MOVEMENT
1612 I've Found Someone Of My Own .... Decca 32818
BOBBY FREEMAN
1589 C'mon And Swim .... Autumn 2
1651 Do You Want To Dance .... Josie 835
ERNIE FREEMAN
1374 Raunchy .... Imperial 5474
GLENN FREY
839 The Heat Is On .... MCA 52512
FRIENDS OF DISTINCTION
1149 Grazing In The Grass .... RCA 0107
1823 Love Or Let Me Be Lonely .... RCA 0319

G

GALLERY
1360 Nice To Be With You .... Sussex 232
GALE GARNETT
1242 We'll Sing In The Sunshine .... RCA 8388
MARVIN GAYE
27 I Heard It Through The Grapevine .... Tamla 54176
306 Let's Get It On .... Tamla 54234
511 Got To Give It Up - Pt. 1 .... Tamla 54280
704 What's Going On .... Tamla 54201
945 Sexual Healing .... Columbia 03302
1329 Mercy Mercy Me (The Ecology) .... Tamla 54207
1392 Too Busy Thinking About My Baby .... Tamla 54181
1583 Your Precious Love .... Tamla 54156
MARVIN GAYE & TAMMI TERRELL
1899 How Sweet It Is To Be Loved By You .... Tamla 54107
CRYSTAL GAYLE
671 Don't It Make My Brown Eyes Blue .... United Art. 1016
1955 You And I .... Elektra 69936
EDDIE RABBITT with CRYSTAL GAYLE
GLORIA GAYNOR
158 I Will Survive .... Polydor 14508
DAVID GEDDES
1432 Run Joey Run .... Big Tree 16044
J. GEILS BAND
33 Centerfold .... EMI America 8102
1220 Freeze-Frame .... EMI America 8108
GENESIS
1779 That's All! .... Atlantic 89724
BOBBIE GENTRY
119 Ode To Billie Joe .... Capitol 5950
GENTRYS
1422 Keep On Dancing .... MGM 13379

RANK **Title** . . . Label & No.

BARBARA GEORGE
1129 I Know (You Don't Love Me No More) .... A.F.O. 302
GERRY & THE PACEMAKERS
1331 Don't Let The Sun Catch You Crying .... Laurie 3251
1835 Ferry Across The Mersey .... Laurie 3284
STAN GETZ/ASTRUD GILBERTO
1590 The Girl From Ipanema .... Verve 10323
ANDY GIBB
20 Shadow Dancing .... RSO 893
89 I Just Want To Be Your Everything .... RSO 872
256 (Love Is) Thicker Than Water .... RSO 883
1221 Desire .... RSO 1019
1655 An Everlasting Love .... RSO 904
BARRY GIBB - see BARBRA STREISAND
NICK GILDER
416 Hot Child In The City .... Chrysalis 2226
TERRY GILKYSON & THE EASY RIDERS
1367 Marianne .... Columbia 40817
JIMMY GILMER & THE FIREBALLS
81 Sugar Shack .... Dot 16487
GO-GO'S
689 We Got The Beat .... I.R.S. 9903
ANDREW GOLD
1962 Lonely Boy .... Asylum 45384
BOBBY GOLDSBORO
82 Honey .... United Art. 50283
DICKIE GOODMAN
1456 Mr. Jaws .... Cash 451
BARRY GORDON with Art Mooney
1954 Nuttin' For Christmas .... MGM 12092
LESLEY GORE
390 It's My Party .... Mercury 72119
719 You Don't Own Me .... Mercury 72206
1597 Judy's Turn To Cry .... Mercury 72143
1670 She's A Fool .... Mercury 72180
CHARLIE GRACIE
331 Butterfly .... Cameo 105
BILLY GRAMMER
1363 Gotta Travel On .... Monument 400
GRAND FUNK RAILROAD
301 The Loco-Motion .... Capitol 3840
539 We're An American Band .... Capitol 3660
1177 Some Kind Of Wonderful .... Capitol 4002
1304 Bad Time .... Capitol 4046
EDDY GRANT
643 Electric Avenue .... Portrait 03793
GOGI GRANT
12 The Wayward Wind .... Era 1013
GRASS ROOTS
1667 Midnight Confessions .... Dunhill 4144
DOBIE GRAY
1621 Drift Away .... Decca 33057

RANK **Title** . . . Label & No.

R.B. GREAVES
872 Take A Letter Maria .... Atco 6714
AL GREEN
550 Let's Stay Together .... Hi 2202
1058 You Ought To Be With Me .... Hi 2227
1092 I'm Still In Love With You.......... Hi 2216
1435 Look What You Done For Me .... Hi 2211
NORMAN GREENBAUM
970 Spirit In The Sky .... Reprise 0885
LORNE GREENE
621 Ringo .... RCA 8444
HENRY GROSS
1738 Shannon .... Lifesong 45002
GUESS WHO
212 American Woman .... RCA 0325
1687 No Time............................ RCA 0300
1881 Clap For The Wolfman .... RCA 0324
1896 These Eyes .... RCA 0102
BONNIE GUITAR
1851 Dark Moon .... Dot 15550

H

BILL HALEY & His Comets
11 Rock Around The Clock...... Decca 29124
1730 See You Later, Alligator...... Decca 29791
DARYL HALL & JOHN OATES
105 Maneater .... RCA 13354
175 Kiss On My List .... RCA 12142
271 Private Eyes .... RCA 12296
272 Out Of Touch...................... RCA 13916
302 Rich Girl .... RCA 10860
463 I Can't Go For That (No Can Do)........ .... RCA 12357
658 Say It Isn't So .... RCA 13654
1256 Sara Smile .... RCA 10530
1482 You Make My Dreams.......... RCA 12217
1638 Method Of Modern Love....... RCA 13970
1878 Family Man .... RCA 13507
1969 One On One .... RCA 13421
1985 She's Gone .... Atlantic 3332
HAMILTON, JOE FRANK & REYNOLDS
543 Fallin' In Love .... Playboy 6024
1311 Don't Pull Your Love........... Dunhill 4276
GEORGE HAMILTON IV
1856 A Rose And A Baby Ruth ABC-Para. 9765
RUSS HAMILTON
1353 Rainbow .... Kapp 184
MARVIN HAMLISCH
1049 The Entertainer ....MCA 40174
ALBERT HAMMOND
1491 It Never Rains In Southern California .. ..Mums 6011
HAPPENINGS
980 I Got Rhythm ..................B.T. Puppy 527
1079 See You In September .....B.T. Puppy 520

RANK **Title** . . . Label & No.

MAJOR HARRIS
1487 Love Won't Let Me Wait ..... Atlantic 3248
RICHARD HARRIS
902 MacArthur Park.................. Dunhill 4134
ROLF HARRIS
1201 Tie Me Kangaroo Down, Sport Epic 9596
THURSTON HARRIS
1742 Little Bitty Pretty One .... Aladdin 3398
GEORGE HARRISON
140 My Sweet Lord .... Apple 2995
603 Give Me Love (Give Me Peace On Earth).............................. Apple 1862
703 All Those Years Ago ..... Dark Horse 49725
WILBERT HARRISON
350 Kansas City......................... Fury 1023
COREY HART
1010 Never Surrender........... EMI America 8268
DAN HARTMAN
1767 I Can Dream About You........MCA 52378
DONNY HATHAWAY - see ROBERTA FLACK
EDWIN HAWKINS' Singers
1339 Oh Happy Day ....Pavilion 20001
ISAAC HAYES
382 Theme From Shaft.......... Enterprise 9038
MURRAY HEAD
1123 One Night In Bangkok .... Chess 13988
ROY HEAD
827 Treat Her Right ....Back Beat 546
HEATWAVE
730 Boogie Nights .... Epic 50370
BOBBY HEBB
793 Sunny.............................. Philips 40365
BOBBY HELMS
1855 Jingle Bell Rock .... Decca 30513
DON HENLEY
also see Stevie Nicks
953 Dirty Laundry................... Asylum 69894
1619 The Boys Of Summer.........Geffen 29141
CLARENCE HENRY
1390 But I Do............................... Argo 5378
HERMAN'S HERMITS
248 Mrs. Brown You've Got A Lovely Daughter.......................... MGM 13341
634 I'm Henry VIII, I Am .... MGM 13367
794 Can't You Hear My Heartbeat........... .... MGM 13310
1205 Listen People..................... MGM 13462
1332 There's A Kind Of Hush....... MGM 13681
1454 Wonderful World .... MGM 13354
1601 Dandy.............................. MGM 13603
1698 Silhouettes .... MGM 13332
AL HIBBLER
1355 He .... Decca 29660
HIGHWAYMEN
337 Michael.......................... United Art. 258

RANK	Title . . . Label & No.
DAN HILL	
992	Sometimes When We Touch .... 20th Century 2355
HILLTOPPERS	
1144	Marianne .... Dot 15537
AL HIRT	
1383	Java .... RCA 8280
HOLLIES	
786	Long Cool Woman (In A Black Dress) .... Epic 10871
1499	Bus Stop .... Imperial 66186
1854	The Air That I Breathe .... Epic 11100
BUDDY HOLLY	
943	Peggy Sue .... Coral 61885
HOLLYWOOD ARGYLES	
589	Alley-Oop .... Lute 5905
EDDIE HOLMAN	
891	Hey There Lonely Girl .... ABC 11240
CLINT HOLMES	
741	Playground In My Mind .... Epic 10891
RUPERT HOLMES	
183	Escape (The Pina Colada Song) .... Infinity 50035
1800	Him .... MCA 41173
HONEYCOMBS	
1702	Have I The Right? .... Interphon 7707
HONEY CONE	
557	Want Ads .... Hot Wax 7011
HONEYDRIPPERS	
1121	Sea Of Love .... Es Paranza 99701
MARY HOPKIN	
711	Those Were The Days .... Apple 1801
JOHNNY HORTON	
44	The Battle Of New Orleans .... Columbia 41339
1132	Sink The Bismarck .... Columbia 41568
1352	North To Alaska .... Columbia 41782
HOT	
1760	Angel In Your Arms .... Big Tree 16085
HOT CHOCOLATE	
946	You Sexy Thing .... Big Tree 16047
1790	Every 1's A Winner .... Infinity 50002
THELMA HOUSTON	
436	Don't Leave Me This Way ... Tamla 54278
WHITNEY HOUSTON	
1118	You Give Good Love .... Arista 9274
HUES CORPORATION	
525	Rock The Boat .... RCA 0232
HUMAN LEAGUE	
155	Don't You Want Me .... A&M 2397
ENGELBERT HUMPERDINCK	
1223	Release Me (And Let Me Love Again) .... Parrot 40011
TAB HUNTER	
45	Young Love .... Dot 15533

RANK	Title . . . Label & No.
FERLIN HUSKY	
1210	Gone .... Capitol 3628
BRIAN HYLAND	
576	Itsy Bitsy Teenie Weenie Yellow Polkadot Bikini .... Leader 805
1012	Gypsy Woman .... Uni 55240
1074	Sealed With A Kiss .... ABC-Para. 10336

I

RANK	Title . . . Label & No.
JANIS IAN	
1011	At Seventeen .... Columbia 10154
IDES OF MARCH	
904	Vehicle .... Warner 7378
BILLY IDOL	
1263	Eyes Without A Face .... Chrysalis 42786
FRANK IFIELD	
1602	I Remember You .... Vee-Jay 457
JULIO IGLESIAS & WILLIE NELSON	
1624	To All The Girls I've Loved Before .... Columbia 04217
IMPALAS	
767	Sorry (I Ran All the Way Home) Cub 9022
IMPRESSIONS	
1409	It's All Right .... ABC-Para. 10487
JORGEN INGMANN	
769	Apache .... Atco 6184
JAMES INGRAM - see PATTI AUSTIN	
LUTHER INGRAM	
1045	(If Loving You Is Wrong) I Don't Want To Be Right .... KoKo 2111
INTRUDERS	
1819	Cowboys To Girls .... Gamble 214
ISLEY BROTHERS	
886	It's Your Thing .... T-Neck 901
1373	Fight The Power .... T-Neck 2256
1735	That Lady .... T-Neck 2251

J

RANK	Title . . . Label & No.
TERRY JACKS	
185	Seasons In The Sun .... Bell 45432
JOE JACKSON	
1727	Steppin' Out .... A&M 2428
MICHAEL JACKSON	
22	Billie Jean .... Epic 03509
41	Say Say Say .... Columbia 04168 *PAUL McCARTNEY & MICHAEL JACKSON*
100	Rock With You .... Epic 50797
165	Beat It .... Epic 03759
476	Don't Stop 'Til You Get Enough .... Epic 50742
567	Ben .... Motown 1207
695	The Girl Is Mine .... Epic 03288 *MICHAEL JACKSON/PAUL McCARTNEY*
811	Rockin' Robin .... Motown 1197
1317	Thriller .... Epic 04364
1402	Got To Be There .... Motown 1191

RANK **Title** . . . Label & No.

1570 Wanna Be Startin' Somethin' . Epic 03914

STONEWALL JACKSON

1245 Waterloo .... Columbia 41393

JACKSON 5

76 I'll Be There .... Motown 1171
383 ABC .... Motown 1163
384 The Love You Save .... Motown 1166
494 I Want You Back .... Motown 1157
721 Never Can Say Goodbye .... Motown 1179
742 Dancing Machine .... Motown 1286
831 Mama's Pearl .... Motown 1177
974 State Of Shock .... Epic 04503
1775 Enjoy Yourself .... Epic 50289
1959 Shake Your Body (Down To The Ground) .... Epic 50656
above 3 shown as The Jacksons

JAGGERZ

901 The Rapper .... Kama Sutra 502

JONI JAMES

1888 You Are My Love .... MGM 12066

SONNY JAMES

462 Young Love .... Capitol 3602

TOMMY JAMES

1419 Draggin' The Line .... Roulette 7103

TOMMY JAMES & THE SHONDELLS

340 Crimson And Clover .... Roulette 7028
407 Hanky Panky .... Roulette 4686
706 Crystal Blue Persuasion .... Roulette 7050
1139 Mony Mony .... Roulette 7008
1381 I Think We're Alone Now ... Roulette 4720

JAN & DEAN

391 Surf City .... Liberty 55580
1199 The Little Old Lady (From Pasadena) .... Liberty 55704

JAY & THE AMERICANS

1062 Come A Little Bit Closer ... United Art. 759
1420 Cara, Mia .... United Art. 881
1682 She Cried .... United Art. 415
1904 This Magic Moment .... United Art. 50475

JAY & THE TECHNIQUES

1803 Apples, Peaches, Pumpkin Pie .... Smash 2086

JAYNETTS

821 Sally, Go 'Round The Roses .... Tuff 369

JEFFERSON AIRPLANE

1675 Somebody To Love .... RCA 9140

JEFFERSON STARSHIP

963 Miracles .... Grunt 10367

JOAN JETT & THE BLACKHEARTS

25 I Love Rock 'N Roll .... Boardwalk 135

JIGSAW

1003 Sky High .... Chelsea 3022

JIVE FIVE

1021 My True Story .... Beltone 1006

RANK **Title** . . . Label & No.

BILLY JOEL

282 It's Still Rock And Roll To Me .... Columbia 11276
512 Tell Her About It .... Columbia 04012
916 Uptown Girl .... Columbia 04149
951 My Life .... Columbia 10853
985 Just The Way You Are .... Columbia 10646
1975 You May Be Right .... Columbia 11231

ELTON JOHN

117 Don't Go Breaking My Heart .... Rocket 40585
ELTON JOHN & KIKI DEE
202 Crocodile Rock .... MCA 40000
222 Island Girl .... MCA 40461
286 Philadelphia Freedom .... MCA 40364
381 Lucy In The Sky With Diamonds .... MCA 40344
509 Bennie And The Jets .... MCA 40198
698 Goodbye Yellow Brick Road .. MCA 40148
796 Don't Let The Sun Go Down On Me .... MCA 40259
875 Daniel .... MCA 40046
923 Little Jeannie .... MCA 41236
1354 I Guess That's Why They Call It The Blues .... Geffen 29460
1411 The Bitch Is Back .... MCA 40297
1426 Someone Saved My Life Tonight .... MCA 40421
1635 Sad Songs (Say So Much) .. Geffen 29292
1751 Sorry Seems To Be The Hardest Word .... MCA/Rocket 40645
1886 Rocket Man .... Uni 55328

ROBERT JOHN

424 Sad Eyes .... EMI America 8015
962 The Lion Sleeps Tonight ..... Atlantic 2846

JOHNNY & THE HURRICANES

1648 Red River Rock .... Warwick 509

SAMMY JOHNS

1653 Chevy Van .... Grc 2046

HOWARD JONES

1616 Things Can Only Get Better. Elektra 69651

JIMMY JONES

852 Handy Man .... Cub 9049
975 Good Timin' .... Cub 9067

JOE JONES

1189 You Talk Too Much .... Roulette 4304

RICKIE LEE JONES

1300 Chuck E.'s In Love .... Warner 8825

TOM JONES

883 She's A Lady .... Parrot 40058
1095 What's New Pussycat? .... Parrot 9765
1596 Without Love (There Is Nothing) .... Parrot 40045
1770 I'll Never Fall In Love Again. Parrot 40018

JANIS JOPLIN

364 Me And Bobby McGee .... Columbia 45314

RANK **Title** . . . Label & No.

JOURNEY
639 Open Arms .... Columbia 02687
1269 Who's Crying Now .... Columbia 02241

BILL JUSTIS
848 Raunchy .... Phillips 3519

K

BERT KAEMPFERT
200 Wonderland By Night .... Decca 31141

KAJAGOOGOO
1637 Too Shy .... EMI America 8161

KALIN TWINS
1566 When .... Decca 30642

KANSAS
1778 Dust In The Wind .... Kirshner 4274

KC & THE SUNSHINE BAND
346 That's The Way (I Like It) .... T.K. 1015
427 Please Don't Go .... T.K. 1035
442 I'm Your Boogie Man .... T.K. 1022
465 (Shake, Shake, Shake) Shake Your Booty .... T.K. 1019
593 Get Down Tonight .... T.K. 1009
686 Keep It Comin' Love .... T.K. 1023
740 Yes, I'm Ready .... Casablanca 2227
TERI DeSARIO with K.C.

ERNIE K-DOE
597 Mother-In-Law .... Minit 623

GRACE KELLY - see BING CROSBY

EDDIE KENDRICKS
307 Keep On Truckin' .... Tamla 54238
766 Boogie Down .... Tamla 54243

CHRIS KENNER
700 I Like It Like That .... Instant 3229

CHAKA KHAN
932 I Feel For You.................. Warner 29195

GREG KIHN Band
842 Jeopardy .... Beserkley 69847

ANDY KIM
522 Rock Me Gently .... Capitol 3895

KING FLOYD
1857 Groove Me .... Chimneyville 435

BEN E. KING
1315 Stand By Me .... Atco 6194
1689 Supernatural Thing .... Atlantic 3241

CAROLE KING
72 It's Too Late .... Ode 66015
870 Jazzman .... Ode 66101

CLAUDE KING
1882 Wolverton Mountain .... Columbia 42352

KINGSMEN
640 Louie Louie .... Wand 143
1442 The Jolly Green Giant .... Wand 172

KINGSTON TRIO
460 Tom Dooley .... Capitol 4049

RANK **Title** . . . Label & No.

KINKS
1802 Come Dancing .... Arista 1054
1839 Tired Of Waiting For You .... Reprise 0347
1976 You Really Got Me .... Reprise 0306
1981 All Day And All Of The Night Reprise 0334

KNACK
42 My Sharona .... Capitol 4731

GLADYS KNIGHT & THE PIPS
308 Midnight Train To Georgia ... Buddah 383
697 I Heard It Through The Grapevine .... Soul 35039
782 Neither One Of Us (Wants To Be The First To Say Goodbye) .... Soul 35098
1140 Best Thing That Ever Happened To Me .... Buddah 403
1291 I've Got To Use My Imagination .... Buddah 393
1555 On And On .... Buddah 423
1919 Every Beat Of My Heart .... Vee-Jay 386
shown only as the Pips

JEAN KNIGHT
778 Mr. Big Stuff .... Stax 0088

BUDDY KNOX
443 Party Doll .... Roulette 4002

KOOL & THE GANG
255 Celebration .... De-Lite 807
838 Joanna .... De-Lite 829
1359 Jungle Boogie .... De-Lite 559
1545 Too Hot .... De-Lite 802
1864 Hollywood Swinging .... De-Lite 561

L

LaBELLE
520 Lady Marmalade .... Epic 50048

FRANKIE LAINE
1112 Moonlight Gambler .... Columbia 40780

MAJOR LANCE
1595 Um, Um, Um, Um, Um, Um .... Okeh 7187

CYNDI LAUPER
296 Time After Time .... Portrait 04432
733 Girls Just Want To Have Fun............ .... Portrait 04120
959 She Bop .... Portrait 04516
1632 All Through The Night .... Portrait 04639

STEVE LAWRENCE
334 Go Away Little Girl .... Columbia 42601
1628 Party Doll .... Coral 61792

VICKI LAWRENCE
300 The Night The Lights Went Out In Georgia .... Bell 45303

LED ZEPPELIN
1391 Whole Lotta Love .... Atlantic 2690

BRENDA LEE
171 I'm Sorry .... Decca 31093
579 I Want To Be Wanted .... Decca 31149
1059 All Alone Am I .... Decca 31424

RANK **Title** . . . Label & No.

1071 Fool #1 ... Decca 31309
1251 Dum Dum ... Decca 31272
1349 Sweet Nothin's ... Decca 30967
1414 Break It To Me Gently ... Decca 31348
1831 You Can Depend On Me ... Decca 31231
1840 Everybody Loves Me But You ... Decca 31379
1911 That's All You Gotta Do ... Decca 31093
1921 Losing You ... Decca 31478

CURTIS LEE
1984 Pretty Little Angel Eyes ... Dunes 2007

DICKEY LEE
1817 Patches ... Smash 1758

JOHNNY LEE
1524 Lookin' For Love ... Full Moon 47004

LEFT BANKE
1699 Walk Away Renee ... Smash 2041

LEMON PIPERS
609 Green Tambourine ... Buddah 23

JOHN LENNON
60 (Just Like) Starting Over ... Geffen 49604
591 Whatever Gets You Thru The Night ... Apple 1874
682 Woman ... Geffen 49644
977 Instant Karma (We All Shine On) ... Apple 1818
1104 Imagine ... Apple 1840
1681 Nobody Told Me ... Polydor 817254

JULIAN LENNON
1652 Too Late For Goodbyes ... Atlantic 89589

KETTY LESTER
1683 Love Letters ... Era 3068

BARBARA LEWIS
1082 Hello Stranger ... Atlantic 2184

BOBBY LEWIS
23 Tossin' And Turnin' ... Beltone 1002

GARY LEWIS & The Playboys
400 This Diamond Ring ... Liberty 55756
828 Count Me In ... Liberty 55778
910 Save Your Heart For Me ... Liberty 55809
930 She's Just My Style ... Liberty 55846
1450 Everybody Loves A Clown ... Liberty 55818

HUEY LEWIS & THE NEWS
309 The Power Of Love ... Chrysalis 42876
1729 The Heart Of Rock & Roll Chrysalis 42782
1783 I Want A New Drug ... Chrysalis 42766
1799 If This Is It ... Chrysalis 42803
1970 Do You Believe In Love ... Chrysalis 2589

JERRY LEE LEWIS
655 Great Balls Of Fire ... Sun 281
984 Whole Lot Of Shakin' Going On Sun 267

RAMSEY LEWIS TRIO
1657 The "In" Crowd ... Argo 5506

RANK **Title** . . . Label & No.

GORDON LIGHTFOOT
524 Sundown ... Reprise 1194
750 The Wreck Of The Edmund Fitzgerald ... Reprise 1369
1496 If You Could Read My Mind Reprise 0974

BOB LIND
1586 Elusive Butterfly ... World Pac. 77808

LIPPS, INC.
110 Funkytown ... Casablanca 2233

LITTLE ANTHONY & THE IMPERIALS
1366 Tears On My Pillow ... End 1027
1749 Goin' Out Of My Head ... DCP 1119

LITTLE EVA
561 The Loco-Motion ... Dimension 1000

LITTLE RICHARD
1863 Long Tall Sally ... Specialty 572

LITTLE RIVER BAND
1009 Reminiscing ... Harvest 4605
1777 The Night Owls ... Capitol 5033
1786 Lonesome Loser ... Capitol 4748

LOBO
808 I'd Love You To Want Me ... Big Tree 147
1584 Me And You And A Dog Named Boo ... Big Tree 112

LOGGINS & MESSINA
1384 Your Mama Don't Dance .. Columbia 45719

DAVE LOGGINS
1549 Please Come To Boston ... Epic 11115

KENNY LOGGINS
176 Footloose ... Columbia 04310
1529 Whenever I Call You 'Friend' ... Columbia 10794
1990 I'm Alright ... Columbia 11317

LOLITA
1639 Sailor (Your Home Is The Sea). Kapp 349

LAURIE LONDON
121 He's Got The Whole World (In His Hands) ... Capitol 3891

LOOKING GLASS
552 Brandy (You're A Fine Girl) ... Epic 10874

TRINI LOPEZ
976 If I Had A Hammer ... Reprise 20198

LOS BRAVOS
1333 Black Is Black ... Press 60002

LOS INDIOS TABAJARAS
1905 Maria Elena ... RCA 8216

LOVE UNLIMITED ORCHESTRA
453 Love's Theme ... 20th Century 2069

LOVIN' SPOONFUL
251 Summer In The City ... Kama Sutra 211
820 Daydream ... Kama Sutra 208
826 Did You Ever Have To Make Up Your Mind? ... Kama Sutra 209

JIM LOWE
161 The Green Door ... Dot 15486

RANK **Title** . . . Label & No.

L.T.D.

1236 (Every Time I Turn Around) Back In Love Again........................A&M 1974

ROBIN LUKE

1647 Susie Darlin'........................Dot 15781

LULU

73 To Sir With Love.................Epic 10187

ARTHUR LYMAN GROUP

1439 Yellow Bird..........................Hi Fi 5024

FRANKIE LYMON & The Teenagers

1734 Why Do Fools Fall In Love......Gee 1002

M

M

434 Pop Muzik............................Sire 49033

BYRON MacGREGOR

1445 Americans......................Westbound 222

MARY MacGREGOR

275 Torn Between Two Lovers Ariola Am. 7638

LONNIE MACK

1696 Memphis........................Fraternity 906

GISELE MacKENZIE

1364 Hard To Get..........................X 0137

MADONNA

47 Like A Virgin........................Sire 29210

472 Crazy For You..................Geffen 29051

771 Material Girl........................Sire 29083

1387 Lucky Star...........................Sire 29177

1654 Angel..................................Sire 29008

MAIN INGREDIENT

1135 Everybody Plays The Fool...... RCA 0731

MAMAS & THE PAPAS

246 Monday, Monday................Dunhill 4026

723 Dedicated To The One I Love Dunhill 4077

1379 California Dreamin'.............Dunhill 4020

1593 Words Of Love...................Dunhill 4057

1723 I Saw Her Again.................Dunhill 4031

1725 Creeque Alley...................Dunhill 4083

MELISSA MANCHESTER

1474 You Should Hear How She Talks About You.........................Arista 0676

1874 Midnight Blue......................Arista 0116

HENRY MANCINI

374 Love Theme From Romeo & Juliet...RCA 0131

MANFRED MANN

385 Do Wah Diddy Diddy............Ascot 2157

MANFRED MANN'S EARTH BAND

481 Blinded By The Light...........Warner 8252

CHUCK MANGIONE

1346 Feels So Good.....................A&M 2001

MANHATTAN TRANSFER

1961 Boy From New York City.... Atlantic 3816

MANHATTANS

260 Kiss And Say Goodbye.... Columbia 10310

1475 Shining Star.................. Columbia 11222

BARRY MANILOW

477 I Write The Songs...............Arista 0157

505 Looks Like We Made It.........Arista 0244

565 Mandy.................................Bell 45613

952 Can't Smile Without You.......Arista 0305

1793 Could It Be Magic...............Arista 0126

MARCELS

236 Blue Moon..........................Colpix 186

LITTLE PEGGY MARCH

237 I Will Follow Him.................RCA 8139

ERNIE MARESCA

1912 Shout! Shout! (Knock Yourself Out)..Seville 117

TEENA MARIE

1350 Lovergirl............................Epic 04619

MARKETTS

1080 Out Of Limits.....................Warner 5391

MAR-KEYS

1072 Last Night..........................Satellite 107

MARTHA & THE VANDELLAS

802 Dancing In The Street..........Gordy 7033

1312 Heat Wave.........................Gordy 7022

DEAN MARTIN

39 Memories Are Made Of This. Capitol 3295

577 Everybody Loves Somebody Reprise 0281

1229 Return To Me......................Capitol 3894

1947 The Door Is Still Open To My Heart..................................Reprise 0307

AL MARTINO

1153 I Love You Because............Capitol 4930

MARVELETTES

445 Please Mr. Postman...........Tamla 54046

MARY JANE GIRLS

1960 In My House.......................Gordy 1741

HUGH MASEKELA

406 Grazing In The Grass...........Uni 55066

BARBARA MASON

1686 Yes, I'm Ready....................Arctic 105

JOHNNY MATHIS

418 Chances Are.................Columbia 40993

523 Too Much, Too Little, Too Late..........................Columbia 10693

JOHNNY MATHIS/DENIECE WILLIAMS

1610 It's Not For Me To Say.... Columbia 40851

1927 Gina.............................Columbia 42582

PAUL MAURIAT

69 Love Is Blue.....................Philips 40495

CURTIS MAYFIELD

1296 Freddie's Dead.................Curtom 1975

C.W. McCALL

568 Convoy............................MGM 14839

PETER McCANN

1517 Do You Wanna Make Love..........................20th Century 2335

RANK	Title . . . Label & No.
PAUL McCARTNEY & WINGS	
26	Ebony And Ivory .... Columbia 02860 *PAUL McCARTNEY & STEVIE WONDER*
41	Say Say Say .... Columbia 04168 *PAUL McCARTNEY & MICHAEL JACKSON*
68	Silly Love Songs .... Capitol 4256
125	My Love .... Apple 1861
182	Coming Up (Live at Glasgow) .... Columbia 11263
324	With A Little Luck .... Capitol 4559
521	Band On The Run.............. Apple 1873
602	Listen To What The Man Said........... ....Capitol 4091
610	Uncle Albert/Admiral Halsey .. Apple 1837
695	The Girl Is Mine .... Epic 03288 *MICHAEL JACKSON/PAUL McCARTNEY*
712	Live And Let Die.................. Apple 1863
929	Let 'Em In ....Capitol 4293
1190	Junior's Farm .... Apple 1875
1492	Goodnight Tonight .... Columbia 10939
1587	Another Day .... Apple 1829
1789	No More Lonely Nights.... Columbia 04581
MARILYN McCOO & BILLY DAVIS, JR.	
428	You Don't Have To Be A Star (To Be In My Show)......................... ABC 12208
VAN McCOY	
507	The Hustle ....Avco 4653
McCOYS	
604	Hang On Sloopy...................Bang 506
GEORGE McCRAE	
339	Rock Your Baby.......................T.K. 1004
GENE McDANIELS	
1054	A Hundred Pounds Of Clay . Liberty 55308
1697	Tower Of Strength ....Liberty 55371
MICHAEL McDONALD	
1235	I Keep Forgettin' (Every Time You're Near)........................... Warner 29933
MAUREEN McGOVERN	
368	The Morning After ....20th Century 2010
McGUIRE SISTERS	
103	Sugartime .... Coral 61924
1677	Something's Gotta Give .... Coral 61423
BARRY McGUIRE	
625	Eve Of Destruction .... Dunhill 4009
SCOTT McKENZIE	
1224	San Francisco (Be Sure To Wear Flowers In Your Hair)........... Ode 103
DON McLEAN	
120	American Pie - Parts I & II............... ....United Art. 50856
1485	Crying .... Millennium 11799
CLYDE McPHATTER	
1847	A Lover's Question .... Atlantic 1199
SISTER JANET MEAD	
1423	The Lord's Prayer................ A&M 1491

RANK	Title . . . Label & No.
MECO	
305	Star Wars Theme/Cantina Band .... Millennium 604
MELANIE	
196	Brand New Key ....Neighborhood 4201
1871	Lay Down (Candles In The Rain) .... Buddah 167
HAROLD MELVIN & THE BLUENOTES	
1041	If You Don't Know Me By Now ....Phil. Int. 3520
MEN AT WORK	
99	Down Under .... Columbia 03303
426	Who Can It Be Now? ...... Columbia 02888
1145	Overkill .... Columbia 03795
1812	It's A Mistake .... Columbia 03959
MEN WITHOUT HATS	
917	The Safety Dance .... Backstreet 52232
SERGIO MENDES	
1215	Never Gonna Let You Go....... A&M 2540
SERGIO MENDES & BRASIL '66	
1408	The Look Of Love .... A&M 924
1926	The Fool On The Hill............. A&M 961
MERCY	
813	Love (Can Make You Happy) . Sundi 6811
MFSB featuring The Three Degrees	
319	TSOP (The Sound Of Philadelphia) ....Phil. Int. 3540
LEE MICHAELS	
1743	Do You Know What I Mean .... A&M 1262
BETTE MIDLER	
937	The Rose .... Atlantic 3656
MITCH MILLER	
46	The Yellow Rose Of Texas............... .... Columbia 40540
NED MILLER	
1828	From A Jack To A King .... Fabor 114
ROGER MILLER	
1415	King Of The Road.............. Smash 1965
STEVE MILLER Band	
262	Abracadabra ....Capitol 5126
479	The Joker ....Capitol 3732
515	Rock'n Me ....Capitol 4323
752	Fly Like An Eagle ....Capitol 4372
FRANK MILLS	
1124	Music Box Dancer .... Polydor 14517
STEPHANIE MILLS	
1765	Never Knew Love Like This Before..... ....20th Century 2460
RONNIE MILSAP	
1458	(There's) No Gettin' Over Me . RCA 12264
GARNET MIMMS & The Enchanters	
1407	Cry Baby......................... United Art. 629
MINDBENDERS	
628	Game Of Love ....Fontana 1509
814	A Groovy Kind Of Love ......Fontana 1541

RANK	Title . . . Label & No.

MIRACLES
343 The Tears Of A Clown........ Tamla 54199
421 Love Machine .... Tamla 54262
867 Shop Around .... Tamla 54034
1246 I Second That Emotion .... Tamla 54159

GUY MITCHELL
2 Singing The Blues .... Columbia 40769
294 Heartaches By The Number .... Columbia 41476

DOMENICO MODUGNO
79 Nel Blu Dipinto Di Blu (Volare) .... Decca 30677

MOMENTS
1053 Love On A Two-Way Street... Stang 5012

MONKEES
29 I'm A Believer .... Colgems 1002
149 Daydream Believer............ Colgems 1012
581 Last Train To Clarksville .... Colgems 1001
911 A Little Bit Me, A Little Bit You .... Colgems 1004
1102 Pleasant Valley Sunday ..... Colgems 1007
1103 Valleri .... Colgems 1019

MONOTONES
1642 Book Of Love .... Argo 5290

LOU MONTE
1721 Pepino The Italian Mouse... Reprise 20106

HUGO MONTENEGRO
843 The Good, The Bad And The Ugly...... .... RCA 9423

CHRIS MONTEZ
1318 Let's Dance .... Monogram 505

MOODY BLUES
762 Nights In White Satin.......... Deram 85023

DORTHY MOORE
922 Misty Blue........................Malaco 1029

JANE MORGAN
1956 Fascination..........................Kapp 191

JAYE P. MORGAN
1891 The Longest Walk................. RCA 6182

MARIA MULDAUR
1848 Midnight At The Oasis........ Reprise 1183

MUNGO JERRY
1180 In The Summertime............... Janus 125

MURMAIDS
1075 Popsicles And Icicles ... Chattahoochee 628

MICHAEL MURPHEY
1020 Wildfire .... Epic 50084

WALTER MURPHY
419 A Fifth Of Beethoven....... Private S. 45073

ANNE MURRAY
431 You Needed Me ....Capitol 4574

MUSIC EXPLOSION
775 Little Bit O'Soul...................Laurie 3380

N

NAPOLEON XIV
1203 They're Coming To Take Me Away, Ha-Haaa! ....Warner 5831

JOHNNY NASH
118 I Can See Clearly Now .... Epic 10902
1568 Hold Me Tight........................JAD 207

DAVID NAUGHTON
1509 Makin' It .... RSO 916

RICKY NELSON
342 Travelin' Man...................Imperial 5741
351 Poor Little Fool ....Imperial 5528
696 Stood Up ....Imperial 5483
850 A Teenager's Romance ....Verve 10047
1119 Be-Bop Baby ....Imperial 5463
1440 Believe What You Say ....Imperial 5503
1700 Young World ....Imperial 5805
1717 Teen Age Idol ....Imperial 5864
1746 Never Be Anyone Else But You.......... ....Imperial 5565
1785 Garden Party .... Decca 32980
1936 It's Up To You ....Imperial 5901
1945 For You .... Decca 31574
1968 Lonesome Town................Imperial 5545

SANDY NELSON
1292 Teen Beat .... Original Sound 5

WILLIE NELSON
1479 Always On My Mind........ Columbia 02741
1624 To All The Girls I've Loved Before...... .... Columbia 04217
JULIO IGLESIAS & WILLIE NELSON

NENA
841 99 Luftballons .... Epic 04108

AARON NEVILLE
892 Tell It Like It Is.................... Par-Lo 101

NEWBEATS
817 Bread And Butter .... Hickory 1269

NEW EDITION
1348 Cool It Now ....MCA 52455

NEW VAUDEVILLE BAND
214 Winchester Cathedral ....Fontana 1562

RANDY NEWMAN
688 Short People ....Warner 8492

JUICE NEWTON
728 Queen Of Hearts ....Capitol 4997
1216 Angel Of The Morning ....Capitol 4976
1987 The Sweetest Thing (I've Ever Known) ....Capitol 5046

WAYNE NEWTON
1277 Daddy Don't You Walk So Fast.......... ....Chelsea 0100

RANK **Title** . . . Label & No.

OLIVIA NEWTON-JOHN
3 Physical .... MCA 51182
107 Magic .... MCA 41247
273 I Honestly Love You .... MCA 40280
437 You're The One That I Want .... RSO 891
JOHN TRAVOLTA & OLIVA NEWTON-JOHN
569 Have You Never Been Mellow MCA 40349
924 Heart Attack .... MCA 52100
1006 A Little More Love .... MCA 40975
1014 Hopelessly Devoted To You .... RSO 903
1055 Please Mr. Please .... MCA 40418
1498 Make A Move On Me .... MCA 52000
1534 If You Love Me (Let Me Know) .... MCA 40209
1542 Twist Of Fate .... MCA 52284
1558 Summer Nights .... RSO 906
JOHN TRAVOLTA & OLIVIA NEWTON-JOHN
1859 Let Me Be There .... MCA 40101

PAUL NICHOLAS
1731 Heaven On The 7th Floor .... RSO 878

STEVIE NICKS
914 Stop Draggin' My Heart Around .... Modern 7336
with Tom Petty
1633 Stand Back .... Modern 99863
1739 Leather And Lace .... Modern 7341
with Don Henley

MAXINE NIGHTINGALE
751 Right Back Where We Started From .... United Art. 752
1514 Lead Me On .... Windsong 11530

NIGHT RANGER
1510 Sister Christian .... MCA 52350

NILSSON
122 Without You .... RCA 0604
1937 Everybody's Talkin' .... RCA 0161

1910 FRUITGUM CO.
1222 Simon Says .... Buddah 24
1581 1, 2, 3, Red Light .... Buddah 54
1694 Indian Giver .... Buddah 91

CLIFF NOBLES & Co.
713 The Horse .... Phil. L.A. 313

KENNY NOLAN
1106 I Like Dreamin' .... 20th Century 2287

CHRIS NORMAN - see SUZI QUATRO

O

OAK RIDGE BOYS
1462 Elvira .... MCA 51084

OCEAN
887 Put Your Hand In The Hand .... Kama Sutra 519

BILLY OCEAN
261 Caribbean Queen .... Jive 9199
846 Loverboy .... Jive 9284

RANK **Title** . . . Label & No.

1267 Suddenly .... Jive 9323

ALAN O'DAY
432 Undercover Angel .... Pacific 001

OHIO EXPRESS
1249 Yummy Yummy Yummy .... Buddah 38

OHIO PLAYERS
545 Fire .... Mercury 73643
553 Love Rollercoaster .... Mercury 73734

O'JAYS
596 Love Train .... Phil. Int. 3524
1162 Back Stabbers .... Phil. Int. 3517
1280 Use Ta Be My Girl .... Phil. Int. 3642
1550 I Love Music .... Phil. Int. 3577

O'KAYSIONS
1470 Girl Watcher .... ABC 11094

OLIVER
798 Jean .... Crewe 334
1088 Good Morning Starshine ...... Jubilee 5659

ROY ORBISON
213 Oh, Pretty Woman .... Monument 851
528 Running Scared .... Monument 438
845 Only The Lonely .... Monument 421
864 Crying .... Monument 447
1446 Dream Baby .... Monument 456
1585 Mean Woman Blues .... Monument 824

ORLEANS
1644 Still The One .... Asylum 45336
1870 Dance With Me .... Asylum 45261

ORLONS
806 The Wah Watusi .... Cameo 218
1185 South Street .... Cameo 243
1399 Don't Hang Up .... Cameo 231

DONNY OSMOND
215 Go Away Little Girl .... MGM 14285
1191 Puppy Love .... MGM 14367

DONNY & MARIE OSMOND
1401 I'm Leaving It (All) Up To You .... MGM 14735

MARIE OSMOND
1560 Paper Roses .... MGM 14609

OSMONDS
83 One Bad Apple .... MGM 14193
978 Yo-Yo .... MGM 14295
1309 Down By The Lazy River ..... MGM 14324

GILBERT O'SULLIVAN
49 Alone Again (Naturally) .... MAM 3619
774 Clair .... MAM 3626

OUTSIDERS
1576 Time Won't Let Me .... Capitol 5573

OZARK MOUNTAIN DAREDEVILS
1005 Jackie Blue .... A&M 1654

P

PABLO CRUISE
1763 Whatcha Gonna Do? .... A&M 1920
1867 Love Will Find A Way .... A&M 2048

RANK	Title . . . Label & No.	
PATTI PAGE		
727	Allegheny Moon	Mercury 70878
1110	Old Cape Cod	Mercury 71101
PAPER LACE		
547	The Night Chicago Died	Mercury 73492
PARIS SISTERS		
1671	I Love How You Love Me	Gregmark 6
RAY PARKER JR.		
186	Ghostbusters	Arista 9212
1270	The Other Woman	Arista 0669
1257	A Woman Needs Love (Just Like You Do)	Arista 0592
ALAN PARSONS Project		
936	Eye In The Sky	Arista 0696
BILL PARSONS		
868	The All American Boy	Fraternity 835
DOLLY PARTON		
259	9 To 5	RCA 12133
263	Islands In The Stream *KENNY ROGERS & DOLLY PARTON*	RCA 13615
1019	Here You Come Again	RCA 11123
PARTRIDGE FAMILY		
190	I Think I Love You	Bell 910
1925	Doesn't Somebody Want To Be Wanted	Bell 963
PATIENCE & PRUDENCE		
1344	Tonight You Belong To Me	Liberty 55022
PAUL & PAULA		
218	Hey Paula	Philips 40084
1951	Young Lovers	Philips 40096
BILLY PAUL		
209	Me And Mrs. Jones	Phil. Int. 3521
FREDA PAYNE		
1120	Band Of Gold	Invictus 9075
PEACHES & HERB		
109	Reunited	Polydor 14547
1463	Shake Your Groove Thing	Polydor 14514
EMILIO PERICOLI		
1909	Al Di La'	Warner 5259
CARL PERKINS		
651	Blue Suede Shoes	Sun 234
STEVE PERRY		
1122	Oh Sherrie	Columbia 04391
PETER & GORDON		
619	A World Without Love	Capitol 5175
1910	Lady Godiva	Capitol 5740
PETER, PAUL & MARY		
526	Leaving On A Jet Plane	Warner 7340
876	Blowin' In The Wind	Warner 5368
893	Puff The Magic Dragon	Warner 5348
PAUL PETERSEN		
1884	My Dad	Colpix 663
TOM PETTY - see STEVIE NICKS		
PHIL PHILLIPS		
764	Sea Of Love	Mercury 71465

RANK	Title . . . Label & No.	
BOBBY 'BORIS' PICKETT & The Crypt-Kickers		
252	Monster Mash	Garpax 44167
WILSON PICKETT		
1948	Land Of 1000 Dances	Atlantic 2348
PILOT		
1629	Magic	EMI 3992
PIPS - see GLADYS KNIGHT		
PINK FLOYD		
98	Another Brick In The Wall (Part II)	Columbia 11187
GENE PITNEY		
894	Only Love Can Break A Heart	Musicor 1022
1434	(The Man Who Shot) Liberty Valance	Musicor 1020
PLATTERS		
57	My Prayer	Mercury 70893
191	Smoke Gets In Your Eyes	Mercury 71383
265	The Great Pretender	Mercury 70753
529	Twilight Time	Mercury 71289
1230	(You've Got) The Magic Touch	Mercury 70819
1481	Only You (And You Alone)	Mercury 70633
PLAYER		
153	Baby Come Back	RSO 879
PLAYMATES		
1298	Beep Beep	Roulette 4115
POINTER SISTERS		
677	Slow Hand	Planet 47929
738	Fire	Planet 45901
933	He's So Shy	Planet 47916
989	Jump (For My Love)	Planet 13780
1626	Automatic	Planet 13730
1732	Neutron Dance	Planet 13951
POLICE		
15	Every Breath You Take	A&M 2542
1015	Every Little Thing She Does Is Magic	A&M 2371
1047	King Of Pain	A&M 2569
POPPY FAMILY featuring Susan Jacks		
770	Which Way You Goin' Billy?	London 129
POWER STATION		
1792	Some Like It Hot	Capitol 5444
PEREZ PRADO		
461	Patricia	RCA 7245
PRATT & McCLAIN		
1580	Happy Days	Reprise 1351
ELVIS PRESLEY		
1	Don't Be Cruel/Hound Dog	RCA 6604
5	All Shook Up	RCA 6870
13	Heartbreak Hotel	RCA 6420
19	Jailhouse Rock	RCA 7035
21	(Let Me Be Your) Teddy Bear	RCA 7000
52	Are You Lonesome To-night?	RCA 7810
58	Love Me Tender	RCA 6643

RANK	Title . . . Label & No.
63	It's Now Or Never .... RCA 7777
64	Don't .... RCA 7150
131	Stuck On You .... RCA 7740
203	Too Much .... RCA 6800
345	Hard Headed Woman .... RCA 7280
380	A Big Hunk O' Love .... RCA 7600
392	Good Luck Charm .... RCA 7992
401	Surrender .... RCA 7850
435	I Want You, I Need You, I Love You ... . RCA 6540
580	Suspicious Minds .... RCA 9764
644	Return To Sender .... RCA 8100
756	Love Me .... RCA 992
871	Wear My Ring Around Your Neck....... .... RCA 7240
878	Burning Love .... RCA 0769
881	(Now and Then There's) A Fool Such As I .... RCA 7506
884	Can't Help Falling In Love ...... RCA 7968
1099	(You're the) Devil In Disguise.. RCA 8188
1171	Crying In The Chapel .... RCA 0643
1182	In The Ghetto .... RCA 9741
1284	One Night .... RCA 7410
1430	I Need Your Love Tonight ...... RCA 7506
1452	(Marie's the Name) His Latest Flame... .... RCA 7908
1701	Little Sister .... RCA 7908
1719	She's Not You .... RCA 8041
1726	I Feel So Bad .... RCA 7880
1917	Don't Cry Daddy .... RCA 9768

BILLY PRESTON

280	Will It Go Round In Circles ..... A&M 1411
513	Nothing From Nothing .... A&M 1544
857	Outa-Space .... A&M 1320
1282	Space Race .... A&M 1463

BILLY PRESTON & SYREETA

1209 With You I'm Born Again .... Motown 1477

JOHNNY PRESTON

160 Running Bear .... Mercury 71474

PRETENDERS

1477 Back On The Chain Gang ...... Sire 29840

LLOYD PRICE

116	Stagger Lee .... ABC-Para. 9972
690	Personality .... ABC-Para. 10018
1070	I'm Gonna Get Married ... ABC-Para. 10032

PRINCE

61	When Doves Cry .... Warner 29286
312	Let's Go Crazy .... Warner 29216
783	Purple Rain .... Warner 29174
858	Raspberry Beret .... Paisley P. 28972
1772	Little Red Corvette .... Warner 29746

PROCOL HARUM

1588 A Whiter Shade Of Pale .... Deram 7507

GARY PUCKETT & THE UNION GAP

705	Young Girl .... Columbia 44450
812	Lady Willpower .... Columbia 44547

RANK	Title . . . Label & No.
1241	Woman, Woman .... Columbia 44297

JAMES & BOBBY PURIFY

1821 I'm Your Puppet .... Bell 648

Q

QUARTERFLASH

988 Harden My Heart .... Geffen 49824

SUZI QUATRO & CHRIS NORMAN

1262 Stumblin' In .... RSO 917

QUEEN

113	Crazy Little Thing Called Love .... Elektra 46579
154	Another One Bites The Dust Elektra 47031
1225	We Are The Champions ...... Elektra 45441

? (QUESTION MARK) & THE MYSTERIANS

582 96 Tears .... Cameo 428

QUIET RIOT

1523 Cum On Feel The Noize ..... Pasha 04005

R

EDDIE RABBITT

258	I Love A Rainy Night .... Elektra 47066
1505	Drivin' My Life Away .... Elektra 46656
1518	Step By Step .... Elektra 47174
1955	You And I .... Elektra 69936
	EDDIE RABBITT with CRYSTAL GAYLE

GERRY RAFFERTY

638 Baker Street .... United Art. 1192

RARE EARTH

1274 Get Ready .... Rare Earth 5012

RASCALS

84	People Got To Be Free .... Atlantic 2537
147	Groovin' .... Atlantic 2401
600	Good Lovin' .... Atlantic 2321
1086	A Beautiful Morning .... Atlantic 2493
1337	How Can I Be Sure .... Atlantic 2438

RASPBERRIES

1548 Go All The Way .... Capitol 3348

LOU RAWLS

749 You'll Never Find Another Love Like Mine .... Phil. Int. 3592

RAY, GOODMAN & BROWN

1543 Special Lady .... Polydor 2033

JOHNNIE RAY

834 Just Walking In The Rain . Columbia 40729

RAYS

1007 Silhouettes .... Cameo 117

REDBONE

1511 Come And Get Your Love ..... Epic 11035

OTIS REDDING

130 (Sittin' On) The Dock Of The Bay .... Volt 157

HELEN REDDY

457	I Am Woman .... Capitol 3350
485	Delta Dawn .... Capitol 3645
540	Angie Baby .... Capitol 3972

RANK **Title** . . . Label & No.

1048 Leave Me Alone (Ruby Red Dress) ..... Capitol 3768

DELLA REESE

853 Don't You Know .... RCA 7591

JIM REEVES

679 He'll Have To Go .... RCA 7643

REFLECTIONS

1933 (Just Like) Romeo & Juliet Golden World 9

DIANE RENAY

1834 Navy Blue .... 20th Century 456

MIKE RENO & ANN WILSON

1999 Almost Paradise...Love Theme From Footloose .... Columbia 04418

REO SPEEDWAGON

198 Can't Fight This Feeling .... Epic 04713
420 Keep On Loving You .... Epic 50953
1530 Take It On The Run .... Epic 01054
1972 Keep The Fire Burnin' .... Epic 02967

PAUL REVERE & THE RAIDERS

455 Indian Reservation (The Lament Of The Cherokee Reservation Indian).... Columbia 45332
1328 Good Thing .... Columbia 43907
1403 Kicks .... Columbia 43556
1724 Him Or Me - What's It Gonna Be?...... Columbia 44094
1949 Hungry .... Columbia 43678

DEBBIE REYNOLDS

56 Tammy .... Coral 61851

JODY REYNOLDS

1551 Endless Sleep .... Demon 1507

RHYTHM HERITAGE

439 Theme From S.W.A.T. .... ABC 12135

CHARLIE RICH

274 The Most Beautiful Girl......... Epic 11040

CLIFF RICHARD

1733 Devil Woman .... Rocket 40574
1998 We Don't Talk Anymore. EMI America 8025

LIONEL RICHIE

6 Endless Love .... Motown 1519
DIANA ROSS & LIONEL RICHIE
101 All Night Long (All Night)..... Motown 1698
267 Hello .... Motown 1722
320 Truly .... Motown 1644
1018 Stuck On You .... Motown 1746
1281 You Are .... Motown 1657
1658 My Love .... Motown 1677

NELSON RIDDLE

90 Lisbon Antigua .... Capitol 3287

RIGHTEOUS BROTHERS

243 (You're My) Soul And Inspiration........ Verve 10383
347 You've Lost That Lovin' Feelin'......... Philles 124

RANK **Title** . . . Label & No.

1043 Rock And Roll Heaven .... Haven 7002
1322 Unchained Melody .... Philles 129
1609 Ebb Tide .... Philles 130

JEANNIE C. RILEY

608 Harper Valley P.T.A. .... Plantation 3

RIP CHORDS

1313 Hey Little Cobra .... Columbia 42921

MINNIE RIPERTON

518 Lovin' You............................ Epic 50057

JOHNNY RIVERS

583 Poor Side Of Town .... Imperial 66205
822 Memphis .... Imperial 66032
1100 Baby I Need Your Lovin'.... Imperial 66227
1200 Secret Agent Man............ Imperial 66159
1860 Rockin' Pneumonia - Boogie Woogie Flu .... United Art. 50960
1983 Seventh Son .... Imperial 66112

RIVIERAS

1720 California Sun .... Riviera 1401

MARTY ROBBINS

276 El Paso .... Columbia 41511
836 A White Sport Coat (And A Pink Carnation) .... Columbia 40864
1163 Don't Worry .... Columbia 41922

DON ROBERTSON

1737 The Happy Whistler .... Capitol 3391

SMOKEY ROBINSON

674 Being With You .... Tamla 54321
1211 Cruisin' .... Tamla 54306

ROCKWELL

691 Somebody's Watching Me... Motown 1702

JIMMIE RODGERS

93 Honeycomb .... Roulette 4015
961 Secretly .... Roulette 4070
1116 Kisses Sweeter Than Wine. Roulette 4031

TOMMY ROE

138 Dizzy .... ABC 11164
378 Sheila .... ABC-Para. 10329
1076 Everybody .... ABC-Para. 10478
1918 Hooray For Hazel .... ABC 10852

KENNY ROGERS

35 Lady .... Liberty 1380
263 Islands In The Stream .... RCA 13615
KENNY ROGERS & DOLLY PARTON
926 Coward Of The County.... United Art. 1327
1024 I Don't Need You............... Liberty 1415
1233 Don't Fall In Love With A Dreamer ..... United Art. 1345
KENNY ROGERS with KIM CARNES
1539 Lucille .... United Art. 929
1557 She Believes In Me......... United Art. 1273
1740 We've Got Tonight............. Liberty 1492
KENNY ROGERS & SHEENA EASTON

RANK	Title . . . Label & No.
KENNY ROGERS & THE FIRST EDITION	
1606	Just Dropped In (To See What Condition My Condition Was In) .... Reprise 0655
1827	Ruby, Don't Take Your Love To Town .... Reprise 0829
ROLLING STONES	
134	Honky Tonk Women .... London 910
142	(I Can't Get No) Satisfaction London 9766
398	Brown Sugar .... Rolling S. 19100
404	Get Off Of My Cloud .... London 9792
409	Paint It, Black .... London 901
478	Miss You .... Rolling S. 19307
555	Angie .... Rolling S. 19105
623	Ruby Tuesday.................... London 904
676	Start Me Up.................. Rolling S. 21003
724	19th Nervous Breakdown.... London 9823
982	Jumpin' Jack Flash .... London 908
1016	Emotional Rescue........... Rolling S. 20001
1755	Time Is On My Side .... London 9708
1953	As Tears Go By .... London 9808
ROMANTICS	
935	Talking In Your Sleep ...... Nemperor 04135
DON RONDO	
2000	White Silver Sands............. Jubilee 5288
RONETTES	
718	Be My Baby .... Philles 116
RONNY & THE DAYTONAS	
1427	G.T.O. .... Mala 481
LINDA RONSTADT	
570	You're No Good .... Capitol 3990
787	When Will I Be Loved.......... Capitol 4050
921	Blue Bayou .... Asylum 45431
1467	It's So Easy.................... Asylum 45438
1674	Heat Wave .... Asylum 45282
ROOFTOP SINGERS	
393	Walk Right In .... Vanguard 35017
ROSE ROYCE	
446	Car Wash .... MCA 40615
DAVID ROSE	
535	The Stripper .... MGM 13064
ROSIE & The Originals	
1690	Angel Baby..................... Highland 1011
DIANA ROSS	
6	Endless Love.................... Motown 1519 *DIANA ROSS & LIONEL RICHIE*
92	Upside Down .... Motown 1494
227	Ain't No Mountain High Enough .... Motown 1169
321	Love Hangover.................. Motown 1392
466	Touch Me In The Morning... Motown 1239
537	Theme From Mahogany (Do You Know Where You're Going To) .... Motown 1377
1480	I'm Coming Out................. Motown 1491
1965	Why Do Fools Fall In Love .... RCA 12349

RANK	Title . . . Label & No.
DAVID LEE ROTH	
1155	California Girls .... Warner 29102
ROYAL GUARDSMEN	
664	Snoopy Vs. The Red Baron... Laurie 3366
ROYAL TEENS	
1051	Short Shorts .... ABC-Para. 9882
RUBY & THE ROMANTICS	
617	Our Day Will Come .... Kapp 501
RUFUS	
966	Tell Me Something Good ...... ABC 11427
1625	Sweet Thing .... ABC 12149
TODD RUNDGREN	
1630	Hello It's Me .... Bearsville 0009
MERRILEE RUSH & The Turnabouts	
1973	Angel Of The Morning .... Bell 705
BOBBY RYDELL	
865	Wild One............................ Cameo 171
1388	Forget Him .... Cameo 280
1400	Volare .... Cameo 179
1710	Swingin' School .... Cameo 175
1798	We Got Love .... Cameo 169
MITCH RYDER & The Detroit Wheels	
1219	Devil With A Blue Dress On & Good Golly Miss Molly........... New Voice 817
1942	Sock It To Me-Baby! .... New Voice 820

S

RANK	Title . . . Label & No.
SADE	
1533	Smooth Operator............. Portrait 04807
SSgt BARRY SADLER	
86	The Ballad Of The Green Berets .... RCA 8739
SAFARIS	
1795	Image Of A Girl .... Eldo 101
CRISPIAN ST. PETERS	
1252	The Pied Piper .... Jamie 1320
KYU SAKAMOTO	
232	Sukiyaki .... Capitol 4945
SAM & DAVE	
708	Soul Man .... Stax 231
SAM THE SHAM & The Pharaohs	
759	Wooly Bully .... MGM 13322
803	Lil' Red Riding Hood .... MGM 13506
TOMMY SANDS	
772	Teen-Age Crush .... Capitol 3639
SAMANTHA SANG	
986	Emotion .... Private S. 45178
SANTANA	
1319	Black Magic Woman .... Columbia 45270
SANTO & JOHNNY	
322	Sleep Walk .... Canadian A. 103
LEO SAYER	
464	You Make Me Feel Like Dancing .... Warner 8283
486	When I Need You .... Warner 8332
642	More Than I Can Say .... Warner 49565

RANK	Title . . . Label & No.	
BOZ SCAGGS		
993	Lowdown	Columbia 10367
SCANDAL featuring Patty Smyth		
1993	The Warrior	Columbia 04424
JOEY SCARBURY		
731	Theme From 'Greatest American Hero' (Believe It Or Not)	Elektra 47147
JACK SCOTT		
1040	Burning Bridges	Top Rank 2041
1126	My True Love	Carlton 462
1468	What In The World's Come Over You..	Top Rank 2028
LINDA SCOTT		
1174	I've Told Every Little Star	Canadian A. 123
SEALS & CROFTS		
1762	Get Closer	Warner 8190
1794	Diamond Girl	Warner 7708
1796	Summer Breeze	Warner 7606
SEARCHERS		
1077	Love Potion Number Nine	Kapp 27
JOHN SEBASTIAN		
605	Welcome Back	Reprise 1349
NEIL SEDAKA		
234	Bad Blood	Rocket 40460
375	Breaking Up Is Hard To Do	RCA 8046
482	Laughter In The Rain	Rocket 40313
1398	Calendar Girl	RCA 7829
1600	Next Door To An Angel	RCA 8086
1750	Happy Birthday, Sweet Sixteen	RCA 7957
SEEKERS		
781	Georgy Girl	Capitol 5756
1428	I'll Never Find Another You	Capitol 5383
BOB SEGER		
650	Shame On The Moon	Capitol 5187
1273	Night Moves	Capitol 4369
1375	Still The Same	Capitol 4581
1490	Against The Wind	Capitol 4863
1540	Tryin' To Live My Life Without You	Capitol 5042
1808	Fire Lake	Capitol 4836
MICHAEL SEMBELLO		
277	Maniac	Casablanca 812516
SENSATIONS		
1283	Let Me In	Argo 5405
SERENDIPITY SINGERS		
1818	Don't Let The Rain Come Down (Crooked Little Man)	Philips 40175
DAVID SEVILLE		
189	Witch Doctor	Liberty 55132
SHANGRI-LAS		
622	Leader Of The Pack	Red Bird 014
1504	Remember (Walkin' In The Sand)	Red Bird 008
1837	I Can Never Go Home Anymore	Red Bird 043
DEL SHANNON		
129	Runaway	Big Top 3067
1582	Hats Off To Larry	Big Top 3075
DEE DEE SHARP		
758	Mashed Potato Time	Cameo 212
1703	Ride!	Cameo 230
SHEP & THE LIMELITES		
895	Daddy's Home	Hull 740
ALLAN SHERMAN		
725	Hello Mudduh, Hello Fadduh!	Warner 5378
BOBBY SHERMAN		
1087	Little Woman	Metromedia 121
1495	Julie, Do Ya Love Me	Metromedia 194
SHIRELLES		
229	Soldier Boy	Scepter 1228
310	Will You Love Me Tomorrow	Scepter 1211
1008	Dedicated To The One I Love	Scepter 1203
1338	Mama Said	Scepter 1217
1412	Foolish Little Girl	Scepter 1248
SHOCKING BLUE		
594	Venus	Colossus 108
TROY SHONDELL		
1916	This Time	Liberty 55353
SILHOUETTES		
361	Get A Job	Ember 1029
SILVER CONVENTION		
205	Fly, Robin, Fly	Midland I. 10339
681	Get Up And Boogie (That's Right)	Midland I. 10571
SIMON & GARFUNKEL		
54	Bridge Over Troubled Water	Columbia 45079
241	Mrs. Robinson	Columbia 44511
376	The Sounds Of Silence	Columbia 43396
1097	I Am A Rock	Columbia 43617
1417	Cecilia	Columbia 45133
1591	Homeward Bound	Columbia 43511
CARLY SIMON		
201	You're So Vain	Elektra 45824
675	Nobody Does It Better	Elektra 45413
1656	Mockingbird *CARLY SIMON & JAMES TAYLOR*	Elektra 45880
1797	You Belong To Me	Elektra 45477
PAUL SIMON		
206	50 Ways To Leave Your Lover	Columbia 10270
804	Kodachrome	Columbia 45859
863	Loves Me Like A Rock	Columbia 45907
1424	Mother And Child Reunion	Columbia 45547
1627	Slip Slidin' Away	Columbia 10630
1745	Late In The Evening	Warner 49511
SIMPLE MINDS		
458	Don't You (Forget About Me)	A&M 2703

RANK **Title** . . . Label & No.

FRANK SINATRA

148 Somethin' Stupid .... Reprise 0561
NANCY & FRANK SINATRA
281 Learnin' The Blues .... Capitol 3102
590 Strangers In The Night .... Reprise 0470
833 All The Way .... Capitol 3793
1125 Hey! Jealous Lover .... Capitol 3552
1335 That's Life .... Reprise 0531
1488 Love And Marriage .... Capitol 3260
1876 Witchcraft .... Capitol 3859

NANCY SINATRA

148 Somethin' Stupid .... Reprise 0561
NANCY & FRANK SINATRA
601 These Boots Are Made For Walkin' .... Reprise 0432
1502 Sugar Town .... Reprise 0527

SINGING NUN

144 Dominique .... Philips 40152

SISTER SLEDGE

757 We Are Family .... Cotillion 44251

PERCY SLEDGE

397 When A Man Loves A Woman .... Atlantic 2326

SLY & THE FAMILY STONE

123 Everyday People .... Epic 10407
228 Family Affair .... Epic 10805
387 Thank You (Falettinme Be Mice Elf Agin) .... Epic 10555
779 Hot Fun In The Summertime.. Epic 10497

MILLIE SMALL

906 My Boy Lollipop .... Smash 1893

SMITH

1497 Baby It's You .... Dunhill 4206

HURRICANE SMITH

1165 Oh, Babe, What Would You Say? .... Capitol 3383

O.C. SMITH

861 Little Green Apples .... Columbia 44616

PHOEBE SNOW

1645 Poetry Man .... Shelter 40353

SONNY & CHER

238 I Got You Babe .... Atco 6359
1838 The Beat Goes On .... Atco 6461

S.O.S. BAND

1001 Take Your Time (Do It Right) .. Tabu 5522

SOUL SURVIVORS

1394 Expressway To Your Heart Crimson 1010

DAVID SOUL

503 Don't Give Up On Us ...... Private S. 45129

JIMMY SOUL

379 If You Wanna Be Happy .... S.P.Q.R. 3305

J.D. SOUTHER

1963 You're Only Lonely .... Columbia 11079

SPANDAU BALLET

1218 True .... Chrysalis 42720

SPINNERS

496 Then Came You .... Atlantic 3202
DIONNE WARWICKE & SPINNERS
680 The Rubberband Man .... Atlantic 3355
732 Working My Way Back To You/Forgive Me, Girl .... Atlantic 3637
1061 I'll Be Around .... Atlantic 2904
1232 Cupid/I've Loved You For A Long Time .... Atlantic 3664
1301 Could It Be I'm Falling In Love .... Atlantic 2927
1547 They Just Can't Stop It the (Games People Play) .... Atlantic 3284

DUSTY SPRINGFIELD

1431 You Don't Have To Say You Love Me. .... Philips 40371
1754 Wishin' And Hopin' .... Philips 40207

RICK SPRINGFIELD

253 Jessie's Girl .... RCA 12201
653 Don't Talk To Strangers .... RCA 13070
1562 Love Somebody .... RCA 13738

BRUCE SPRINGSTEEN

654 Dancing In The Dark .... Columbia 04463
1459 Hungry Heart .... Columbia 11391
1641 Glory Days .... Columbia 04924
1781 I'm On Fire .... Columbia 04772

JIM STAFFORD

1111 Spiders & Snakes .... MGM 14648

TERRY STAFFORD

1063 Suspicion .... Crusader 101

STAPLE SINGERS

572 I'll Take You There .... Stax 0125
584 Let's Do It Again .... Curtom 0109

STARBUCK

997 Moonlight Feels Right ..... Private S. 45039

STARLAND VOCAL BAND

299 Afternoon Delight .... Windsong 10588

EDWIN STARR

216 War .... Gordy 7101
1913 Twenty-Five Miles .... Gordy 7083

KAY STARR

31 Rock And Roll Waltz .... RCA 6359

RINGO STARR

563 Photograph .... Apple 1865
585 You're Sixteen .... Apple 1870
1083 No No Song .... Apple 1880
1327 It Don't Come Easy .... Apple 1831
1684 Oh My My .... Apple 1872
1922 Only You .... Apple 1876

STARS ON 45

473 Stars on 45 (Medley) .... Radio 3810

STATLER BROTHERS

1433 Flowers On The Wall .... Columbia 43315

STEALERS WHEEL

1866 Stuck In The Middle With You. A&M 1416

RANK **Title** . . . Label & No.

STEAM
349 Na Na Hey Hey Kiss Him Goodbye..... .... Fontana 1667

STEELY DAN
1371 Rikki Don't Lose That Number........... .... ABC 11439
1744 Do It Again........ ABC 11338

STEPPENWOLF
715 Born To Be Wild .... Dunhill 4138
1146 Magic Carpet Ride........ Dunhill 4161

CAT STEVENS
1820 Morning Has Broken........ A&M 1335
1914 Another Saturday Night .... A&M 1602
1979 Peace Train........ A&M 1291

CONNIE STEVENS
1109 Sixteen Reasons .... Warner 5137
1321 Kookie Kookie (Lend Me Your Comb) . ... Warner 5047
EDWARD BYRNES & CONNIE STEVENS

DODIE STEVENS
1017 Pink Shoe Laces .... Crystalette 724

RAY STEVENS
207 The Streak .... Barnaby 600
362 Everything Is Beautiful........ Barnaby 2011
1598 Ahab, The Arab........ Mercury 71966

AMII STEWART
488 Knock On Wood........ Ariola 7736

JOHN STEWART
1546 Gold........ RSO 931

ROD STEWART
14 Tonight's The Night (Gonna Be Alright) .... Warner 8262
71 Maggie May .... Mercury 73224
115 Da Ya Think I'm Sexy?........ Warner 8724
1228 You're In My Heart (The Final Acclaim) .... Warner 8475
1464 Young Turks........ Warner 49843
1527 Passion .... Warner 49617
1791 Infatuation........ Warner 29256

STING
1026 If You Love Somebody Set Them Free .... A&M 2738

MORRIS STOLOFF
157 Moonglow and Theme From 'Picnic' ... . Decca 29888

STORIES
317 Brother Louie........ Kama Sutra 577

GALE STORM
693 I Hear You Knocking........ Dot 15412
1351 Dark Moon........ Dot 15558
1663 Memories Are Made Of This... Dot 15436
1787 Ivory Tower........ Dot 15458
1810 Teen Age Prayer .... Dot 15436

STRAWBERRY ALARM CLOCK
554 Incense And Peppermints ...... Uni 55018

RANK **Title** . . . Label & No.

STRAY CATS
956 Stray Cat Strut........ EMI America 8122
1569 (She's) Sexy + 17........ EMI America 8168

BARBRA STREISAND
164 Love Theme From 'A Star Is Born' (Evergreen) .... Columbia 10450
167 Woman In Love........ Columbia 11364
174 The Way We Were........ Columbia 45944
329 You Don't Bring Me Flowers .... Columbia 10840
BARBRA STREISAND & NEIL DIAMOND
357 No More Tears (Enough Is Enough).... .... Columbia 11125
BARBRA STREISAND/DONNA SUMMER
927 The Main Event/Fight...... Columbia 11008
994 Guilty .... Columbia 11390
BARBRA STREISAND & BARRY GIBB
1285 My Heart Belongs To Me. Columbia 10555
1541 People........ Columbia 42965
1868 Stoney End .... Columbia 45236

STRING-A-LONGS
1046 Wheels .... Warwick 603

STYLISTICS
734 You Make Me Feel Brand New Avco 4634
1142 Betcha By Golly, Wow........ Avco 4591
1688 Break Up To Make Up .... Avco 4611

STYX
311 Babe........ A&M 2188
925 The Best Of Times .... A&M 2300
1022 Mr. Roboto........ A&M 2525
1804 Lady........ Wooden N. 10102
1877 Don't Let It End........ A&M 2543

SUGARLOAF
1037 Green-Eyed Lady........ Liberty 56183

DONNA SUMMER
65 Bad Girls .... Casablanca 988
180 Hot Stuff........ Casablanca 978
187 MacArthur Park........ Casablanca 939
357 No More Tears (Enough Is Enough).... .... Columbia 11125
BARBRA STREISAND/DONNA SUMMER
747 Dim All The Lights .... Casablanca 2201
763 Love To Love You Baby .... Oasis 401
944 She Works Hard For The Money........ .... Mercury 812370
950 The Wanderer........ Geffen 49563
1002 Last Dance........ Casablanca 926
1234 Heaven Knows........ Casablanca 959
1552 On The Radio .... Casablanca 2236
1850 I Feel Love .... Casablanca 884

SUPERTRAMP
1728 The Logical Song .... A&M 2128

SUPREMES
146 Baby Love........ Motown 1066
341 Love Child........ Motown 1135
371 Come See About Me........ Motown 1068

RANK	Title . . . Label & No.
372	Where Did Our Love Go ..... Motown 1060
389	You Can't Hurry Love......... Motown 1097
405	Stop! In The Name Of Love. Motown 1074
408	You Keep Me Hangin' On ... Motown 1101
413	I Hear A Symphony........... Motown 1083
551	Someday We'll Be Together Motown 1156
626	Love Is Here And Now You're Gone ... . Motown 1103
627	The Happening .... Motown 1107
629	Back In My Arms Again ...... Motown 1075
810	I'm Gonna Make You Love Me.......... .... Motown 1137 *SUPREMES & TEMPTATIONS*
825	Reflections .... Motown 1111
1603	My World Is Empty Without You......... .... Motown 1089

SURFARIS

832	Wipe Out............................ Dot 16479

SURVIVOR

37	Eye Of The Tiger .... Scotti Br. 02912
1362	The Search Is Over......... Scotti Br. 04871

BILLY SWAN

327	I Can Help..................... Monument 8621

SWEET

942	Little Willy .... Bell 45251
1614	Ballroom Blitz .... Capitol 4055
1659	Fox On The Run .... Capitol 4157

SYLVERS

471	Boogie Fever .... Capitol 4179
1508	Hot Line.......................... Capitol 4336

SYLVIA

1004	Pillow Talk .... Vibration 521

SYREETA - see BILLY PRESTON

T

TACO

1271	Puttin' On The Ritz .... RCA 13574

TARRIERS

1365	The Banana Boat Song .... Glory 249

TASTE OF HONEY

173	Boogie Oogie Oogie........... Capitol 4565
938	Sukiyaki.......................... Capitol 4953

JAMES TAYLOR

598	You've Got A Friend .... Warner 7498
967	Fire And Rain .... Warner 7423
1278	Handy Man.................... Columbia 10557
1573	How Sweet It Is (To Be Loved By You)............................. Warner 8109
1656	Mockingbird .... Elektra 45880 *CARLY SIMON & JAMES TAYLOR*

JOHNNIE TAYLOR

124	Disco Lady .... Columbia 10281
1577	Who's Making Love .... Stax 0009

R. DEAN TAYLOR

1567	Indiana Wants Me.......... Rare Earth 5013

T-BONES

1181	No Matter What Shape (Your Stomach's In) .... Liberty 55836

TEARS FOR FEARS

193	Shout .... Mercury 880294
268	Everybody Wants To Rule The World.. .... Mercury 58130

TEDDY BEARS

172	To Know Him, Is To Love Him . Dore 503

TEE SET

1708	Ma Belle Amie .... Colossus 107

NINO TEMPO & APRIL STEVENS

586	Deep Purple .... Atco 6273

TEMPTATIONS

328	I Can't Get Next To You .... Gordy 7093
358	Just My Imagination............ Gordy 7105
564	Papa Was A Rollin' Stone ..... Gordy 7121
612	My Girl .... Gordy 7038
810	I'm Gonna Make You Love Me.......... .... Motown 1137 *SUPREMES & TEMPTATIONS*
971	Ball Of Confusion .... Gordy 7099
1197	Beauty Is Only Skin Deep ..... Gordy 7055
1248	I Wish It Would Rain .... Gordy 7068
1829	Run Away Child, Running Wild.......... .... Gordy 7084
1830	Cloud Nine .... Gordy 7081
1928	You're My Everything .... Gordy 7063

10cc

699	I'm Not In Love .... Mercury 73678
1537	The Things We Do For Love............ .... Mercury 73875

TAMMI TERRELL - see MARVIN GAYE

JOE TEX

746	I Gotcha.............................. Dial 1010
1604	Hold What You've Got............ Dial 4001

B.J. THOMAS

111	Raindrops Keep Fallin' On My Head ... . Scepter 12265
514	(Hey Won't You Play) Another Somebody Done Somebody Wrong Song .... ABC 12054
1563	Hooked On A Feeling .... Scepter 12230

TIMMY THOMAS

1168	Why Can't We Live Together Glades 1703

THOMPSON TWINS

999	Hold Me Now .... Arista 9164

SUE THOMPSON

1152	Norman .... Hickory 1159
1680	Sad Movies (Make Me Cry) . Hickory 1153

THREE DEGREES

319	TSOP (The Sound Of Philadelphia) .... Phil. Int. 3540 *MFSB featuring The Three Degrees*
856	When Will I See You Again.. Phil. Int. 3550

RANK	Title . . . Label & No.
THREE DOG NIGHT	
51	Joy To The World.............. Dunhill 4272
359	Mama Told Me (Not To Come)........... Dunhill 4239
632	Black & White.................... Dunhill 4317
1148	Shambala.......................... Dunhill 4352
1255	An Old Fashioned Love Song Dunhill 4294
1320	Easy To Be Hard................ Dunhill 4203
1370	The Show Must Go On........ Dunhill 4382
1494	One.................................. Dunhill 4191
1592	Never Been To Spain.......... Dunhill 4299
JOHNNY THUNDER	
1448	Loop De Loop................... Diamond 129
JOHNNY TILLOTSON	
877	Poetry In Motion............... Cadence 1384
1170	It Keeps Right On A-Hurtin' Cadence 1418
ART & DOTTY TODD	
1879	Chanson D'Amour (Song Of Love)...... Era 1064
TOKENS	
217	The Lion Sleeps Tonight........ RCA 7954
TOMMY TUTONE	
1226	867-5309/Jenny .... Columbia 02646
TORNADOES	
210	Telstar.............................. London 9561
TOTO	
467	Africa .... Columbia 03335
641	Rosanna .... Columbia 02811
1521	Hold The Line .... Columbia 10830
TOYS	
709	A Lover's Concerto.......... DynoVoice 209
TRASHMEN	
1325	Surfin' Bird........................ Garrett 4002
JOHN TRAVOLTA - see OLIVIA NEWTON-JOHN	
TROGGS	
410	Wild Thing.........................Fontana 1548
ANDREA TRUE Connection	
1345	More, More, More .... Buddah 515
TUNE WEAVERS	
1634	Happy, Happy Birthday Baby Checker 872
IKE & TINA TURNER	
1421	Proud Mary ....Liberty 56216
SAMMY TURNER	
1131	Lavender-Blue ....Big Top 3016
TINA TURNER	
156	What's Love Got To Do With It .... Capitol 5354
1525	Better Be Good To Me ....Capitol 5387
TURTLES	
219	Happy Together .... White Whale 244
1101	She'd Rather Be With Me White Whale 249
1931	Elenore .... White Whale 276
1934	You Showed Me............ White Whale 292

RANK	Title . . . Label & No.
CONWAY TWITTY	
283	It's Only Make Believe......... MGM 12677
1889	Lonely Blue Boy................. MGM 12857
BONNIE TYLER	
91	Total Eclipse Of The Heart Columbia 03906
1000	It's A Heartache .... RCA 11249
TYMES	
587	So Much In Love .... Parkway 871
U	
UNDISPUTED TRUTH	
1029	Smiling Faces Sometimes .....Gordy 7108
USA for AFRICA	
126	We Are The World .... Columbia 04839
V	
RITCHIE VALENS	
736	Donna .... Del-Fi 4110
FRANKIE VALLI	
279	Grease .... RSO 897
447	My Eyes Adored You ......Private S. 45003
862	Can't Take My Eyes Off You Philips 40446
1915	Swearin' To God ....Private S. 45021
LEROY VAN DYKE	
1493	Walk On By .... Mercury 71834
VAN HALEN	
62	Jump.............................. Warner 29384
VANGELIS	
422	Chariots Of Fire - Titles ...... Polydor 2189
VANILLA FUDGE	
1875	You Keep Me Hangin' On ...... Atco 6590
VANITY FARE	
1519	Hitchin' A Ride ....Page One 21029
GINO VANNELLI	
1272	I Just Wanna Stop .... A&M 2072
1736	Living Inside Myself .... Arista 0588
RANDY VANWARMER	
1276	Just When I Needed You Most .... Bearsville 0334
BILLY VAUGHN	
1469	The Shifting Whispering Sands Dot 15409
1473	Sail Along Silvery Moon......... Dot 15661
BOBBY VEE	
225	Take Good Care Of My Baby .... Liberty 55354
873	Run To Him......................Liberty 55388
968	Come Back When You Grow Up .... Liberty 55964
1078	The Night Has A Thousand Eyes........ Liberty 55521
1784	Devil Or Angel...................Liberty 55270
1897	Rubber Ball ....Liberty 55287
VENTURES	
854	Walk--Don't Run..................Dolton 25
1413	Hawaii Five-O ....Liberty 56068
LARRY VERNE	
616	Mr. Custer........................... Era 3024

RANK	Title . . . Label & No.
VILLAGE PEOPLE	
670	Y.M.C.A. .... Casablanca 945
1030	In The Navy .... Casablanca 973
VILLAGE STOMPERS	
888	Washington Square .... Epic 9617
GENE VINCENT & His Blue Caps	
1964	Be-Bop-A-Lula .... Capitol 3450
BOBBY VINTON	
137	Roses Are Red (My Love) ...... Epic 9509
145	There! I've Said It Again .... Epic 9638
221	Blue Velvet .... Epic 9614
571	Mr. Lonely .... Epic 9730
1042	My Melody Of Love .... ABC 12022
1186	Blue On Blue .... Epic 9593
1752	Please Love Me Forever .... Epic 10228
VIRTUES	
1561	Guitar Boogie Shuffle .... Hunt 324
VOGUES	
1310	Five O'Clock World .... Co & Ce 232
1443	You're The One .... Co & Ce 229

W

RANK	Title . . . Label & No.
ADAM WADE	
1599	The Writing On The Wall .... Coed 550
JACK WAGNER	
744	All I Need .... Qwest 29238
JOHN WAITE	
438	Missing You .... EMI America 8212
JR. WALKER & THE ALL STARS	
1316	Shotgun .... Soul 35008
1389	What Does It Take (To Win Your Love) .... Soul 35062
WAR	
792	The Cisco Kid .... United Art. 163
1117	Spill The Wine .... MGM 14118 *ERIC BURDON & WAR*
1858	Why Can't We Be Friends? United Art. 629
ANITA WARD	
288	Ring My Bell .... Juana 3422
JENNIFER WARNES	
177	Up Where We Belong .... Island 99996 *JOE COCKER & JENNIFER WARNES*
1773	Right Time Of The Night .... Arista 0223
DIONNE WARWICK	
496	Then Came You .... Atlantic 3202 *DIONNE WARWICKE & SPINNERS*
663	(Theme From) Valley Of The Dolls .... Scepter 12203
1429	I Say A Little Prayer .... Scepter 12203
1507	I'll Never Love This Way Again .... Arista 0419
1822	Walk On By .... Scepter 1274
1940	I'll Never Fall In Love Again Scepter 12273
1978	This Girl's In Love With You .... Scepter 12241

RANK	Title . . . Label & No.
DINAH WASHINGTON - see BROOK BENTON	
GROVER WASHINGTON, JR./BILL WITHERS	
678	Just The Two Of Us .... Elektra 47103
THOMAS WAYNE	
1465	Tragedy .... Fernwood 109
WE FIVE	
1161	You Were On My Mind .... A&M 770
ERIC WEISSBERG & STEVE MANDELL	
662	Dueling Banjos .... Warner 7659
LENNY WELCH	
1294	Since I Fell For You .... Cadence 1439
LAWRENCE WELK	
332	Calcutta .... Dot 16161
MARY WELLS	
360	My Guy .... Motown 1056
WHAM!	
170	Wake Me Up Before You Go-Go .... Columbia 04552
181	Careless Whisper .... Columbia 04691
303	Everything She Wants ..... Columbia 04840
BARRY WHITE	
624	Can't Get Enough Of Your Love, Babe .... 20th Century 2120
789	You're The First, The Last, My Everything .... 20th Century 2133
1133	I'm Gonna Love You Just A Little More Baby .... 20th Century 2018
1268	It's Ecstasy When You Lay Down Next To Me .... 20th Century 2350
WILD CHERRY	
166	Play That Funky Music .... Epic 50225
MATTHEW WILDER	
1472	Break My Stride .... Private I 04113
ANDY WILLIAMS	
188	Butterfly .... Cadence 1308
661	Can't Get Used To Losing You .... Columbia 42674
1138	Are You Sincere .... Cadence 1340
1661	Lonely Street .... Cadence 1370
1989	Canadian Sunset .... Cadence 1297
BILLY WILLIAMS	
918	I'm Gonna Sit Right Down And Write Myself A Letter .... Coral 61830
DENIECE WILLIAMS	
313	Let's Hear It For The Boy Columbia 04417
523	Too Much, Too Little, Too Late.......... .... Columbia 10693 *JOHNNY MATHIS/DENIECE WILLIAMS*
LARRY WILLIAMS	
1620	Short Fat Fannie .... Specialty 608
MASON WILLIAMS	
807	Classical Gas .... Warner 7190
MAURICE WILLIAMS & The Zodiacs	
516	Stay .... Herald 552

RANK **Title** . . . Label & No.

ROGER WILLIAMS
96 Autumn Leaves .... Kapp 116
AL WILSON
454 Show And Tell .... Rocky Road 30073
ANN WILSON - see MIKE RENO
J. FRANK WILSON & The Cavaliers
849 Last Kiss .... Josie 923
JACKIE WILSON
1288 Night .... Brunswick 55166
1503 Baby Workout .... Brunswick 55239
1833 (Your Love Keeps Lifting Me) Higher And Higher .... Brunswick 55336
1991 Lonely Teardrops .... Brunswick 55105
WINGS - see PAUL McCARTNEY
EDGAR WINTER GROUP
487 Frankenstein .... Epic 10967
HUGO WINTERHALTER/EDDIE HEYWOOD
726 Canadian Sunset .... RCA 6537
BILL WITHERS
192 Lean On Me .... Sussex 235
678 Just The Two Of Us .... Elektra 47103
GROVER WASHINGTON, JR./BILL WITHERS
823 Use Me .... Sussex 241
1050 Ain't No Sunshine .... Sussex 219
STEVIE WONDER
26 Ebony And Ivory .... Columbia 02860
PAUL McCARTNEY & STEVIE WONDER
163 I Just Called To Say I Love You .... Motown 1745
204 Sir Duke .... Tamla 54281
223 Fingertips - Pt 2 .... Tamla 54080
500 You Haven't Done Nothin.... Tamla 54252
527 I Wish .... Tamla 54274
538 You Are The Sunshine Of My Life .... Tamla 54232
558 Superstition .... Tamla 54226
790 I Was Made To Love Her .... Tamla 54151
797 For Once In My Life .... Tamla 54174
1035 Boogie On Reggae Woman . Tamla 54254
1067 Signed, Sealed, Delivered I'm Yours ... . Tamla 54196

RANK **Title** . . . Label & No.

1084 Uptight (Everything's Alright) Tamla 54124
1217 Send One Your Love .... Tamla 54303
1238 That Girl .... Tamla 1602
1314 My Cherie Amour .... Tamla 54180
1404 Higher Ground .... Tamla 54235
1478 Master Blaster (Jammin') .... Tamla 54317
SHEB WOOLEY
53 The Purple People Eater ...... MGM 12651
BETTY WRIGHT
1893 Clean Up Woman .... Alston 4601
GARY WRIGHT
685 Dream Weaver .... Warner 8167
729 Love Is Alive .... Warner 8143

Y

YARDBIRDS
1935 For Your Love .... Epic 9790
YES
270 Owner Of A Lonely Heart ...... Atco 99817
YOUNGBLOODS
1506 Get Together .... RCA 9752
YOUNG-HOLT UNLIMITED
1178 Soulful Strut .... Brunswick 55391
JOHN PAUL YOUNG
1994 Love Is In The Air .... Scotti Br. 402
KATHY YOUNG with The Innocents
1136 A Thousand Stars .... Indigo 108
NEIL YOUNG
595 Heart Of Gold .... Reprise 1065
PAUL YOUNG
444 Everytime You Go Away .. Columbia 04867
TIMI YURO
1441 Hurt .... Liberty 55343

Z

JOHN ZACHERLE
1923 Dinner With Drac .... Cameo 130
ZAGER & EVANS
55 In The Year 2525 .... RCA 0174
ZOMBIES
874 She's Not There .... Parrot 9695
1089 Time Of The Season .... Date 1628
1841 Tell Her No .... Parrot 9723

THE SONG TITLES

This section lists, alphabetically, all titles listed in the Top 2000 ranking. The artist's name is listed next to each title along with its Top 2000 ranking.

A song with more than one charted version is listed once, with the artist's names listed below it in rank order. Songs that have the same title, but are different tunes, are listed separately, with the highest ranked song listed first.

RANK	**Title** . . . Artist
	A
383	**ABC** . . . *Jackson 5*
262	**Abracadabra** . . . *Steve Miller Band*
1306	**Abraham, Martin And John** . . . *Dion*
467	**Africa** . . . *Toto*
768	**After The Love Has Gone** . . . *Earth, Wind & Fire*
299	**Afternoon Delight** . . . *Starland Vocal Band*
169	**Against All Odds (Take A Look At Me Now)** . . . *Phil Collins*
1490	**Against The Wind** . . . *Bob Seger*
1598	**Ahab, The Arab** . . . *Ray Stevens*
227	**Ain't No Mountain High Enough** . . . *Diana Ross*
1050	**Ain't No Sunshine** . . . *Bill Withers*
1299	**Ain't No Woman (Like The One I've Got)** . . . *Four Tops*
292	**Ain't That A Shame** . . . *Pat Boone*
1854	**Air That I Breathe** . . . *Hollies*
1909	**Al Di La'** . . . *Emilio Pericoli*
1059	**All Alone Am I** . . . *Brenda Lee*
868	**All American Boy** . . . *Bill Parsons*
692	**All By Myself** . . . *Eric Carmen*
1981	**All Day And All Of The Night** . . . *Kinks*
66	**All I Have To Do Is Dream** . . . *Everly Brothers*
744	**All I Need** . . . *Jack Wagner*
101	**All Night Long (All Night)** . . . *Lionel Richie*
648	**All Out Of Love** . . . *Air Supply*
1382	**All Right Now** . . . *Free*
5	**All Shook Up** . . . *Elvis Presley*
833	**All The Way** . . . *Frank Sinatra*
703	**All Those Years Ago** . . . *George Harrison*
1632	**All Through The Night** . . . *Cyndi Lauper*
630	**All You Need Is Love** . . . *Beatles*
727	**Allegheny Moon** . . . *Patti Page*
589	**Alley-Oop** . . . *Hollywood Argyles*
1999	**Almost Paradise...Love Theme From Footloose** . . . *Mike Reno & Ann Wilson*
49	**Alone Again (Naturally)** . . . *Gilbert O'Sullivan*
903	**Also Sprach Zarathustra (2001)** . . . *Deodato*
1064	**Alvin's Harmonica** . . . *Chipmunks*
1479	**Always On My Mind** . . . *Willie Nelson*
120	**American Pie** . . . *Don McLean*
212	**American Woman** . . . *Guess Who*
1445	**Americans** . . . *Byron MacGregor*
896	**And When I Die** . . . *Blood, Sweat & Tears*
1654	**Angel** . . . *Madonna*
1690	**Angel Baby** . . . *Rosie & The Originals*
1760	**Angel In Your Arms** . . . *Hot*
	Angel Of The Morning
1216	*Juice Newton*
1973	*Merrilee Rush & The Turnabouts*
555	**Angie** . . . *Rolling Stones*
540	**Angie Baby** . . . *Helen Reddy*
338	**Annie's Song** . . . *John Denver*
98	**Another Brick In The Wall (Part II)** . . . *Pink Floyd*
1587	**Another Day** . . . *Paul McCartney*
154	**Another One Bites The Dust** . . . *Queen*
1914	**Another Saturday Night** . . . *Cat Stevens*
769	**Apache** . . . *Jorgen Ingmann*
1803	**Apples, Peaches, Pumpkin Pie** . . . *Jay & The Techniques*
30	**April Love** . . . *Pat Boone*
50	**Aquarius/Let The Sunshine In** . . . *5th Dimension*
52	**Are You Lonesome To-night?** . . . *Elvis Presley*
1138	**Are You Sincere** . . . *Andy Williams*
168	**Arthur's Theme (Best That You Can Do)** . . . *Christopher Cross*
1953	**As Tears Go By** . . . *Rolling Stones*
1011	**At Seventeen** . . . *Janis Ian*
24	**At The Hop** . . . *Danny & The Juniors*
1626	**Automatic** . . . *Pointer Sisters*
96	**Autumn Leaves** . . . *Roger Williams*
958	**Axel F** . . . *Harold Faltermeyer*
	B
311	**Babe** . . . *Styx*
153	**Baby Come Back** . . . *Player*
254	**Baby, Come To Me** . . . *Patti Austin & James Ingram*
199	**Baby Don't Get Hooked On Me** . . . *Mac Davis*
1449	**Baby I Love You** . . . *Aretha Franklin*
1100	**Baby I Need Your Lovin'** . . . *Johnny Rivers*
1094	**Baby I'm-A Want You** . . . *Bread*
1497	**Baby It's You** . . . *Smith*
146	**Baby Love** . . . *Supremes*
1908	**Baby Sittin' Boogie** . . . *Buzz Clifford*
1378	**Baby, What A Big Surprise** . . . *Chicago*

RANK	**Title** . . . Artist
1503	**Baby Workout** . . . *Jackie Wilson*
1665	**Baby (You've Got What It Takes)** . . . *Dinah Washington & Brook Benton*
1565	**Back Home Again** . . . *John Denver*
629	**Back In My Arms Again** . . . *Supremes*
1477	**Back On The Chain Gang** . . . *Pretenders*
1162	**Back Stabbers** . . . *O'Jays*
278	**Bad, Bad Leroy Brown** . . . *Jim Croce*
234	**Bad Blood** . . . *Neil Sedaka*
65	**Bad Girls** . . . *Donna Summer*
890	**Bad Moon Rising** . . . *Creedence Clearwater Revival*
1304	**Bad Time** . . . *Grand Funk*
638	**Baker Street** . . . *Gerry Rafferty*
971	**Ball Of Confusion** . . . *Temptations*
86	**Ballad Of The Green Berets** . . . *SSgt Barry Sadler*
1614	**Ballroom Blitz** . . . *Sweet*
1457	**Banana Boat (Day-O)** . . . *Harry Belafonte*
1365	**Banana Boat Song** . . . *Tarriers*
1120	**Band Of Gold** . . . *Freda Payne*
1358	**Band Of Gold** . . . *Don Cherry*
521	**Band On The Run** . . . *Paul McCartney & Wings*
907	**Bang Bang (My Baby Shot Me Down)** . . . *Cher*
829	**Barbara Ann** . . . *Beach Boys*
44	**Battle Of New Orleans** . . . *Johnny Horton*
1964	**Be-Bop-A-Lula** . . . *Gene Vincent & His Blue Caps*
1119	**Be-Bop Baby** . . . *Ricky Nelson*
718	**Be My Baby** . . . *Ronettes*
1376	**Be Thankful For What You Got** . . . *William DeVaughn*
1938	**Be True To Your School** . . . *Beach Boys*
1289	**Beach Baby** . . . *First Class*
1838	**Beat Goes On** . . . *Sonny & Cher*
165	**Beat It** . . . *Michael Jackson*
1086	**Beautiful Morning** . . . *Rascals*
1197	**Beauty Is Only Skin Deep** . . . *Temptations*
1202	**Because** . . . *Dave Clark Five*
1303	**Because They're Young** . . . *Duane Eddy*
1298	**Beep Beep** . . . *Playmates*
470	**Before The Next Teardrop Falls** . . . *Freddy Fender*
674	**Being With You** . . . *Smokey Robinson*

RANK	**Title** . . . Artist
	Believe It or Not...see: Theme From "Greatest American Hero"
1440	**Believe What You Say** . . . *Ricky Nelson*
567	**Ben** . . . *Michael Jackson*
1578	**Bend Me, Shape Me** . . . *American Breed*
509	**Bennie And The Jets** . . . *Elton John*
1341	**Bernadette** . . . *Four Tops*
59	**Best Of My Love** . . . *Emotions*
501	**Best Of My Love** . . . *Eagles*
925	**Best Of Times** . . . *Styx*
	Best That You Can Do...see: Arthur's Theme
1140	**Best Thing That Ever Happened To Me** . . . *Gladys Knight & The Pips*
1142	**Betcha By Golly, Wow** . . . *Stylistics*
8	**Bette Davis Eyes** . . . *Kim Carnes*
1525	**Better Be Good To Me** . . . *Tina Turner*
1898	**Beyond The Sea** . . . *Bobby Darin*
78	**Big Bad John** . . . *Jimmy Dean*
77	**Big Girls Don't Cry** . . . *4 Seasons*
380	**Big Hunk O' Love** . . . *Elvis Presley*
1033	**Big Hurt** . . . *Miss Toni Fisher*
1065	**Big Man** . . . *Four Preps*
954	**Biggest Part Of Me** . . . *Ambrosia*
22	**Billie Jean** . . . *Michael Jackson*
315	**Billy, Don't Be A Hero** . . . *Bo Donaldson & The Heywoods*
510	**Bird Dog** . . . *Everly Brothers*
1069	**Birds And The Bees** . . . *Jewel Akens*
1411	**Bitch Is Back** . . . *Elton John*
1254	**Bits And Pieces** . . . *Dave Clark Five*
632	**Black & White** . . . *Three Dog Night*
1939	**Black Denim Trousers** . . . *Cheers*
1333	**Black Is Black** . . . *Los Bravos*
1319	**Black Magic Woman** . . . *Santana*
541	**Black Water** . . . *Doobie Brothers*
481	**Blinded By The Light** . . . *Manfred Mann's Earth Band*
847	**Blossom Fell** . . . *Nat King Cole*
876	**Blowin' In The Wind** . . . *Peter, Paul & Mary*
921	**Blue Bayou** . . . *Linda Ronstadt*
1643	**Blue Monday** . . . *Fats Domino*
236	**Blue Moon** . . . *Marcels*
1186	**Blue On Blue** . . . *Bobby Vinton*
651	**Blue Suede Shoes** . . . *Carl Perkins*
221	**Blue Velvet** . . . *Bobby Vinton*

RANK	**Title** . . . Artist
669	**Blueberry Hill** . . . *Fats Domino*
928	**Bobby's Girl** . . . *Marcie Blane*
701	**Boll Weevil Song** . . . *Brook Benton*
766	**Boogie Down** . . . *Eddie Kendricks*
471	**Boogie Fever** . . . *Sylvers*
730	**Boogie Nights** . . . *Heatwave*
1035	**Boogie On Reggae Woman** . . . *Stevie Wonder*
173	**Boogie Oogie Oogie** . . . *Taste Of Honey*
1806	**Boogie Wonderland** . . . *Earth, Wind & Fire with The Emotions*
1642	**Book Of Love** . . . *Monotones*
715	**Born To Be Wild** . . . *Steppenwolf*
1526	**Born To Be With You** . . . *Chordettes*
1961	**Boy From New York City** . . . *Manhattan Transfer*
720	**Boy Named Sue** . . . *Johnny Cash*
1619	**Boys Of Summer** . . . *Don Henley*
196	**Brand New Key** . . . *Melanie*
552	**Brandy (You're A Fine Girl)** . . . *Looking Glass*
817	**Bread And Butter** . . . *Newbeats*
1414	**Break It To Me Gently** . . . *Brenda Lee*
1472	**Break My Stride** . . . *Matthew Wilder*
1688	**Break Up To Make Up** . . . *Stylistics*
375	**Breaking Up Is Hard To Do** . . . *Neil Sedaka*
1660	**Brick House** . . . *Commodores*
	Bridge Over Troubled Water
54	*Simon & Garfunkel*
1924	*Aretha Franklin*
773	**Bristol Stomp** . . . *Dovells*
317	**Brother Louie** . . . *Stories*
398	**Brown Sugar** . . . *Rolling Stones*
972	**Build Me Up Buttercup** . . . *Foundations*
1040	**Burning Bridges** . . . *Jack Scott*
878	**Burning Love** . . . *Elvis Presley*
1499	**Bus Stop** . . . *Hollies*
1250	**Busted** . . . *Ray Charles*
1390	**But I Do** . . . *Clarence Henry*
	Butterfly
188	*Andy Williams*
331	*Charlie Gracie*
647	**Bye Bye Love** . . . *Everly Brothers*

C

RANK	**Title** . . . Artist
	C'mon...see: Come On
332	**Calcutta** . . . *Lawrence Welk*
1398	**Calendar Girl** . . . *Neil Sedaka*
1379	**California Dreamin'** . . . *Mamas & The Papas*
	California Girls
1098	*Beach Boys*
1155	*David Lee Roth*
1720	**California Sun** . . . *Rivieras*
36	**Call Me** . . . *Blondie*
1815	**Call On Me** . . . *Chicago*
1695	**Can I Change My Mind** . . . *Tyrone Davis*
88	**Can't Buy Me Love** . . . *Beatles*
198	**Can't Fight This Feeling** . . . *REO Speedwagon*
1669	**Can't Get Enough** . . . *Bad Company*
624	**Can't Get Enough Of Your Love, Babe** . . . *Barry White*
661	**Can't Get Used To Losing You** . . . *Andy Williams*
884	**Can't Help Falling In Love** . . . *Elvis Presley*
952	**Can't Smile Without You** . . . *Barry Manilow*
862	**Can't Take My Eyes Off You** . . . *Frankie Valli*
794	**Can't You Hear My Heartbeat** . . . *Herman's Hermits*
1453	**Can't You See That She's Mine** . . . *Dave Clark Five*
	Canadian Sunset
726	*Hugo Winterhalter/Eddie Heywood*
1989	*Andy Williams*
1027	**Candida** . . . *Dawn*
1184	**Candy Girl** . . . *Four Seasons*
184	**Candy Man** . . . *Sammy Davis, Jr.*
446	**Car Wash** . . . *Rose Royce*
1420	**Cara, Mia** . . . *Jay & The Americans*
181	**Careless Whisper** . . . *Wham!*
261	**Caribbean Queen (No More Love On The Run)** . . . *Billy Ocean*
508	**Cat's In The Cradle** . . . *Harry Chapin*
441	**Catch A Falling Star** . . . *Perry Como*
1336	**Catch Us If You Can** . . . *Dave Clark Five*
75	**Cathy's Clown** . . . *Everly Brothers*
1417	**Cecilia** . . . *Simon & Garfunkel*
255	**Celebration** . . . *Kool & The Gang*
33	**Centerfold** . . . *J. Geils Band*
777	**Chain Gang** . . . *Sam Cooke*
816	**Chain Of Fools** . . . *Aretha Franklin*
418	**Chances Are** . . . *Johnny Mathis*
1879	**Chanson D'Amour (Song Of Love)** . . . *Art & Dotty Todd*
1764	**Chantilly Lace** . . . *Big Bopper*

RANK	**Title** . . . Artist
244	**Chapel Of Love** . . . *Dixie Cups*
422	**Chariots Of Fire - Titles** . . . *Vangelis*
707	**Charlie Brown** . . . *Coasters*
233	**Cherish** . . . *Association*
1932	**Cherry, Cherry** . . . *Neil Diamond*
1653	**Chevy Van** . . . *Sammy Johns*
94	**Chipmunk Song** . . . *Chipmunks*
1300	**Chuck E.'s In Love** . . . *Rickie Lee Jones*
792	**Cisco Kid** . . . *War*
774	**Clair** . . . *Gilbert O'Sullivan*
1881	**Clap For The Wolfman** . . . *Guess Who*
807	**Classical Gas** . . . *Mason Williams*
1893	**Clean Up Woman** . . . *Betty Wright*
753	**Closer I Get To You** . . . *Roberta Flack with Donny Hathaway*
1830	**Cloud Nine** . . . *Temptations*
1852	**Cold As Ice** . . . *Foreigner*
	Come...also see: Cum
1062	**Come A Little Bit Closer** . . . *Jay & The Americans*
1511	**Come And Get Your Love** . . . *Redbone*
968	**Come Back When You Grow Up** . . . *Bobby Vee*
1802	**Come Dancing** . . . *Kinks*
1343	**Come Go With Me** . . . *Dell-Vikings*
1589	**C'mon And Swim** . . . *Bobby Freeman*
1811	**Come On Down To My Boat** . . . *Every Mothers' Son*
448	**Come On Eileen** . . . *Dexys Midnight Runners*
371	**Come See About Me** . . . *Supremes*
133	**Come Softly To Me** . . . *Fleetwoods*
548	**Come Together** . . . *Beatles*
182	**Coming Up (Live at Glasgow)** . . . *Paul McCartney & Wings*
568	**Convoy** . . . *C.W. McCall*
1348	**Cool It Now** . . . *New Edition*
1301	**Could It Be I'm Falling In Love** . . . *Spinners*
1793	**Could It Be Magic** . . . *Barry Manilow*
1113	**Couldn't Get It Right** . . . *Climax Blues Band*
828	**Count Me In** . . . *Gary Lewis & The Playboys*
1782	**Cover Of "Rolling Stone"** . . . *Dr. Hook*
926	**Coward Of The County** . . . *Kenny Rogers*
1819	**Cowboys To Girls** . . . *Intruders*
574	**Cracklin' Rosie** . . . *Neil Diamond*

RANK	**Title** . . . Artist
472	**Crazy For You** . . . *Madonna*
113	**Crazy Little Thing Called Love** . . . *Queen*
1725	**Creeque Alley** . . . *Mamas & The Papas*
340	**Crimson And Clover** . . . *Tommy James & The Shondells*
202	**Crocodile Rock** . . . *Elton John*
	Crooked Little Man...see: Don't Let The Rain Come Down
1211	**Cruisin'** . . . *Smokey Robinson*
1407	**Cry Baby** . . . *Garnet Mimms & The Enchanters*
791	**Cry Like A Baby** . . . *Box Tops*
	Crying
864	*Roy Orbison*
1485	*Don McLean*
1171	**Crying In The Chapel** . . . *Elvis Presley*
1826	**Crying In The Rain** . . . *Everly Brothers*
1890	**Crying Time** . . . *Ray Charles*
706	**Crystal Blue Persuasion** . . . *Tommy James & The Shondells*
1523	**Cum On Feel The Noize** . . . *Quiet Riot*
1232	**Cupid/I've Loved You For A Long Time** . . . *Spinners*

D

RANK	**Title** . . . Artist
	Da Doo Ron Ron
459	*Shaun Cassidy*
1188	*Crystals*
115	**Da Ya Think I'm Sexy?** . . . *Rod Stewart*
1277	**Daddy Don't You Walk So Fast** . . . *Wayne Newton*
895	**Daddy's Home** . . . *Shep & The Limelites*
1759	**Dance, Dance, Dance (Yowsah, Yowsah, Yowsah)** . . . *Chic*
1870	**Dance With Me** . . . *Orleans*
654	**Dancing In The Dark** . . . *Bruce Springsteen*
802	**Dancing In The Street** . . . *Martha & The Vandellas*
742	**Dancing Machine** . . . *Jackson 5*
456	**Dancing Queen** . . . *Abba*
1601	**Dandy** . . . *Herman's Hermits*
875	**Daniel** . . . *Elton John*
562	**Dark Lady** . . . *Cher*
	Dark Moon
1351	*Gale Storm*
1851	*Bonnie Guitar*
979	**Dawn (Go Away)** . . . *Four Seasons*
1405	**Day After Day** . . . *Badfinger*

RANK	**Title** . . . Artist
1705	**Day Dreaming** . . . *Aretha Franklin*
1722	**Day Tripper** . . . *Beatles*
820	**Daydream** . . . *Lovin' Spoonful*
149	**Daydream Believer** . . . *Monkees*
998	**Dazz** . . . *Brick*
159	**December, 1963 (Oh, What a Night)** . . . *Four Seasons*
	Dedicated To The One I Love
723	*Mamas & The Papas*
1008	*Shirelles*
586	**Deep Purple** . . . *Nino Tempo & April Stevens*
485	**Delta Dawn** . . . *Helen Reddy*
1522	**Der Kommissar** . . . *After The Fire*
1221	**Desire** . . . *Andy Gibb*
1784	**Devil Or Angel** . . . *Bobby Vee*
1031	**Devil Went Down To Georgia** . . . *Charlie Daniels Band*
1219	**Devil With A Blue Dress On & Good Golly Miss Molly** . . . *Mitch Ryder & The Detroit Wheels*
1733	**Devil Woman** . . . *Cliff Richard*
1794	**Diamond Girl** . . . *Seals & Crofts*
417	**Diana** . . . *Paul Anka*
826	**Did You Ever Have To Make Up Your Mind?** . . . *Lovin' Spoonful*
747	**Dim All The Lights** . . . *Donna Summer*
1923	**Dinner With Drac** . . . *John Zacherle*
953	**Dirty Laundry** . . . *Don Henley*
433	**Disco Duck** . . . *Rick Dees*
124	**Disco Lady** . . . *Johnnie Taylor*
138	**Dizzy** . . . *Tommy Roe*
760	**Do It ('Til You're Satisfied)** . . . *B.T. Express*
1744	**Do It Again** . . . *Steely Dan*
423	**Do That To Me One More Time** . . . *Captain & Tennille*
385	**Do Wah Diddy Diddy** . . . *Manfred Mann*
	Do You...also see: Da Ya
1970	**Do You Believe In Love** . . . *Huey Lewis & The News*
	Do You Know Where You're Going To...see: Theme From Mahogany
1743	**Do You Know What I Mean** . . . *Lee Michaels*
960	**Do You Love Me** . . . *Contours*
672	**Do You Really Want To Hurt Me** . . . *Culture Club*
1517	**Do You Wanna Make Love** . . . *Peter McCann*
1651	**Do You Want To Dance** . . . *Bobby Freeman*

RANK	**Title** . . . Artist
908	**Do You Want To Know A Secret** . . . *Beatles*
1715	**Does Your Chewing Gum Lose It's Flavor (On The Bedpost Over Night)** . . . *Lonnie Donegan*
1925	**Doesn't Somebody Want To Be Wanted** . . . *Partridge Family*
144	**Dominique** . . . *Singing Nun*
64	**Don't** . . . *Elvis Presley*
1	**Don't Be Cruel** . . . *Elvis Presley*
613	**Don't Break The Heart That Loves You** . . . *Connie Francis*
1305	**Don't Bring Me Down** . . . *Electric Light Orchestra*
1917	**Don't Cry Daddy** . . . *Elvis Presley*
1233	**Don't Fall In Love With A Dreamer** . . . *Kenny Rogers with Kim Carnes*
450	**Don't Forbid Me** . . . *Pat Boone*
503	**Don't Give Up On Us** . . . *David Soul*
117	**Don't Go Breaking My Heart** . . . *Elton John & Kiki Dee*
1399	**Don't Hang Up** . . . *Orlons*
671	**Don't It Make My Brown Eyes Blue** . . . *Crystal Gayle*
436	**Don't Leave Me This Way** . . . *Thelma Houston*
1877	**Don't Let It End** . . . *Styx*
1818	**Don't Let The Rain Come Down (Crooked Little Man)** . . . *Serendipity Singers*
1331	**Don't Let The Sun Catch You Crying** . . . *Gerry & The Pacemakers*
796	**Don't Let The Sun Go Down On Me** . . . *Elton John*
1323	**Don't Look Back** . . . *Boston*
1311	**Don't Pull Your Love** . . . *Hamilton, Joe Frank & Reynolds*
1607	**Don't Sleep In The Subway** . . . *Petula Clark*
1025	**Don't Stop** . . . *Fleetwood Mac*
476	**Don't Stop 'Til You Get Enough** . . . *Michael Jackson*
653	**Don't Talk To Strangers** . . . *Rick Springfield*
1163	**Don't Worry** . . . *Marty Robbins*
1907	**Don't You Care** . . . *Buckinghams*
458	**Don't You (Forget About Me)** . . . *Simple Minds*
853	**Don't You Know** . . . *Della Reese*
155	**Don't You Want Me** . . . *Human League*
736	**Donna** . . . *Ritchie Valens*
1836	**Donna The Prima Donna** . . . *Dion*

RANK	**Title** . . . Artist
1947	**Door Is Still Open To My Heart** . . . *Dean Martin*
754	**Double Vision** . . . *Foreigner*
1309	**Down By The Lazy River** . . . *Osmonds*
1159	**Down On The Corner** . . . *Creedence Clearwater Revival*
99	**Down Under** . . . *Men At Work*
355	**Downtown** . . . *Petula Clark*
1419	**Draggin' The Line** . . . *Tommy James*
1446	**Dream Baby (How Long Must I Dream)** . . . *Roy Orbison*
859	**Dream Lover** . . . *Bobby Darin*
1846	**Dream On** . . . *Aerosmith*
685	**Dream Weaver** . . . *Gary Wright*
502	**Dreams** . . . *Fleetwood Mac*
1621	**Drift Away** . . . *Dobie Gray*
1944	**Drip Drop** . . . *Dion*
955	**Drive** . . . *Cars*
1505	**Drivin' My Life Away** . . . *Eddie Rabbitt*
662	**Dueling Banjos** . . . *Eric Weissberg & Steve Mandell*
224	**Duke Of Earl** . . . *Gene Chandler*
1251	**Dum Dum** . . . *Brenda Lee*
1778	**Dust In The Wind** . . . *Kansas*
	E
395	**Easier Said Than Done** . . . *Essex*
1265	**Easy** . . . *Commodores*
739	**Easy Lover** . . . *Philip Bailey with Phil Collins*
1320	**Easy To Be Hard** . . . *Three Dog Night*
1609	**Ebb Tide** . . . *Righteous Brothers*
26	**Ebony And Ivory** . . . *Paul McCartney & Stevie Wonder*
415	**Eight Days A Week** . . . *Beatles*
122	**867-5309/Jenny** . . . *Tommy Tutone*
276	**El Paso** . . . *Marty Robbins*
643	**Electric Avenue** . . . *Eddy Grant*
1931	**Elenore** . . . *Turtles*
1586	**Elusive Butterfly** . . . *Bob Lind*
1462	**Elvira** . . . *Oak Ridge Boys*
986	**Emotion** . . . *Samantha Sang*
1016	**Emotional Rescue** . . . *Rolling Stones*
860	**End Of The World** . . . *Skeeter Davis*
6	**Endless Love** . . . *Diana Ross & Lionel Richie*
1551	**Endless Sleep** . . . *Jody Reynolds*
1775	**Enjoy Yourself** . . . *Jacksons*
1049	**Entertainer, The** . . . *Marvin Hamlisch*
183	**Escape (The Pina Colada Song)** . . . *Rupert Holmes*
625	**Eve Of Destruction** . . . *Barry McGuire*
1544	**Even The Nights Are Better** . . . *Air Supply*
	Evergreen...see: Love Theme From "A Star Is Born"
1655	**Everlasting Love** . . . *Andy Gibb*
1813	**Everlasting Love** . . . *Carl Carlton*
1919	**Every Beat Of My Heart** . . . *Pips*
15	**Every Breath You Take** . . . *Police*
1015	**Every Little Thing She Does Is Magic** . . . *Police*
1236	**(Every Time I Turn Around) Back In Love Again** . . . *L.T.D.*
1617	**Every Woman In The World** . . . *Air Supply*
1076	**Everybody** . . . *Tommy Roe*
1450	**Everybody Loves A Clown** . . . *Gary Lewis & The Playboys*
1894	**Everybody Loves A Lover** . . . *Doris Day*
1840	**Everybody Loves Me But You** . . . *Brenda Lee*
577	**Everybody Loves Somebody** . . . *Dean Martin*
1135	**Everybody Plays The Fool** . . . *Main Ingredient*
268	**Everybody Wants To Rule The World** . . . *Tears For Fears*
316	**Everybody's Somebody's Fool** . . . *Connie Francis*
1937	**Everybody's Talkin'** . . . *Nilsson*
123	**Everyday People** . . . *Sly & The Family Stone*
1790	**Every 1's A Winner** . . . *Hot Chocolate*
1501	**Everything I Own** . . . *Bread*
362	**Everything Is Beautiful** . . . *Ray Stevens*
303	**Everything She Wants** . . . *Wham!*
444	**Everytime You Go Away** . . . *Paul Young*
844	**Exodus** . . . *Ferrante & Teicher*
1247	**Express** . . . *B.T. Express*
1394	**Expressway To Your Heart** . . . *Soul Survivors*
936	**Eye In The Sky** . . . *Alan Parsons Project*
37	**Eye Of The Tiger** . . . *Survivor*
1263	**Eyes Without A Face** . . . *Billy Idol*
	F
543	**Fallin' In Love** . . . *Hamilton, Joe Frank & Reynolds*

RANK	**Title** . . . Artist
291	**Fame** . . . *David Bowie*
1258	**Fame** . . . *Irene Cara*
228	**Family Affair** . . . *Sly & The Family Stone*
1878	**Family Man** . . . *Daryl Hall & John Oates*
1956	**Fascination** . . . *Jane Morgan*
556	**Feel Like Makin' Love** . . . *Roberta Flack*
1845	**Feelings** . . . *Morris Albert*
1266	**Feels Like The First Time** . . . *Foreigner*
1346	**Feels So Good** . . . *Chuck Mangione*
1835	**Ferry Across The Mersey** . . . *Gerry & The Pacemakers*
419	**Fifth Of Beethoven** . . . *Walter Murphy*
206	**50 Ways To Leave Your Lover** . . . *Paul Simon*
	Fight...see: Main Event
1373	**Fight The Power** . . . *Isley Brothers*
223	**Fingertips - Pt 2** . . . *Little Stevie Wonder*
545	**Fire** . . . *Ohio Players*
738	**Fire** . . . *Pointer Sisters*
899	**Fire** . . . *Arthur Brown*
967	**Fire And Rain** . . . *James Taylor*
1808	**Fire Lake** . . . *Bob Seger*
48	**First Time Ever I Saw Your Face** . . . *Roberta Flack*
1310	**Five O'Clock World** . . . *Vogues*
32	**Flashdance...What A Feeling** . . . *Irene Cara*
784	**Float On** . . . *Floaters*
1433	**Flowers On The Wall** . . . *Statler Brothers*
752	**Fly Like An Eagle** . . . *Steve Miller*
205	**Fly, Robin, Fly** . . . *Silver Convention*
1183	**Flying Saucer (Parts 1 & 2)** . . . *Buchanan & Goodman*
1992	**Fool** . . . *Sanford Clark*
1071	**Fool #1** . . . *Brenda Lee*
1926	**Fool On The Hill** . . . *Sergio Mendes & Brasil '66*
1039	**Fooled Around And Fell In Love** . . . *Elvin Bishop*
1412	**Foolish Little Girl** . . . *Shirelles*
176	**Footloose** . . . *Kenny Loggins*
1085	**For All We Know** . . . *Carpenters*
797	**For Once In My Life** . . . *Stevie Wonder*
1945	**For You** . . . *Rick Nelson*
1213	**For Your Eyes Only** . . . *Sheena Easton*
1935	**For Your Love** . . . *Yardbirds*
1388	**Forget Him** . . . *Bobby Rydell*
	Forgive Me, Girl...see: Working My Way Back To You
1659	**Fox On The Run** . . . *Sweet*
487	**Frankenstein** . . . *Edgar Winter Group*
1296	**Freddie's Dead** . . . *Curtis Mayfield*
1127	**Freeway Of Love** . . . *Aretha Franklin*
1220	**Freeze-Frame** . . . *J. Geils Band*
1869	**Freight Train** . . . *Rusty Draper*
1615	**Friendly Persuasion (Thee I Love)** . . . *Pat Boone*
1828	**From A Jack To A King** . . . *Ned Miller*
1712	**Fun, Fun, Fun** . . . *Beach Boys*
110	**Funkytown** . . . *Lipps, Inc.*
1532	**Funny Face** . . . *Donna Fargo*

G

RANK	**Title** . . . Artist
1427	**G.T.O.** . . . *Ronny & The Daytonas*
1438	**Galveston** . . . *Glen Campbell*
628	**Game Of Love** . . . *Mindbenders*
1785	**Garden Party** . . . *Rick Nelson*
618	**Georgia On My Mind** . . . *Ray Charles*
781	**Georgy Girl** . . . *Seekers*
361	**Get A Job** . . . *Silhouettes*
87	**Get Back** . . . *Beatles*
1762	**Get Closer** . . . *Seals & Crofts*
593	**Get Down Tonight** . . . *K.C. & The Sunshine Band*
404	**Get Off Of My Cloud** . . . *Rolling Stones*
1274	**Get Ready** . . . *Rare Earth*
1506	**Get Together** . . . *Youngbloods*
681	**Get Up And Boogie (That's Right)** . . . *Silver Convention*
186	**Ghostbusters** . . . *Ray Parker Jr.*
1927	**Gina** . . . *Johnny Mathis*
1590	**Girl From Ipanema** . . . *Stan Getz/Astrud Gilberto*
695	**Girl Is Mine** . . . *Michael Jackson/Paul McCartney*
1470	**Girl Watcher** . . . *O'Kaysions*
733	**Girls Just Want To Have Fun** . . . *Cyndi Lauper*
1166	**Give Me Just A Little More Time** . . . *Chairmen Of The Board*
603	**Give Me Love (Give Me Peace On Earth)** . . . *George Harrison*
1260	**Give Me The Night** . . . *George Benson*
1895	**Glad All Over** . . . *Dave Clark Five*
667	**Gloria** . . . *Laura Branigan*
1641	**Glory Days** . . . *Bruce Springsteen*

RANK	**Title** . . . Artist
1548	**Go All The Way** . . . *Raspberries*
	Go Away Little Girl
215	*Donny Osmond*
334	*Steve Lawrence*
1662	**Go, Jimmy, Go** . . . *Jimmy Clanton*
1749	**Goin' Out Of My Head** . . . *Little Anthony & The Imperials*
1546	**Gold** . . . *John Stewart*
1210	**Gone** . . . *Ferlin Husky*
490	**Gonna Fly Now (Theme From "Rocky")** . . . *Bill Conti*
	Good Golly Miss Molly...see: Devil With A Blue Dress On
600	**Good Lovin'** . . . *Young Rascals*
392	**Good Luck Charm** . . . *Elvis Presley*
1088	**Good Morning Starshine** . . . *Oliver*
843	**Good, The Bad And The Ugly** . . . *Hugo Montenegro*
1328	**Good Thing** . . . *Paul Revere & The Raiders*
498	**Good Times** . . . *Chic*
975	**Good Timin'** . . . *Jimmy Jones*
599	**Good Vibrations** . . . *Beach Boys*
1038	**Goodbye Cruel World** . . . *James Darren*
698	**Goodbye Yellow Brick Road** . . . *Elton John*
1492	**Goodnight Tonight** . . . *Wings*
1402	**Got To Be There** . . . *Michael Jackson*
1974	**Got To Get You Into My Life** . . . *Beatles*
511	**Got To Give It Up** . . . *Marvin Gaye*
1363	**Gotta Travel On** . . . *Billy Grammer*
	Grazing In The Grass
406	*Hugh Masekela*
1149	*Friends Of Distinction*
279	**Grease** . . . *Frankie Valli*
655	**Great Balls Of Fire** . . . *Jerry Lee Lewis*
265	**Great Pretender** . . . *Platters*
	Greatest American Hero...see: Theme From
	Green Berets...see: Ballad Of
161	**Green Door** . . . *Jim Lowe*
1037	**Green-Eyed Lady** . . . *Sugarloaf*
1151	**Green Onions** . . . *Booker T. & The MG's*
898	**Green River** . . . *Creedence Clearwater Revival*
609	**Green Tambourine** . . . *Lemon Pipers*
657	**Greenfields** . . . *Brothers Four*
1857	**Groove Me** . . . *King Floyd*
147	**Groovin'** . . . *Young Rascals*
814	**Groovy Kind Of Love** . . . *Mindbenders*
994	**Guilty** . . . *Barbra Streisand & Barry Gibb*
1561	**Guitar Boogie Shuffle** . . . *Virtues*
1012	**Gypsy Woman** . . . *Brian Hyland*
344	**Gypsys, Tramps & Thieves** . . . *Cher*

H

RANK	**Title** . . . Artist
785	**Hair** . . . *Cowsills*
298	**Half-Breed** . . . *Cher*
	Handy Man
852	*Jimmy Jones*
1278	*James Taylor*
604	**Hang On Sloopy** . . . *McCoys*
407	**Hanky Panky** . . . *Tommy James & The Shondells*
627	**Happening** . . . *Supremes*
1750	**Happy Birthday, Sweet Sixteen** . . . *Neil Sedaka*
1580	**Happy Days** . . . *Pratt & McClain*
1634	**Happy, Happy Birthday Baby** . . . *Tune Weavers*
532	**Happy Organ** . . . *Dave "Baby" Cortez*
219	**Happy Together** . . . *Turtles*
1737	**Happy Whistler** . . . *Don Robertson*
386	**Hard Day's Night** . . . *Beatles*
987	**Hard Habit To Break** . . . *Chicago*
345	**Hard Headed Woman** . . . *Elvis Presley*
1364	**Hard To Get** . . . *Gisele MacKenzie*
266	**Hard To Say I'm Sorry** . . . *Chicago*
988	**Harden My Heart** . . . *Quarterflash*
608	**Harper Valley P.T.A.** . . . *Jeannie C. Riley*
1582	**Hats Off To Larry** . . . *Del Shannon*
1702	**Have I The Right?** . . . *Honeycombs*
569	**Have You Never Been Mellow** . . . *Olivia Newton-John*
1066	**Have You Seen Her** . . . *Chi-Lites*
1413	**Hawaii Five-O** . . . *Ventures*
1355	**He** . . . *Al Hibbler*
239	**He Don't Love You (Like I Love You)** . . . *Tony Orlando & Dawn*
	He'll Have To Go (Stay)
679	*Jim Reeves*
1334	*Jeanne Black*
325	**He's A Rebel** . . . *Crystals*
121	**He's Got The Whole World (In His Hands)** . . . *Laurie London*
139	**He's So Fine** . . . *Chiffons*
933	**He's So Shy** . . . *Pointer Sisters*
924	**Heart Attack** . . . *Olivia Newton-John*

RANK **Title** . . . Artist

474 **Heart Of Glass** . . . *Blondie*
595 **Heart Of Gold** . . . *Neil Young*
1729 **Heart Of Rock & Roll** . . . *Huey Lewis & The News*
575 **Heartache Tonight** . . . *Eagles*
294 **Heartaches By The Number** . . . *Guy Mitchell*
1137 **Heartbeat - It's A Lovebeat** . . . *DeFranco Family featuring Tony DeFranco*
13 **Heartbreak Hotel** . . . *Elvis Presley*
1466 **Heartlight** . . . *Neil Diamond*
839 **Heat Is On** . . . *Glenn Frey*
1239 **Heat Of The Moment** . . . *Asia*
Heat Wave
1312 *Martha & The Vandellas*
1674 *Linda Ronstadt*
314 **Heaven** . . . *Bryan Adams*
1234 **Heaven Knows** . . . *Donna Summer*
1731 **Heaven On The 7th Floor** . . . *Paul Nicholas*
267 **Hello** . . . *Lionel Richie*
1807 **Hello Again** . . . *Neil Diamond*
449 **Hello, Dolly!** . . . *Louis Armstrong & The All Stars*
250 **Hello Goodbye** . . . *Beatles*
399 **Hello, I Love You** . . . *The Doors*
1630 **Hello It's Me** . . . *Todd Rundgren*
725 **Hello Mudduh, Hello Fadduh!** . . . *Allan Sherman*
1082 **Hello Stranger** . . . *Barbara Lewis*
242 **Help!** . . . *Beatles*
377 **Help Me, Rhonda** . . . *Beach Boys*
1946 **Her Royal Majesty** . . . *James Darren*
1275 **Here Comes The Rain Again** . . . *Eurythmics*
1483 **Here I Am (Just When I Thought I Was Over You)** . . . *Air Supply*
1019 **Here You Come Again** . . . *Dolly Parton*
220 **Hey! Baby** . . . *Bruce Channel*
1125 **Hey! Jealous Lover** . . . *Frank Sinatra*
10 **Hey Jude** . . . *Beatles*
1313 **Hey Little Cobra** . . . *Rip Chords*
218 **Hey Paula** . . . *Paul & Paula*
891 **Hey There Lonely Girl** . . . *Eddie Holman*
514 **(Hey Won't You Play) Another Somebody Done Somebody Wrong Song** . . . *B.J. Thomas*
1404 **Higher Ground** . . . *Stevie Wonder*
1800 **Him** . . . *Rupert Holmes*
1724 **Him Or Me - What's It Gonna Be?** . . . *Paul Revere & The Raiders*
388 **Hit The Road Jack** . . . *Ray Charles*
1519 **Hitchin' A Ride** . . . *Vanity Fare*
1206 **Hold Me** . . . *Fleetwood Mac*
999 **Hold Me Now** . . . *Thompson Twins*
1568 **Hold Me Tight** . . . *Johnny Nash*
1521 **Hold The Line** . . . *Toto*
1604 **Hold What You've Got** . . . *Joe Tex*
1572 **Hold Your Head Up** . . . *Argent*
1892 **Holly Holy** . . . *Neil Diamond*
1864 **Hollywood Swinging** . . . *Kool & The Gang*
1591 **Homeward Bound** . . . *Simon & Garfunkel*
82 **Honey** . . . *Bobby Goldsboro*
93 **Honeycomb** . . . *Jimmie Rodgers*
666 **Honky Tonk (Parts 1 & 2)** . . . *Bill Doggett*
134 **Honky Tonk Women** . . . *Rolling Stones*
Hooked On A Feeling
531 *Blue Swede*
1563 *B.J. Thomas*
1918 **Hooray For Hazel** . . . *Tommy Roe*
1014 **Hopelessly Devoted To You** . . . *Olivia Newton-John*
713 **Horse** . . . *Cliff Nobles & Co.*
230 **Horse With No Name** . . . *America*
1034 **Hot Blooded** . . . *Foreigner*
416 **Hot Child In The City** . . . *Nick Gilder*
440 **Hot Diggity (Dog Ziggity Boom)** . . . *Perry Como*
779 **Hot Fun In The Summertime** . . . *Sly & The Family Stone*
1508 **Hot Line** . . . *Sylvers*
180 **Hot Stuff** . . . *Donna Summer*
495 **Hotel California** . . . *Eagles*
1192 **Hotel Happiness** . . . *Brook Benton*
1 **Hound Dog** . . . *Elvis Presley*
249 **House Of The Rising Sun** . . . *Animals*
1843 **House That Jack Built** . . . *Aretha Franklin*
1337 **How Can I Be Sure** . . . *Young Rascals*
136 **How Can You Mend A Broken Heart** . . . *Bee Gees*
152 **How Deep Is Your Love** . . . *Bee Gees*
1052 **How Long** . . . *Ace*
948 **How Much I Feel** . . . *Ambrosia*
How Sweet It Is (To Be Loved By You)
1573 *James Taylor*
1899 *Marvin Gaye*

RANK	**Title** . . . Artist
1054	**Hundred Pounds Of Clay** . . . *Gene McDaniels*
1949	**Hungry** . . . *Paul Revere & The Raiders*
1459	**Hungry Heart** . . . *Bruce Springsteen*
941	**Hungry Like The Wolf** . . . *Duran Duran*
1706	**Hurdy Gurdy Man** . . . *Donovan*
1441	**Hurt** . . . *Timi Yuro*
818	**Hurting Each Other** . . . *Carpenters*
646	**Hurts So Good** . . . *John Cougar*
1340	**Hush** . . . *Deep Purple*
507	**Hustle, The** . . . *Van McCoy*
	I
102	**I Almost Lost My Mind** . . . *Pat Boone*
1097	**I Am A Rock** . . . *Simon & Garfunkel*
1455	**I Am...I Said** . . . *Neil Diamond*
457	**I Am Woman** . . . *Helen Reddy*
1767	**I Can Dream About You** . . . *Dan Hartman*
327	**I Can Help** . . . *Billy Swan*
1837	**I Can Never Go Home Anymore** . . . *Shangri-Las*
118	**I Can See Clearly Now** . . . *Johnny Nash*
328	**I Can't Get Next To You** . . . *Temptations*
142	**(I Can't Get No) Satisfaction** . . . *Rolling Stones*
463	**I Can't Go For That (No Can Do)** . . . *Daryl Hall & John Oates*
370	**I Can't Help Myself** . . . *Four Tops*
70	**I Can't Stop Loving You** . . . *Ray Charles*
1776	**I Cried A Tear** . . . *LaVern Baker*
1024	**I Don't Need You** . . . *Kenny Rogers*
247	**I Feel Fine** . . . *Beatles*
932	**I Feel For You** . . . *Chaka Khan*
1850	**I Feel Love** . . . *Donna Summer*
1726	**I Feel So Bad** . . . *Elvis Presley*
353	**I Get Around** . . . *Beach Boys*
1958	**I Go Crazy** . . . *Paul Davis*
980	**I Got Rhythm** . . . *Happenings*
1832	**I Got The Feelin'** . . . *James Brown*
238	**I Got You Babe** . . . *Sonny & Cher*
983	**I Got You (I Feel Good)** . . . *James Brown*
746	**I Gotcha** . . . *Joe Tex*
1354	**I Guess That's Why They Call It The Blues** . . . *Elton John*

RANK	**Title** . . . Artist
413	**I Hear A Symphony** . . . *Supremes*
	I Hear You Knocking
693	*Gale Storm*
1330	*Dave Edmunds*
	I Heard It Through The Grapevine
27	*Marvin Gaye*
697	*Gladys Knight & The Pips*
273	**I Honestly Love You** . . . *Olivia Newton-John*
163	**I Just Called To Say I Love You** . . . *Stevie Wonder*
1272	**I Just Wanna Stop** . . . *Gino Vannelli*
89	**I Just Want To Be Your Everything** . . . *Andy Gibb*
1235	**I Keep Forgettin' (Every Time You're Near)** . . . *Michael McDonald*
1193	**I Know A Place** . . . *Petula Clark*
1129	**I Know (You Don't Love Me No More)** . . . *Barbara George*
1106	**I Like Dreamin'** . . . *Kenny Nolan*
700	**I Like It Like That** . . . *Chris Kenner*
258	**I Love A Rainy Night** . . . *Eddie Rabbitt*
1671	**I Love How You Love Me** . . . *Paris Sisters*
1550	**I Love Music** . . . *O'Jays*
25	**I Love Rock 'N Roll** . . . *Joan Jett & The Blackhearts*
1471	**I Love The Nightlife (Disco 'Round)** . . . *Alicia Bridges*
1153	**I Love You Because** . . . *Al Martino*
1430	**I Need Your Love Tonight** . . . *Elvis Presley*
1602	**I Remember You** . . . *Frank Ifield*
1723	**I Saw Her Again** . . . *Mamas & The Papas*
1429	**I Say A Little Prayer** . . . *Dionne Warwick*
1246	**I Second That Emotion** . . . *Miracles*
607	**I Shot The Sheriff** . . . *Eric Clapton*
1943	**I Started A Joke** . . . *Bee Gees*
190	**I Think I Love You** . . . *Partridge Family*
1381	**I Think We're Alone Now** . . . *Tommy James & The Shondells*
1783	**I Want A New Drug** . . . *Huey Lewis & The News*
579	**I Want To Be Wanted** . . . *Brenda Lee*
28	**I Want To Hold Your Hand** . . . *Beatles*

RANK	**Title** . . . Artist
287	**I Want To Know What Love Is** . . . *Foreigner*
494	**I Want You Back** . . . *Jackson 5*
435	**I Want You, I Need You, I Love You** . . . *Elvis Presley*
790	**I Was Made To Love Her** . . . *Stevie Wonder*
237	**I Will Follow Him** . . . *Little Peggy March*
158	**I Will Survive** . . . *Gloria Gaynor*
527	**I Wish** . . . *Stevie Wonder*
1248	**I Wish It Would Rain** . . . *Temptations*
477	**I Write The Songs** . . . *Barry Manilow*
808	**I'd Love You To Want Me** . . . *Lobo*
735	**I'd Really Love To See You Tonight** . . . *England Dan & John Ford Coley*
1061	**I'll Be Around** . . . *Spinners*
964	**I'll Be Good To You** . . . *Brothers Johnson*
1357	**I'll Be Home** . . . *Pat Boone*
76	**I'll Be There** . . . *Jackson 5*
1770	**I'll Never Fall In Love Again** . . . *Tom Jones*
1940	**I'll Never Fall In Love Again** . . . *Dionne Warwick*
1428	**I'll Never Find Another You** . . . *Seekers*
1507	**I'll Never Love This Way Again** . . . *Dionne Warwick*
572	**I'll Take You There** . . . *Staple Singers*
29	**I'm A Believer** . . . *Monkees*
1990	**I'm Alright** . . . *Kenny Loggins*
1480	**I'm Coming Out** . . . *Diana Ross*
1070	**I'm Gonna Get Married** . . . *Lloyd Price*
1133	**I'm Gonna Love You Just A Little More Baby** . . . *Barry White*
810	**I'm Gonna Make You Love Me** . . . *Supremes & Temptations*
918	**I'm Gonna Sit Right Down And Write Myself A Letter** . . . *Billy Williams*
634	**I'm Henry VIII, I Am** . . . *Herman's Hermits*
991	**I'm In Love Again** . . . *Fats Domino*
687	**I'm In You** . . . *Peter Frampton*
	I'm Leaving It Up To You
366	*Dale & Grace*
1401	*Donny & Marie Osmond*
699	**I'm Not In Love** . . . *10cc*
1286	**I'm Not Lisa** . . . *Jessi Colter*
1781	**I'm On Fire** . . . *Bruce Springsteen*
171	**I'm Sorry** . . . *Brenda Lee*
517	**I'm Sorry** . . . *John Denver*
1092	**I'm Still In Love With You** . . . *Al Green*
411	**I'm Telling You Now** . . . *Freddie & The Dreamers*
1347	**I'm Walkin'** . . . *Fats Domino*
442	**I'm Your Boogie Man** . . . *KC & The Sunshine Band*
1821	**I'm Your Puppet** . . . *James & Bobby Purify*
1612	**I've Found Someone Of My Own** . . . *Free Movement*
1622	**I've Got Love On My Mind** . . . *Natalie Cole*
1291	**I've Got To Use My Imagination** . . . *Gladys Knight & The Pips*
1809	**I've Had It** . . . *Bell Notes*
	I've Loved You For A Long Time...see: Cupid
931	**I've Never Been To Me** . . . *Charlene*
1174	**I've Told Every Little Star** . . . *Linda Scott*
1436	**If** . . . *Bread*
451	**If I Can't Have You** . . . *Yvonne Elliman*
976	**If I Had A Hammer** . . . *Trini Lopez*
1045	**(If Loving You Is Wrong) I Don't Want To Be Right** . . . *Luther Ingram*
1799	**If This Is It** . . . *Huey Lewis & The News*
1496	**If You Could Read My Mind** . . . *Gordon Lightfoot*
1041	**If You Don't Know Me By Now** . . . *Harold Melvin & The Blue Notes*
285	**If You Leave Me Now** . . . *Chicago*
1534	**If You Love Me (Let Me Know)** . . . *Olivia Newton-John*
1026	**If You Love Somebody Set Them Free** . . . *Sting*
379	**If You Wanna Be Happy** . . . *Jimmy Soul*
1795	**Image Of A Girl** . . . *Safaris*
1104	**Imagine** . . . *John Lennon*
1657	**"In" Crowd** . . . *Ramsey Lewis Trio*
1960	**In My House** . . . *Mary Jane Girls*
1182	**In The Ghetto** . . . *Elvis Presley*
1368	**In The Mood** . . . *Ernie Fields*
1030	**In The Navy** . . . *Village People*
1693	**In The Rain** . . . *Dramatics*
1180	**In The Summertime** . . . *Mungo Jerry*

RANK	**Title** . . . Artist
55	**In The Year 2525** . . . *Zager & Evans*
554	**Incense And Peppermints** . . . *Strawberry Alarm Clock*
1694	**Indian Giver** . . . *1910 Fruitgum Co.*
455	**Indian Reservation (The Lament Of The Cherokee Reservation Indian)** . . . *Raiders*
1567	**Indiana Wants Me** . . . *R. Dean Taylor*
1791	**Infatuation** . . . *Rod Stewart*
977	**Instant Karma (We All Shine On)** . . . *John Ono Lennon*
1380	**Is There Something I Should Know** . . . *Duran Duran*
222	**Island Girl** . . . *Elton John*
263	**Islands In The Stream** . . . *Kenny Rogers & Dolly Parton*
1327	**It Don't Come Easy** . . . *Ringo Starr*
1170	**It Keeps Right On A-Hurtin'** . . . *Johnny Tillotson*
1060	**It Must Be Him** . . . *Vikki Carr*
1491	**It Never Rains In Southern California** . . . *Albert Hammond*
1000	**It's A Heartache** . . . *Bonnie Tyler*
1812	**It's A Mistake** . . . *Men At Work*
40	**It's All In The Game** . . . *Tommy Edwards*
1409	**It's All Right** . . . *Impressions*
1268	**It's Ecstasy When You Lay Down Next To Me** . . . *Barry White*
1130	**It's Just A Matter Of Time** . . . *Brook Benton*
390	**It's My Party** . . . *Lesley Gore*
1610	**It's Not For Me To Say** . . . *Johnny Mathis*
63	**It's Now Or Never** . . . *Elvis Presley*
283	**It's Only Make Believe** . . . *Conway Twitty*
1467	**It's So Easy** . . . *Linda Ronstadt*
282	**It's Still Rock And Roll To Me** . . . *Billy Joel*
1608	**It's The Same Old Song** . . . *Four Tops*
1395	**It's Time To Cry** . . . *Paul Anka*
72	**It's Too Late** . . . *Carole King*
1936	**It's Up To You** . . . *Rick Nelson*
886	**It's Your Thing** . . . *Isley Brothers*
576	**Itsy Bitsy Teenie Weenie Yellow Polkadot Bikini** . . . *Brian Hyland*
	Ivory Tower
837	*Cathy Carr*
1787	*Gale Storm*

J

RANK	**Title** . . . Artist
114	**Jack & Diane** . . . *John Cougar*
1005	**Jackie Blue** . . . *Ozark Mountain Daredevils*
19	**Jailhouse Rock** . . . *Elvis Presley*
1383	**Java** . . . *Al Hirt*
870	**Jazzman** . . . *Carole King*
798	**Jean** . . . *Oliver*
	Jenny...see: 867-5309
842	**Jeopardy** . . . *Greg Kihn Band*
253	**Jessie's Girl** . . . *Rick Springfield*
1855	**Jingle Bell Rock** . . . *Bobby Helms*
335	**Jive Talkin'** . . . *Bee Gees*
838	**Joanna** . . . *Kool & The Gang*
356	**Johnny Angel** . . . *Shelley Fabares*
479	**Joker** . . . *Steve Miller Band*
1442	**Jolly Green Giant** . . . *Kingsmen*
1903	**Joy** . . . *Apollo 100 featuring Tom Parker*
51	**Joy To The World** . . . *Three Dog Night*
348	**Judy In Disguise (With Glasses)** . . . *John Fred & His Playboy Band*
1597	**Judy's Turn To Cry** . . . *Lesley Gore*
1495	**Julie, Do Ya Love Me** . . . *Bobby Sherman*
62	**Jump** . . . *Van Halen*
989	**Jump (For My Love)** . . . *Pointer Sisters*
982	**Jumpin' Jack Flash** . . . *Rolling Stones*
1359	**Jungle Boogie** . . . *Kool & The Gang*
1190	**Junior's Farm** . . . *Paul McCartney & Wings*
1237	**Just A Dream** . . . *Jimmy Clanton*
1995	**Just A Song Before I Go** . . . *Crosby, Stills & Nash*
1606	**Just Dropped In (To See What Condition My Condition Was In)** . . . *First Edition*
1933	**(Just Like) Romeo & Juliet** . . . *Reflections*
60	**(Just Like) Starting Over** . . . *John Lennon*
358	**Just My Imagination (Running Away With Me)** . . . *Temptations*
678	**Just The Two Of Us** . . . *Grover Washington, Jr./Bill Withers*

RANK	Title . . . Artist
985	**Just The Way You Are** . . . *Billy Joel*
834	**Just Walking In The Rain** . . . *Johnnie Ray*
1276	**Just When I Needed You Most** . . . *Randy Vanwarmer*
1279	**Just You 'N' Me** . . . *Chicago*

K

RANK	Title . . . Artist
350	**Kansas City** . . . *Wilbert Harrison*
179	**Karma Chameleon** . . . *Culture Club*
686	**Keep It Comin' Love** . . . *KC & The Sunshine Band*
1422	**Keep On Dancing** . . . *Gentrys*
420	**Keep On Loving You** . . . *REO Speedwagon*
307	**Keep On Truckin'** . . . *Eddie Kendricks*
1972	**Keep The Fire Burnin'** . . . *REO Speedwagon*
1747	**Kewpie Doll** . . . *Perry Como*
1403	**Kicks** . . . *Paul Revere & The Raiders*
80	**Killing Me Softly With His Song** . . . *Roberta Flack*
394	**Kind Of A Drag** . . . *Buckinghams*
1047	**King Of Pain** . . . *Police*
1415	**King Of The Road** . . . *Roger Miller*
260	**Kiss And Say Goodbye** . . . *Manhattans*
175	**Kiss On My List** . . . *Daryl Hall & John Oates*
104	**Kiss You All Over** . . . *Exile*
1116	**Kisses Sweeter Than Wine** . . . *Jimmie Rodgers*
488	**Knock On Wood** . . . *Amii Stewart*
194	**Knock Three Times** . . . *Dawn*
804	**Kodachrome** . . . *Paul Simon*
1321	**Kookie, Kookie (Lend Me Your Comb)** . . . *Edward Byrnes & Connie Stevens*
323	**Kung Fu Fighting** . . . *Carl Douglas*

L

RANK	Title . . . Artist
1393	**La - La - Means I Love You** . . . *Delfonics*
35	**Lady** . . . *Kenny Rogers*
1804	**Lady** . . . *Styx*
1910	**Lady Godiva** . . . *Peter & Gordon*
1253	**Lady Madonna** . . . *Beatles*
520	**Lady Marmalade** . . . *LaBelle*
812	**Lady Willpower** . . . *Gary Puckett & The Union Gap*
1948	**Land Of 1000 Dances** . . . *Wilson Pickett*
1002	**Last Dance** . . . *Donna Summer*
656	**Last Date** . . . *Floyd Cramer*
849	**Last Kiss** . . . *J. Frank Wilson & The Cavaliers*
1072	**Last Night** . . . *Mar-Keys*
1032	**Last Song** . . . *Edward Bear*
581	**Last Train To Clarksville** . . . *Monkees*
1745	**Late In The Evening** . . . *Paul Simon*
482	**Laughter In The Rain** . . . *Neil Sedaka*
1131	**Lavender-Blue** . . . *Sammy Turner*
1871	**Lay Down (Candles In The Rain)** . . . *Melanie*
940	**Lay Down Sally** . . . *Eric Clapton*
34	**Le Freak** . . . *Chic*
1514	**Lead Me On** . . . *Maxine Nightingale*
622	**Leader Of The Pack** . . . *Shangri-Las*
192	**Lean On Me** . . . *Bill Withers*
281	**Learnin' The Blues** . . . *Frank Sinatra*
1739	**Leather And Lace** . . . *Stevie Nicks with Don Henley*
1048	**Leave Me Alone (Ruby Red Dress)** . . . *Helen Reddy*
526	**Leaving On A Jet Plane** . . . *Peter, Paul & Mary*
929	**Let 'Em In** . . . *Wings*
369	**Let It Be** . . . *Beatles*
1692	**Let It Be Me** . . . *Betty Everett & Jerry Butler*
1513	**Let It Whip** . . . *Dazz Band*
1859	**Let Me Be There** . . . *Olivia Newton-John*
21	**(Let Me Be Your) Teddy Bear** . . . *Elvis Presley*
1283	**Let Me In** . . . *Sensations*
	Let The Sunshine In...see: Aquarius
	Let Them...see: Let 'Em
506	**Let Your Love Flow** . . . *Bellamy Brothers*
483	**Let's Dance** . . . *David Bowie*
1318	**Let's Dance** . . . *Chris Montez*
584	**Let's Do It Again** . . . *Staple Singers*
306	**Let's Get It On** . . . *Marvin Gaye*
312	**Let's Go Crazy** . . . *Prince & the Revolution*
1880	**Let's Go, Let's Go, Let's Go** . . . *Hank Ballard & The Midnighters*
915	**Let's Groove** . . . *Earth, Wind & Fire*
1150	**Let's Hang On!** . . . *Four Seasons*
313	**Let's Hear It For The Boy** . . . *Deniece Williams*

RANK	**Title** . . . Artist
550	**Let's Stay Together** . . . *Al Green*
	Letter, The
132	*Box Tops*
1982	*Joe Cocker*
	Light My Fire
178	*The Doors*
981	*Jose Feliciano*
592	**Lightnin' Strikes** . . . *Lou Christie*
824	**Like A Rolling Stone** . . . *Bob Dylan*
47	**Like A Virgin** . . . *Madonna*
803	**Lil' Red Riding Hood** . . . *Sam The Sham & The Pharaohs*
737	**Limbo Rock** . . . *Chubby Checker*
	Lion Sleeps Tonight
217	*Tokens*
962	*Robert John*
1489	**Lipstick On Your Collar** . . . *Connie Francis*
90	**Lisbon Antigua** . . . *Nelson Riddle*
1205	**Listen People** . . . *Herman's Hermits*
602	**Listen To What The Man Said** . . . *Wings*
	Little...also see: Lil'
911	**Little Bit Me, A Little Bit You** . . . *Monkees*
775	**Little Bit O'Soul** . . . *Music Explosion*
1742	**Little Bitty Pretty One** . . . *Thurston Harris*
636	**Little Darlin'** . . . *Diamonds*
861	**Little Green Apples** . . . *O.C. Smith*
923	**Little Jeannie** . . . *Elton John*
1006	**Little More Love** . . . *Olivia Newton-John*
1199	**Little Old Lady (From Pasadena)** . . . *Jan & Dean*
1451	**Little Ole Man (Uptight-Everything's Alright)** . . . *Bill Cosby*
1772	**Little Red Corvette** . . . *Prince*
1701	**Little Sister** . . . *Elvis Presley*
493	**Little Star** . . . *Elegants*
942	**Little Willy** . . . *Sweet*
1087	**Little Woman** . . . *Bobby Sherman*
712	**Live And Let Die** . . . *Wings*
1736	**Living Inside Myself** . . . *Gino Vannelli*
	Loco-Motion, The
301	*Grand Funk*
561	*Little Eva*
1728	**Logical Song** . . . *Supertramp*
788	**Lollipop** . . . *Chordettes*
1889	**Lonely Blue Boy** . . . *Conway Twitty*
135	**Lonely Boy** . . . *Paul Anka*
1962	**Lonely Boy** . . . *Andrew Gold*
1900	**Lonely Bull** . . . *Tijuana Brass featuring Herb Alpert*
1173	**Lonely Days** . . . *Bee Gees*
957	**Lonely Night (Angel Face)** . . . *Captain & Tennille*
1685	**Lonely People** . . . *America*
1661	**Lonely Street** . . . *Andy Williams*
1991	**Lonely Teardrops** . . . *Jackie Wilson*
1786	**Lonesome Loser** . . . *Little River Band*
1968	**Lonesome Town** . . . *Ricky Nelson*
412	**Long And Winding Road** . . . *Beatles*
786	**Long Cool Woman (In A Black Dress)** . . . *Hollies*
1863	**Long Tall Sally** . . . *Little Richard*
743	**Longer** . . . *Dan Fogelberg*
1891	**Longest Walk** . . . *Jaye P. Morgan*
1575	**Longfellow Serenade** . . . *Neil Diamond*
1408	**Look Of Love** . . . *Sergio Mendes & Brasil '66*
1435	**Look What You Done For Me** . . . *Al Green*
1524	**Lookin' For Love** . . . *Johnny Lee*
897	**Lookin' Out My Back Door** . . . *Creedence Clearwater Revival*
1535	**Looking Back** . . . *Nat King Cole*
505	**Looks Like We Made It** . . . *Barry Manilow*
1448	**Loop De Loop** . . . *Johnny Thunder*
1423	**Lord's Prayer** . . . *Sister Janet Mead*
1921	**Losing You** . . . *Brenda Lee*
919	**Lost In Love** . . . *Air Supply*
640	**Louie Louie** . . . *Kingsmen*
1488	**Love And Marriage** . . . *Frank Sinatra*
813	**Love (Can Make You Happy)** . . . *Mercy*
341	**Love Child** . . . *Supremes*
1500	**Love Grows (Where My Rosemary Goes)** . . . *Edison Lighthouse*
321	**Love Hangover** . . . *Diana Ross*
1618	**Love Is A Battlefield** . . . *Pat Benatar*
43	**Love Is A Many-Splendored Thing** . . . *Four Aces*
729	**Love Is Alive** . . . *Gary Wright*
69	**Love Is Blue** . . . *Paul Mauriat*
626	**Love Is Here And Now You're Gone** . . . *Supremes*

RANK	**Title** . . . Artist
1994	**Love Is In The Air** . . . *John Paul Young*
256	**(Love Is) Thicker Than Water** . . . *Andy Gibb*
1683	**Love Letters** . . . *Ketty Lester*
18	**Love Letters In The Sand** . . . *Pat Boone*
421	**Love Machine** . . . *Miracles*
756	**Love Me** . . . *Elvis Presley*
606	**Love Me Do** . . . *Beatles*
58	**Love Me Tender** . . . *Elvis Presley*
1164	**Love Me With All Your Heart** . . . *Ray Charles Singers*
1053	**Love On A Two-Way Street** . . . *Moments*
683	**Love On The Rocks** . . . *Neil Diamond*
1823	**Love Or Let Me Be Lonely** . . . *Friends Of Distinction*
1077	**Love Potion Number Nine** . . . *Searchers*
553	**Love Rollercoaster** . . . *Ohio Players*
920	**Love So Right** . . . *Bee Gees*
1562	**Love Somebody** . . . *Rick Springfield*
164	**Love Theme From "A Star Is Born" (Evergreen)** . . . *Barbra Streisand*
	Love Theme From "Footloose"...see: Almost Paradise
374	**Love Theme From Romeo & Juliet** . . . *Henry Mancini*
763	**Love To Love You Baby** . . . *Donna Summer*
596	**Love Train** . . . *O'Jays*
1867	**Love Will Find A Way** . . . *Pablo Cruise*
108	**Love Will Keep Us Together** . . . *Captain & Tennille*
1487	**Love Won't Let Me Wait** . . . *Major Harris*
504	**Love You Inside Out** . . . *Bee Gees*
384	**Love You Save** . . . *Jackson 5*
453	**Love's Theme** . . . *Love Unlimited Orchestra*
709	**Lover's Concerto** . . . *Toys*
1847	**Lover's Question** . . . *Clyde McPhatter*
846	**Loverboy** . . . *Billy Ocean*
1350	**Lovergirl** . . . *Teena Marie*
1196	**Lovers Who Wander** . . . *Dion*
863	**Loves Me Like A Rock** . . . *Paul Simon*
518	**Lovin' You** . . . *Minnie Riperton*

RANK	**Title** . . . Artist
993	**Lowdown** . . . *Boz Scaggs*
1539	**Lucille** . . . *Kenny Rogers*
1387	**Lucky Star** . . . *Madonna*
381	**Lucy In The Sky With Diamonds** . . . *Elton John*
805	**Lyin' Eyes** . . . *Eagles*

M

RANK	**Title** . . . Artist
1708	**Ma Belle Amie** . . . *Tee Set*
	MacArthur Park
187	*Donna Summer*
902	*Richard Harris*
7	**Mack The Knife** . . . *Bobby Darin*
71	**Maggie May** . . . *Rod Stewart*
107	**Magic** . . . *Olivia Newton-John*
1629	**Magic** . . . *Pilot*
1146	**Magic Carpet Ride** . . . *Steppenwolf*
1385	**Magic Moments** . . . *Perry Como*
927	**Main Event/Fight** . . . *Barbra Streisand*
1498	**Make A Move On Me** . . . *Olivia Newton-John*
534	**Make It With You** . . . *Bread*
1906	**Make The World Go Away** . . . *Eddy Arnold*
1509	**Makin' It** . . . *David Naughton*
673	**Making Love Out Of Nothing At All** . . . *Air Supply*
1338	**Mama Said** . . . *Shirelles*
359	**Mama Told Me (Not To Come)** . . . *Three Dog Night*
831	**Mama's Pearl** . . . *Jackson 5*
1434	**(Man Who Shot) Liberty Valance** . . . *Gene Pitney*
565	**Mandy** . . . *Barry Manilow*
105	**Maneater** . . . *Daryl Hall & John Oates*
277	**Maniac** . . . *Michael Sembello*
1905	**Maria Elena** . . . *Los Indios Tabajaras*
	Marianne
1144	*Hilltoppers*
1367	*Terry Gilkyson & The Easy Riders*
1452	**(Marie's the Name) His Latest Flame** . . . *Elvis Presley*
758	**Mashed Potato Time** . . . *Dee Dee Sharp*
1478	**Master Blaster (Jammin')** . . . *Stevie Wonder*
771	**Material Girl** . . . *Madonna*
1711	**Maybellene** . . . *Chuck Berry*
364	**Me And Bobby McGee** . . . *Janis Joplin*
209	**Me And Mrs. Jones** . . . *Billy Paul*
1584	**Me And You And A Dog Named Boo** . . . *Lobo*

RANK	Title . . . Artist
1585	**Mean Woman Blues** . . . *Roy Orbison*
722	**Mellow Yellow** . . . *Donovan*
1484	**Melodie D'Amour** . . . *Ames Brothers*
	Memories Are Made Of This
39	*Dean Martin*
1663	*Gale Storm*
	Memphis
822	*Johnny Rivers*
1696	*Lonnie Mack*
1952	**Men In My Little Girl's Life** . . . *Mike Douglas*
1329	**Mercy Mercy Me (The Ecology)** . . . *Marvin Gaye*
1707	**Mercy, Mercy, Mercy** . . . *Buckinghams*
1638	**Method Of Modern Love** . . . *Daryl Hall & John Oates*
337	**Michael** . . . *Highwaymen*
425	**Mickey** . . . *Toni Basil*
1848	**Midnight At The Oasis** . . . *Maria Muldaur*
1874	**Midnight Blue** . . . *Melissa Manchester*
1667	**Midnight Confessions** . . . *Grass Roots*
885	**Midnight In Moscow** . . . *Kenny Ball & his Jazzmen*
308	**Midnight Train To Georgia** . . . *Gladys Knight & The Pips*
1571	**Million To One** . . . *Jimmy Charles*
963	**Miracles** . . . *Jefferson Starship*
1559	**Miss Me Blind** . . . *Culture Club*
478	**Miss You** . . . *Rolling Stones*
438	**Missing You** . . . *John Waite*
	Mister...see: Mr.
922	**Misty Blue** . . . *Dorthy Moore*
1656	**Mockingbird** . . . *Carly Simon & James Taylor*
637	**Moments To Remember** . . . *Four Lads*
246	**Monday, Monday** . . . *Mama's & The Papa's*
252	**Monster Mash** . . . *Bobby "Boris" Pickett & The Crypt-Kickers*
1139	**Mony Mony** . . . *Tommy James & The Shondells*
588	**Moody River** . . . *Pat Boone*
	Moonglow and Theme From "Picnic"
157	*Morris Stoloff*
1356	*George Cates*
997	**Moonlight Feels Right** . . . *Starbuck*

RANK	Title . . . Artist
1112	**Moonlight Gambler** . . . *Frankie Laine*
1372	**More** . . . *Perry Como*
1345	**More, More, More** . . . *Andrea True Connection*
1536	**More Than A Feeling** . . . *Boston*
642	**More Than I Can Say** . . . *Leo Sayer*
368	**Morning After** . . . *Maureen McGovern*
1820	**Morning Has Broken** . . . *Cat Stevens*
290	**Morning Train (Nine To Five)** . . . *Sheena Easton*
274	**Most Beautiful Girl** . . . *Charlie Rich*
1424	**Mother And Child Reunion** . . . *Paul Simon*
597	**Mother-In-Law** . . . *Ernie K-Doe*
795	**Mountain's High** . . . *Dick & DeeDee*
778	**Mr. Big Stuff** . . . *Jean Knight*
491	**Mr. Blue** . . . *Fleetwoods*
616	**Mr. Custer** . . . *Larry Verne*
1456	**Mr. Jaws** . . . *Dickie Goodman*
1768	**Mr. Lee** . . . *Bobbettes*
571	**Mr. Lonely** . . . *Bobby Vinton*
1022	**Mr. Roboto** . . . *Styx*
614	**Mr. Tambourine Man** . . . *Byrds*
248	**Mrs. Brown You've Got A Lovely Daughter** . . . *Herman's Hermits*
241	**Mrs. Robinson** . . . *Simon & Garfunkel*
1640	**Mule Skinner Blues** . . . *Fendermen*
1124	**Music Box Dancer** . . . *Frank Mills*
1208	**Muskrat Love** . . . *Captain & Tennille*
906	**My Boy Lollipop** . . . *Millie Small*
231	**My Boyfriend's Back** . . . *Angels*
1314	**My Cherie Amour** . . . *Stevie Wonder*
1884	**My Dad** . . . *Paul Petersen*
336	**My Ding-A-Ling** . . . *Chuck Berry*
447	**My Eyes Adored You** . . . *Frankie Valli*
612	**My Girl** . . . *Temptations*
360	**My Guy** . . . *Mary Wells*
761	**My Happiness** . . . *Connie Francis*
1285	**My Heart Belongs To Me** . . . *Barbra Streisand*
330	**My Heart Has A Mind Of Its Own** . . . *Connie Francis*
939	**My Heart Is An Open Book** . . . *Carl Dobkins, Jr.*
951	**My Life** . . . *Billy Joel*

RANK	**Title** . . . Artist
125	**My Love** . . . *Paul McCartney & Wings*
396	**My Love** . . . *Petula Clark*
1658	**My Love** . . . *Lionel Richie*
1042	**My Melody Of Love** . . . *Bobby Vinton*
57	**My Prayer** . . . *Platters*
42	**My Sharona** . . . *Knack*
140	**My Sweet Lord** . . . *George Harrison*
1126	**My True Love** . . . *Jack Scott*
1021	**My True Story** . . . *Jive Five*
1603	**My World Is Empty Without You** . . . *Supremes*

N

RANK	**Title** . . . Artist
349	**Na Na Hey Hey Kiss Him Goodbye** . . . *Steam*
1081	**Name Game** . . . *Shirley Ellis*
1834	**Navy Blue** . . . *Diane Renay*
782	**Neither One Of Us (Wants To Be The First To Say Goodbye)** . . . *Gladys Knight & The Pips*
	Nel Blu Dipinto Di Blu...see: Volare
1732	**Neutron Dance** . . . *Pointer Sisters*
1746	**Never Be Anyone Else But You** . . . *Ricky Nelson*
1592	**Never Been To Spain** . . . *Three Dog Night*
721	**Never Can Say Goodbye** . . . *Jackson 5*
1215	**Never Gonna Let You Go** . . . *Sergio Mendes*
1765	**Never Knew Love Like This Before** . . . *Stephanie Mills*
799	**Never My Love** . . . *Association*
1010	**Never Surrender** . . . *Corey Hart*
578	**New Kid In Town** . . . *Eagles*
1901	**New Orleans** . . . *Gary "U.S." Bonds*
1600	**Next Door To An Angel** . . . *Neil Sedaka*
1360	**Nice To Be With You** . . . *Gallery*
1288	**Night** . . . *Jackie Wilson*
547	**Night Chicago Died** . . . *Paper Lace*
17	**Night Fever** . . . *Bee Gees*
1078	**Night Has A Thousand Eyes** . . . *Bobby Vee*
1273	**Night Moves** . . . *Bob Seger*
1777	**Night Owls** . . . *Little River Band*
300	**Night The Lights Went Out In Georgia** . . . *Vicki Lawrence*
1158	**Night They Drove Old Dixie Down** . . . *Joan Baez*
762	**Nights In White Satin** . . . *Moody Blues*
1114	**Nightshift** . . . *Commodores*
259	**9 To 5** . . . *Dolly Parton*
724	**19th Nervous Breakdown** . . . *Rolling Stones*
582	**96 Tears** . . . *? (Question Mark) & The Mysterians*
841	**99 Luftballons** . . . *Nena*
1181	**No Matter What Shape (Your Stomach's In)** . . . *T-Bones*
1789	**No More Lonely Nights** . . . *Paul McCartney*
	No More Love On The Run...see: Caribbean Queen
357	**No More Tears (Enough Is Enough)** . . . *Barbra Streisand/Donna Summer*
1083	**No No Song** . . . *Ringo Starr*
649	**No, Not Much!** . . . *Four Lads*
1687	**No Time** . . . *Guess Who*
675	**Nobody Does It Better** . . . *Carly Simon*
1681	**Nobody Told Me** . . . *John Lennon*
1152	**Norman** . . . *Sue Thompson*
1352	**North To Alaska** . . . *Johnny Horton*
513	**Nothing From Nothing** . . . *Billy Preston*
881	**(Now and Then There's) A Fool Such As I** . . . *Elvis Presley*
1204	**Nowhere Man** . . . *Beatles*
1954	**Nuttin' For Christmas** . . . *Barry Gordon*

O

RANK	**Title** . . . Artist
1849	**Obsession** . . . *Animotion*
119	**Ode To Billie Joe** . . . *Bobbie Gentry*
1165	**Oh, Babe, What Would You Say?** . . . *Hurricane Smith*
573	**Oh Girl** . . . *Chi-Lites*
1339	**Oh Happy Day** . . . *Edwin Hawkin's Singers*
1486	**Oh Julie** . . . *Crescendos*
1684	**Oh My My** . . . *Ringo Starr*
1231	**Oh No** . . . *Commodores*
213	**Oh, Pretty Woman** . . . *Roy Orbison*
1122	**Oh Sherrie** . . . *Steve Perry*
	Oh, What A Night...see: December, 1963
1110	**Old Cape Cod** . . . *Patti Page*
1605	**Old Days** . . . *Chicago*
1255	**Old Fashioned Love Song** . . . *Three Dog Night*
1668	**Old Lamplighter** . . . *Browns*
1714	**Old Rivers** . . . *Walter Brennan*
1555	**On And On** . . . *Gladys Knight & The Pips*

RANK	**Title** . . . Artist
1986	**On The Dark Side** . . . *John Cafferty & The Beaver Brown Band*
1552	**On The Radio** . . . *Donna Summer*
1418	**On The Rebound** . . . *Floyd Cramer*
1212	**On The Street Where You Live** . . . *Vic Damone*
1494	**One** . . . *Three Dog Night*
83	**One Bad Apple** . . . *Osmonds*
1718	**One Fine Day** . . . *Chiffons*
755	**One Less Bell To Answer** . . . *5th Dimension*
326	**One More Night** . . . *Phil Collins*
1284	**One Night** . . . *Elvis Presley*
1123	**One Night In Bangkok** . . . *Murray Head*
530	**One Of These Nights** . . . *Eagles*
1969	**One On One** . . . *Daryl Hall & John Oates*
499	**One That You Love** . . . *Air Supply*
1369	**One Thing Leads To Another** . . . *Fixx*
882	**1-2-3** . . . *Len Barry*
1581	**1, 2, 3, Red Light** . . . *1910 Fruitgum Co.*
894	**Only Love Can Break A Heart** . . . *Gene Pitney*
1774	**Only Sixteen** . . . *Dr. Hook*
845	**Only The Lonely (Know How I Feel)** . . . *Roy Orbison*
1416	**Only The Strong Survive** . . . *Jerry Butler*
1326	**Only Yesterday** . . . *Carpenters*
	Only You (And You Alone)
1481	*Platters*
1922	*Ringo Starr*
639	**Open Arms** . . . *Journey*
1270	**Other Woman** . . . *Ray Parker Jr.*
617	**Our Day Will Come** . . . *Ruby & The Romantics*
1080	**Out Of Limits** . . . *Marketts*
272	**Out Of Touch** . . . *Daryl Hall & John Oates*
857	**Outa-Space** . . . *Billy Preston*
620	**Over And Over** . . . *Dave Clark Five*
1145	**Overkill** . . . *Men At Work*
270	**Owner Of A Lonely Heart** . . . *Yes*

P

RANK	**Title** . . . Artist
409	**Paint It, Black** . . . *Rolling Stones*
1056	**Palisades Park** . . . *Freddy Cannon*
564	**Papa Was A Rollin' Stone** . . . *Temptations*
	Paper Roses
1560	*Marie Osmond*
1650	*Anita Bryant*
414	**Paperback Writer** . . . *Beatles*
	Party Doll
443	*Buddy Knox*
1628	*Steve Lawrence*
1673	**Party Lights** . . . *Claudine Clark*
1527	**Passion** . . . *Rod Stewart*
1307	**Patches** . . . *Clarence Carter*
1817	**Patches** . . . *Dickey Lee*
461	**Patricia** . . . *Perez Prado*
1979	**Peace Train** . . . *Cat Stevens*
943	**Peggy Sue** . . . *Buddy Holly*
633	**Penny Lane** . . . *Beatles*
1541	**People** . . . *Barbra Streisand*
84	**People Got To Be Free** . . . *Rascals*
1721	**Pepino The Italian Mouse** . . . *Lou Monte*
195	**Peppermint Twist - Part I** . . . *Joey Dee & the Starliters*
690	**Personality** . . . *Lloyd Price*
1672	**Petite Fleur (Little Flower)** . . . *Chris Barber's Jazz Band*
286	**Philadelphia Freedom** . . . *Elton John Band*
563	**Photograph** . . . *Ringo Starr*
3	**Physical** . . . *Olivia Newton-John*
536	**Pick Up The Pieces** . . . *Average White Band*
1252	**Pied Piper** . . . *Crispian St. Peters*
1004	**Pillow Talk** . . . *Sylvia*
1017	**Pink Shoe Laces** . . . *Dodie Stevens*
1295	**Pipeline** . . . *Chantay's*
166	**Play That Funky Music** . . . *Wild Cherry*
741	**Playground In My Mind** . . . *Clint Holmes*
1102	**Pleasant Valley Sunday** . . . *Monkees*
1549	**Please Come To Boston** . . . *Dave Loggins*
427	**Please Don't Go** . . . *K.C. & The Sunshine Band*
1752	**Please Love Me Forever** . . . *Bobby Vinton*
1055	**Please Mr. Please** . . . *Olivia Newton-John*
	Please Mr. Postman
445	*Marvelettes*
544	*Carpenters*
1090	**Please Please Me** . . . *Beatles*
877	**Poetry In Motion** . . . *Johnny Tillotson*
1645	**Poetry Man** . . . *Phoebe Snow*
208	**Pony Time** . . . *Chubby Checker*
351	**Poor Little Fool** . . . *Ricky Nelson*

RANK	**Title** . . . Artist
38	**Poor People Of Paris** . . . *Les Baxter*
583	**Poor Side Of Town** . . . *Johnny Rivers*
434	**Pop Muzik** . . . *M*
1075	**Popsicles And Icicles** . . . *Murmaids*
309	**Power Of Love** . . . *Huey Lewis & The News*
1057	**Precious And Few** . . . *Climax*
1984	**Pretty Little Angel Eyes** . . . *Curtis Lee*
271	**Private Eyes** . . . *Daryl Hall & John Oates*
880	**Problems** . . . *Everly Brothers*
	Proud Mary
710	*Creedence Clearwater Revival*
1421	*Ike & Tina Turner*
1594	**Psychotic Reaction** . . . *Count Five*
893	**Puff The Magic Dragon** . . . *Peter, Paul & Mary*
	Puppy Love
801	*Paul Anka*
1191	*Donny Osmond*
53	**Purple People Eater** . . . *Sheb Wooley*
783	**Purple Rain** . . . *Prince & the Revolution*
1410	**Put A Little Love In Your Heart** . . . *Jackie DeShannon*
887	**Put Your Hand In The Hand** . . . *Ocean*
694	**Put Your Head On My Shoulder** . . . *Paul Anka*
1271	**Puttin' On The Ritz** . . . *Taco*
	Q
363	**Quarter To Three** . . . *U.S. Bonds*
728	**Queen Of Hearts** . . . *Juice Newton*
1290	**Quiet Village** . . . *Martin Denny*
	R
402	**Rag Doll** . . . *4 Seasons*
780	**Rain, The Park & Other Things** . . . *Cowsills*
1353	**Rainbow** . . . *Russ Hamilton*
869	**Raindrops** . . . *Dee Clark*
111	**Raindrops Keep Fallin' On My Head** . . . *B.J. Thomas*
912	**Rainy Day Women #12 & 35** . . . *Bob Dylan*
815	**Rainy Days And Mondays** . . . *Carpenters*
1302	**Rainy Night In Georgia** . . . *Brook Benton*
866	**Ramblin Man** . . . *Allman Brothers Band*

RANK	**Title** . . . Artist
776	**Ramblin' Rose** . . . *Nat King Cole*
901	**Rapper, The** . . . *Jaggerz*
297	**Rapture** . . . *Blondie*
858	**Raspberry Beret** . . . *Prince & the Revolution*
	Raunchy
848	*Bill Justis*
1374	*Ernie Freeman*
367	**Reach Out I'll Be There** . . . *Four Tops*
1564	**Real Love** . . . *Doobie Brothers*
1816	**Rebel-'Rouser** . . . *Duane Eddy*
1648	**Red River Rock** . . . *Johnny & The Hurricanes*
900	**Red Rubber Ball** . . . *Cyrkle*
825	**Reflections** . . . *Supremes*
289	**Reflex, The** . . . *Duran Duran*
1223	**Release Me (And Let Me Love Again)** . . . *Engelbert Humperdinck*
1504	**Remember (Walkin' In The Sand)** . . . *Shangri-Las*
1853	**Remember You're Mine** . . . *Pat Boone*
1009	**Reminiscing** . . . *Little River Band*
1425	**Rescue Me** . . . *Fontella Bass*
403	**Respect** . . . *Aretha Franklin*
1229	**Return To Me** . . . *Dean Martin*
644	**Return To Sender** . . . *Elvis Presley*
109	**Reunited** . . . *Peaches & Herb*
269	**Rhinestone Cowboy** . . . *Glen Campbell*
995	**Rhythm Of The Night** . . . *DeBarge*
1143	**Rhythm Of The Rain** . . . *Cascades*
302	**Rich Girl** . . . *Daryl Hall & John Oates*
1703	**Ride!** . . . *Dee Dee Sharp*
1396	**Ride Captain Ride** . . . *Blues Image*
652	**Ride Like The Wind** . . . *Christopher Cross*
751	**Right Back Where We Started From** . . . *Maxine Nightingale*
1773	**Right Time Of The Night** . . . *Jennifer Warnes*
1371	**Rikki Don't Lose That Number** . . . *Steely Dan*
288	**Ring My Bell** . . . *Anita Ward*
621	**Ringo** . . . *Lorne Greene*
264	**Rise** . . . *Herb Alpert*
1043	**Rock And Roll Heaven** . . . *Righteous Brothers*
1649	**Rock And Roll Music** . . . *Beach Boys*
31	**Rock And Roll Waltz** . . . *Kay Starr*
11	**Rock Around The Clock** . . . *Bill Haley & His Comets*
522	**Rock Me Gently** . . . *Andy Kim*

RANK	Title . . . Artist
1613	**Rock On** . . . *David Essex*
525	**Rock The Boat** . . . *Hues Corporation*
100	**Rock With You** . . . *Michael Jackson*
339	**Rock Your Baby** . . . *George McCrae*
1886	**Rocket Man** . . . *Elton John*
515	**Rock'n Me** . . . *Steve Miller*
1860	**Rockin' Pneumonia - Boogie Woogie Flu** . . . *Johnny Rivers*
	Rockin' Robin
745	*Bobby Day*
811	*Michael Jackson*
	Romeo & Juliet...see: Love Theme From
1950	**Ronnie** . . . *4 Seasons*
641	**Rosanna** . . . *Toto*
937	**Rose, The** . . . *Bette Midler*
1856	**Rose And A Baby Ruth** . . . *George Hamilton IV*
1036	**Rose Garden** . . . *Lynn Anderson*
137	**Roses Are Red (My Love)** . . . *Bobby Vinton*
257	**Round And Round** . . . *Perry Como*
1897	**Rubber Ball** . . . *Bobby Vee*
680	**Rubberband Man** . . . *Spinners*
717	**Ruby Baby** . . . *Dion*
1827	**Ruby, Don't Take Your Love To Town** . . . *Kenny Rogers & The First Edition*
623	**Ruby Tuesday** . . . *Rolling Stones*
1829	**Run Away Child, Running Wild** . . . *Temptations*
1432	**Run Joey Run** . . . *David Geddes*
873	**Run To Him** . . . *Bobby Vee*
1861	**Run To You** . . . *Bryan Adams*
373	**Runaround Sue** . . . *Dion*
129	**Runaway** . . . *Del Shannon*
160	**Running Bear** . . . *Johnny Preston*
528	**Running Scared** . . . *Roy Orbison*

S

RANK	Title . . . Artist
	S.W.A.T. ...see: Theme From
424	**Sad Eyes** . . . *Robert John*
1680	**Sad Movies (Make Me Cry)** . . . *Sue Thompson*
1635	**Sad Songs (Say So Much)** . . . *Elton John*
917	**Safety Dance** . . . *Men Without Hats*
1473	**Sail Along Silvery Moon** . . . *Billy Vaughn*
1287	**Sail On** . . . *Commodores*
475	**Sailing** . . . *Christopher Cross*
1639	**Sailor (Your Home Is The Sea)** . . . *Lolita*
821	**Sally, Go 'Round The Roses** . . . *Jaynetts*
1224	**San Francisco (Be Sure To Wear Flowers In Your Hair)** . . . *Scott McKenzie*
1977	**Sara** . . . *Fleetwood Mac*
1256	**Sara Smile** . . . *Daryl Hall & John Oates*
1096	**Saturday In The Park** . . . *Chicago*
542	**Saturday Night** . . . *Bay City Rollers*
197	**Save The Last Dance For Me** . . . *Drifters*
910	**Save Your Heart For Me** . . . *Gary Lewis & The Playboys*
1147	**Say, Has Anybody Seen My Sweet Gypsy Rose** . . . *Dawn*
658	**Say It Isn't So** . . . *Daryl Hall & John Oates*
41	**Say Say Say** . . . *Paul McCartney & Michael Jackson*
934	**School Day** . . . *Chuck Berry*
1713	**School Is Out** . . . *Gary "U.S." Bonds*
1741	**Scorpio** . . . *Dennis Coffey & The Detroit Guitar Band*
	Sea Of Love
764	*Phil Phillips*
1121	*Honeydrippers*
1074	**Sealed With A Kiss** . . . *Brian Hyland*
1362	**Search Is Over** . . . *Survivor*
1107	**Searchin'** . . . *Coasters*
185	**Seasons In The Sun** . . . *Terry Jacks*
1200	**Secret Agent Man** . . . *Johnny Rivers*
961	**Secretly** . . . *Jimmie Rodgers*
1079	**See You In September** . . . *Happenings*
1730	**See You Later, Alligator** . . . *Bill Haley & His Comets*
1259	**Self Control** . . . *Laura Branigan*
1761	**Send For Me** . . . *Nat King Cole*
1217	**Send One Your Love** . . . *Stevie Wonder*
	Seventeen
1156	*Fontane Sisters*
1646	*Boyd Bennett & His Rockets*
1983	**Seventh Son** . . . *Johnny Rivers*
945	**Sexual Healing** . . . *Marvin Gaye*
1520	**Sexy Eyes** . . . *Dr. Hook*
20	**Shadow Dancing** . . . *Andy Gibb*
	Shaft...see: Theme From
1227	**Shake It Up** . . . *Cars*

RANK	**Title** . . . Artist
465	**(Shake, Shake, Shake) Shake Your Booty** . . . *KC & The Sunshine Band*
1959	**Shake Your Body (Down To The Ground)** . . . *Jacksons*
1463	**Shake Your Groove Thing** . . . *Peaches & Herb*
1148	**Shambala** . . . *Three Dog Night*
650	**Shame On The Moon** . . . *Bob Seger*
1738	**Shannon** . . . *Henry Gross*
1771	**Sharing The Night Together** . . . *Dr. Hook*
1557	**She Believes In Me** . . . *Kenny Rogers*
1461	**She Blinded Me With Science** . . . *Thomas Dolby*
959	**She Bop** . . . *Cyndi Lauper*
1682	**She Cried** . . . *Jay & The Americans*
352	**She Loves You** . . . *Beatles*
944	**She Works Hard For The Money** . . . *Donna Summer*
1101	**She'd Rather Be With Me** . . . *Turtles*
1670	**She's A Fool** . . . *Lesley Gore*
883	**She's A Lady** . . . *Tom Jones*
1342	**She's A Woman** . . . *Beatles*
1985	**She's Gone** . . . *Daryl Hall & John Oates*
930	**She's Just My Style** . . . *Gary Lewis & The Playboys*
874	**She's Not There** . . . *Zombies*
1719	**She's Not You** . . . *Elvis Presley*
1569	**(She's) Sexy + 17** . . . *Stray Cats*
378	**Sheila** . . . *Tommy Roe*
85	**Sherry** . . . *4 Seasons*
	Shifting, Whispering Sands
1044	*Rusty Draper*
1469	*Billy Vaughn*
489	**Shining Star** . . . *Earth, Wind & Fire*
1475	**Shining Star** . . . *Manhattans*
1825	**Shoop Shoop Song (It's In His Kiss)** . . . *Betty Everett*
	Shop Around
867	*Miracles*
1386	*Captain & Tennille*
1620	**Short Fat Fannie** . . . *Larry Williams*
688	**Short People** . . . *Randy Newman*
1051	**Short Shorts** . . . *Royal Teens*
1316	**Shotgun** . . . *Jr. Walker & The All Stars*
193	**Shout** . . . *Tears For Fears*
1930	**Shout - Part I** . . . *Joey Dee & The Starliters*
1912	**Shout! Shout! (Knock Yourself Out)** . . . *Ernie Maresca*

RANK	**Title** . . . Artist
454	**Show And Tell** . . . *Al Wilson*
1788	**Show Me The Way** . . . *Peter Frampton*
1370	**Show Must Go On** . . . *Three Dog Night*
1067	**Signed, Sealed, Delivered I'm Yours** . . . *Stevie Wonder*
1134	**Signs** . . . *Five Man Electrical Band*
	Silhouettes
1007	*Rays*
1698	*Herman's Hermits*
68	**Silly Love Songs** . . . *Wings*
1222	**Simon Says** . . . *1910 Fruitgum Co.*
1294	**Since I Fell For You** . . . *Lenny Welch*
1073	**Sing** . . . *Carpenters*
1554	**Sing A Song** . . . *Earth, Wind & Fire*
2	**Singing The Blues** . . . *Guy Mitchell*
1132	**Sink The Bismarck** . . . *Johnny Horton*
204	**Sir Duke** . . . *Stevie Wonder*
1510	**Sister Christian** . . . *Night Ranger*
566	**Sister Golden Hair** . . . *America*
130	**(Sittin' On) The Dock Of The Bay** . . . *Otis Redding*
748	**16 Candles** . . . *Crests*
1109	**Sixteen Reasons** . . . *Connie Stevens*
16	**Sixteen Tons** . . . *Tennessee Ernie Ford*
1780	**'65 Love Affair** . . . *Paul Davis*
1003	**Sky High** . . . *Jigsaw*
322	**Sleep Walk** . . . *Santo & Johnny*
1883	**Slip Away** . . . *Clarence Carter*
1627	**Slip Slidin' Away** . . . *Paul Simon*
1198	**Sloop John B** . . . *Beach Boys*
677	**Slow Hand** . . . *Pointer Sisters*
1169	**Slow Twistin'** . . . *Chubby Checker*
1679	**Smile A Little Smile For Me** . . . *Flying Machine*
1029	**Smiling Faces Sometimes** . . . *Undisputed Truth*
191	**Smoke Gets In Your Eyes** . . . *Platters*
1293	**Smoke On The Water** . . . *Deep Purple*
1128	**Smokin' In The Boy's Room** . . . *Brownsville Station*
1533	**Smooth Operator** . . . *Sade*
664	**Snoopy Vs. The Red Baron** . . . *Royal Guardsmen*
1966	**So In To You** . . . *Atlanta Rhythm Section*
1805	**So Many Ways** . . . *Brook Benton*
587	**So Much In Love** . . . *Tymes*
645	**So Rare** . . . *Jimmy Dorsey*

RANK	**Title** . . . Artist
1942	**Sock It To Me-Baby!** . . . *Mitch Ryder & The Detroit Wheels*
229	**Soldier Boy** . . . *Shirelles*
1177	**Some Kind Of Wonderful** . . . *Grand Funk*
1792	**Some Like It Hot** . . . *Power Station*
1675	**Somebody To Love** . . . *Jefferson Airplane*
1967	**Somebody's Baby** . . . *Jackson Browne*
691	**Somebody's Watching Me** . . . *Rockwell*
551	**Someday We'll Be Together** . . . *Supremes*
1426	**Someone Saved My Life Tonight** . . . *Elton John*
148	**Somethin' Stupid** . . . *Nancy & Frank Sinatra*
548	**Something** . . . *Beatles*
1677	**Something's Gotta Give** . . . *McGuire Sisters*
992	**Sometimes When We Touch** . . . *Dan Hill*
611	**Song Sung Blue** . . . *Neil Diamond*
767	**Sorry (I Ran All the Way Home)** . . . *Impalas*
1751	**Sorry Seems To Be The Hardest Word** . . . *Elton John*
708	**Soul Man** . . . *Sam & Dave*
1178	**Soulful Strut** . . . *Young-Holt Unlimited*
376	**Sounds Of Silence** . . . *Simon & Garfunkel*
1185	**South Street** . . . *Orlons*
469	**Southern Nights** . . . *Glen Campbell*
1282	**Space Race** . . . *Billy Preston*
819	**Spanish Harlem** . . . *Aretha Franklin*
1543	**Special Lady** . . . *Ray, Goodman & Brown*
1753	**Speedy Gonzales** . . . *Pat Boone*
1111	**Spiders & Snakes** . . . *Jim Stafford*
1117	**Spill The Wine** . . . *Eric Burdon & War*
714	**Spinning Wheel** . . . *Blood, Sweat & Tears*
970	**Spirit In The Sky** . . . *Norman Greenbaum*
1160	**Splish Splash** . . . *Bobby Darin*
973	**Spooky** . . . *Classics IV*
116	**Stagger Lee** . . . *Lloyd Price*
1633	**Stand Back** . . . *Stevie Nicks*
1315	**Stand By Me** . . . *Ben E. King*
1842	**Standing In The Shadows Of Love** . . . *Four Tops*
949	**Standing On The Corner** . . . *Four Lads*
305	**Star Wars Theme/Cantina Band** . . . *Meco*
473	**Stars on 45 (Medley)** . . . *Stars on 45*
676	**Start Me Up** . . . *Rolling Stones*
974	**State Of Shock** . . . *Jacksons*
516	**Stay** . . . *Maurice Williams & The Zodiacs*
95	**Stayin' Alive** . . . *Bee Gees*
1769	**Steal Away** . . . *Robbie Dupree*
1518	**Step By Step** . . . *Eddie Rabbitt*
1727	**Steppin' Out** . . . *Joe Jackson*
480	**Still** . . . *Commodores*
1644	**Still The One** . . . *Orleans*
1375	**Still The Same** . . . *Bob Seger*
969	**Stoned Soul Picnic** . . . *5th Dimension*
1868	**Stoney End** . . . *Barbra Streisand*
696	**Stood Up** . . . *Ricky Nelson*
914	**Stop Draggin' My Heart Around** . . . *Stevie Nicks with Tom Petty*
405	**Stop! In The Name Of Love** . . . *Supremes*
1666	**Stormy** . . . *Classics IV*
468	**Stranger On The Shore** . . . *Mr. Acker Bilk*
590	**Strangers In The Night** . . . *Frank Sinatra*
1538	**Strawberry Letter 23** . . . *Brothers Johnson*
956	**Stray Cat Strut** . . . *Stray Cats*
207	**Streak, The** . . . *Ray Stevens*
535	**Stripper, The** . . . *David Rose*
1361	**Stroll, The** . . . *Diamonds*
1866	**Stuck In The Middle With You** . . . *Stealers Wheel*
131	**Stuck On You** . . . *Elvis Presley*
1018	**Stuck On You** . . . *Lionel Richie*
1262	**Stumblin' In** . . . *Suzi Quatro & Chris Norman*
1267	**Suddenly** . . . *Billy Ocean*
1678	**Sugar Moon** . . . *Pat Boone*
81	**Sugar Shack** . . . *Jimmy Gilmer & The Fireballs*
112	**Sugar, Sugar** . . . *Archies*
1502	**Sugar Town** . . . *Nancy Sinatra*
103	**Sugartime** . . . *McGuire Sisters*
	Sukiyaki
232	*Kyu Sakamoto*
938	*Taste Of Honey*
1297	**Sultans Of Swing** . . . *Dire Straits*
1796	**Summer Breeze** . . . *Seals & Crofts*
251	**Summer In The City** . . . *Lovin' Spoonful*
1558	**Summer Nights** . . . *John Travolta & Olivia Newton-John*

RANK	**Title** . . . Artist
1553	**Summer Of '69** . . . *Bryan Adams*
	Summer Place...see: Theme From A
524	**Sundown** . . . *Gordon Lightfoot*
793	**Sunny** . . . *Bobby Hebb*
1244	**Sunshine** . . . *Jonathan Edwards*
1611	**Sunshine Of Your Love** . . . *Cream*
519	**Sunshine On My Shoulders** . . . *John Denver*
615	**Sunshine Superman** . . . *Donovan*
1689	**Supernatural Thing** . . . *Ben E. King*
809	**Superstar** . . . *Carpenters*
558	**Superstition** . . . *Stevie Wonder*
391	**Surf City** . . . *Jan & Dean*
1325	**Surfin' Bird** . . . *Trashmen*
1108	**Surfin' U.S.A.** . . . *Beach Boys*
401	**Surrender** . . . *Elvis Presley*
1647	**Susie Darlin'** . . . *Robin Luke*
1063	**Suspicion** . . . *Terry Stafford*
580	**Suspicious Minds** . . . *Elvis Presley*
533	**Sussudio** . . . *Phil Collins*
1915	**Swearin' To God** . . . *Frankie Valli*
1308	**Sweet Caroline (Good Times Never Seemed So Good)** . . . *Neil Diamond*
1528	**Sweet Dreams** . . . *Air Supply*
430	**Sweet Dreams (Are Made of This)** . . . *Eurythmics*
1844	**Sweet Hitch-Hiker** . . . *Creedence Clearwater Revival*
702	**Sweet Little Sixteen** . . . *Chuck Berry*
1515	**Sweet Love** . . . *Commodores*
1349	**Sweet Nothin's** . . . *Brenda Lee*
1996	**Sweet Old Fashioned Girl** . . . *Teresa Brewer*
879	**Sweet Soul Music** . . . *Arthur Conley*
1460	**(Sweet Sweet Baby) Since You've Been Gone** . . . *Aretha Franklin*
1625	**Sweet Thing** . . . *Rufus featuring Chaka Khan*
1987	**Sweetest Thing (I've Ever Known)** . . . *Juice Newton*
1710	**Swingin' School** . . . *Bobby Rydell*
1574	**Sylvia's Mother** . . . *Dr. Hook*

T

RANK	**Title** . . . Artist
319	**TSOP (The Sound Of Philadelphia)** . . . *MFSB featuring The Three Degrees*
1023	**Take A Chance On Me** . . . *Abba*
872	**Take A Letter Maria** . . . *R.B. Greaves*
225	**Take Good Care Of My Baby** . . . *Bobby Vee*
1530	**Take It On The Run** . . . *REO Speedwagon*
1264	**Take It To The Limit** . . . *Eagles*
840	**Take Me Home, Country Roads** . . . *John Denver*
1001	**Take Your Time (Do It Right)** . . . *S.O.S. Band*
935	**Talking In Your Sleep** . . . *Romantics*
1887	**Tallahassee Lassie** . . . *Freddy Cannon*
	Tammy
56	*Debbie Reynolds*
1476	*Ames Brothers*
1997	**Tea For Two Cha Cha** . . . *Tommy Dorsey Orchestra*
1512	**Tear Fell** . . . *Teresa Brewer*
343	**Tears Of A Clown** . . . *Miracles*
1366	**Tears On My Pillow** . . . *Little Anthony & The Imperials*
772	**Teen-Age Crush** . . . *Tommy Sands*
1717	**Teen Age Idol** . . . *Rick Nelson*
1810	**Teen Age Prayer** . . . *Gale Storm*
318	**Teen Angel** . . . *Mark Dinning*
1292	**Teen Beat** . . . *Sandy Nelson*
1664	**Teenager In Love** . . . *Dion & The Belmonts*
850	**Teenager's Romance** . . . *Ricky Nelson*
1988	**Telephone Line** . . . *Electric Light Orchestra*
512	**Tell Her About It** . . . *Billy Joel*
1841	**Tell Her No** . . . *Zombies*
1324	**Tell Him** . . . *Exciters*
892	**Tell It Like It Is** . . . *Aaron Neville*
966	**Tell Me Something Good** . . . *Rufus*
210	**Telstar** . . . *Tornadoes*
67	**Tequila** . . . *Champs*
497	**Thank God I'm A Country Boy** . . . *John Denver*
387	**Thank You (Falettinme Be Mice Elf Agin)** . . . *Sly & The Family Stone*
1238	**That Girl** . . . *Stevie Wonder*
1735	**That Lady** . . . *Isley Brothers*
452	**That'll Be The Day** . . . *Crickets*
1779	**That's All!** . . . *Genesis*
1911	**That's All You Gotta Do** . . . *Brenda Lee*
1335	**That's Life** . . . *Frank Sinatra*
990	**That's Rock 'N' Roll** . . . *Shaun Cassidy*

RANK	**Title** . . . Artist
346	**That's The Way (I Like It)** . . . *KC & The Sunshine Band*
9	**Theme From "A Summer Place"** . . . *Percy Faith*
731	**Theme From "Greatest American Hero" (Believe It or Not)** . . . *Joey Scarbury*
537	**Theme From Mahogany (Do You Know Where You're Going To)** . . . *Diana Ross*
	Theme From "Picnic"...see: Moonglow
	Theme From "Rocky"...see: Gonna Fly Now
439	**Theme From S.W.A.T.** . . . *Rhythm Heritage*
382	**Theme From Shaft** . . . *Isaac Hayes*
663	**(Theme From) Valley Of The Dolls** . . . *Dionne Warwick*
496	**Then Came You** . . . *Dionne Warwicke & Spinners*
1757	**Then He Kissed Me** . . . *Crystals*
1920	**Then You Can Tell Me Goodbye** . . . *Casinos*
851	**There Goes My Baby** . . . *Drifters*
145	**There! I've Said It Again** . . . *Bobby Vinton*
1332	**There's A Kind Of Hush** . . . *Herman's Hermits*
1175	**There's A Moon Out Tonight** . . . *Capris*
1458	**(There's) No Gettin' Over Me** . . . *Ronnie Milsap*
601	**These Boots Are Made For Walkin'** . . . *Nancy Sinatra*
1896	**These Eyes** . . . *Guess Who*
1547	**They Just Can't Stop It the (Games People Play)** . . . *Spinners*
127	**(They Long To Be) Close To You** . . . *Carpenters*
1203	**They're Coming To Take Me Away, Ha-Haaa!** . . . *Napoleon XIV*
1195	**Things** . . . *Bobby Darin*
1616	**Things Can Only Get Better** . . . *Howard Jones*
1537	**Things We Do For Love** . . . *10cc*
400	**This Diamond Ring** . . . *Gary Lewis & The Playboys*
	This Guy's (Girl's) In Love With You
143	*Herb Alpert*
1978	*Dionne Warwick*
1194	**This Is My Song** . . . *Petula Clark*
1904	**This Magic Moment** . . . *Jay & The Americans*
1916	**This Time** . . . *Troy Shondell*
1873	**This Will Be** . . . *Natalie Cole*
1929	**Those Lazy-Hazy-Crazy Days Of Summer** . . . *Nat King Cole*
711	**Those Were The Days** . . . *Mary Hopkin*
1136	**Thousand Stars** . . . *Kathy Young with The Innocents*
128	**Three Bells** . . . *Browns*
293	**Three Times A Lady** . . . *Commodores*
1317	**Thriller** . . . *Michael Jackson*
631	**Ticket To Ride** . . . *Beatles*
429	**Tide Is High** . . . *Blondie*
106	**Tie A Yellow Ribbon Round The Ole Oak Tree** . . . *Dawn*
1201	**Tie Me Kangaroo Down, Sport** . . . *Rolf Harris*
1091	**Tiger** . . . *Fabian*
354	**Tighten Up** . . . *Archie Bell & The Drells*
1243	**('Til) I Kissed You** . . . *Everly Brothers*
296	**Time After Time** . . . *Cyndi Lauper*
765	**Time (Clock Of The Heart)** . . . *Culture Club*
365	**Time In A Bottle** . . . *Jim Croce*
1755	**Time Is On My Side** . . . *Rolling Stones*
1824	**Time Is Tight** . . . *Booker T. & The MG's*
1089	**Time Of The Season** . . . *Zombies*
1576	**Time Won't Let Me** . . . *Outsiders*
1240	**Tin Man** . . . *America*
1676	**Tina Marie** . . . *Perry Como*
1839	**Tired Of Waiting For You** . . . *Kinks*
1624	**To All The Girls I've Loved Before** . . . *Julio Iglesias & Willie Nelson*
172	**To Know Him, Is To Love Him** . . . *Teddy Bears*
73	**To Sir With Love** . . . *Lulu*
1941	**Together** . . . *Connie Francis*
460	**Tom Dooley** . . . *Kingston Trio*
1344	**Tonight You Belong To Me** . . . *Patience & Prudence*
14	**Tonight's The Night (Gonna Be Alright)** . . . *Rod Stewart*
1392	**Too Busy Thinking About My Baby** . . . *Marvin Gaye*
1545	**Too Hot** . . . *Kool & The Gang*
1652	**Too Late For Goodbyes** . . . *Julian Lennon*

RANK **Title** . . . Artist

800 **Too Late To Turn Back Now** . . . *Cornelius Brothers & Sister Rose*
203 **Too Much** . . . *Elvis Presley*
284 **Too Much Heaven** . . . *Bee Gees*
523 **Too Much, Too Little, Too Late** . . . *Johnny Mathis/Deniece Williams*
1637 **Too Shy** . . . *Kajagoogoo*
295 **Top Of The World** . . . *Carpenters*
947 **Topsy II** . . . *Cozy Cole*
275 **Torn Between Two Lovers** . . . *Mary MacGregor*
23 **Tossin' And Turnin'** . . . *Bobby Lewis*
91 **Total Eclipse Of The Heart** . . . *Bonnie Tyler*
1176 **Touch Me** . . . *The Doors*
466 **Touch Me In The Morning** . . . *Diana Ross*
1697 **Tower Of Strength** . . . *Gene McDaniels*
905 **Traces** . . . *Classics IV*
304 **Tragedy** . . . *Bee Gees*
1465 **Tragedy** . . . *Thomas Wayne*
830 **Travelin' Band** . . . *Creedence Clearwater Revival*
342 **Travelin' Man** . . . *Ricky Nelson*
1028 **Treat Her Like A Lady** . . . *Cornelius Brothers & Sister Rose*
827 **Treat Her Right** . . . *Roy Head*
1756 **Troglodyte (Cave Man)** . . . *Jimmy Castor Bunch*
1218 **True** . . . *Spandau Ballet*
1105 **True Love** . . . *Bing Crosby & Grace Kelly*
320 **Truly** . . . *Lionel Richie*
1540 **Tryin' To Live My Life Without You** . . . *Bob Seger*
1179 **Turn Back The Hands Of Time** . . . *Tyrone Davis*
235 **Turn! Turn! Turn!** . . . *Byrds*
1516 **Turn Your Love Around** . . . *George Benson*
1913 **Twenty-Five Miles** . . . *Edwin Starr*
1437 **25 Or 6 To 4** . . . *Chicago*
684 **26 Miles (Santa Catalina)** . . . *Four Preps*
529 **Twilight Time** . . . *Platters*
151 **Twist, The** . . . *Chubby Checker*
665 **Twist And Shout** . . . *Beatles*
1542 **Twist Of Fate** . . . *Olivia Newton-John*
1814 **Two Faces Have I** . . . *Lou Christie*
2001...see: Also Sprach Zarathustra

RANK **Title** . . . Artist

U

1595 **Um, Um, Um, Um, Um, Um** . . . *Major Lance*
1322 **Unchained Melody** . . . *Righteous Brothers*
610 **Uncle Albert/Admiral Halsey** . . . *Paul & Linda McCartney*
1406 **Under The Boardwalk** . . . *Drifters*
432 **Undercover Angel** . . . *Alan O'Day*
965 **Union Of The Snake** . . . *Duran Duran*
1115 **Until You Come Back To Me (That's What I'm Gonna Do)** . . . *Aretha Franklin*
1447 **Up Around The Bend** . . . *Creedence Clearwater Revival*
1631 **Up On The Roof** . . . *Drifters*
1980 **Up-Up And Away** . . . *5th Dimension*
177 **Up Where We Belong** . . . *Joe Cocker & Jennifer Warnes*
92 **Upside Down** . . . *Diana Ross*
1084 **Uptight (Everything's Alright)** . . . *Stevie Wonder*
916 **Uptown Girl** . . . *Billy Joel*
1214 **Urgent** . . . *Foreigner*
823 **Use Me** . . . *Bill Withers*
1280 **Use Ta Be My Girl** . . . *O'Jays*

V

1103 **Valleri** . . . *Monkees*
1865 **Valley Of Tears** . . . *Fats Domino*
Valley Of The Dolls...see: Theme From
904 **Vehicle** . . . *Ides Of March*
74 **Venus** . . . *Frankie Avalon*
594 **Venus** . . . *Shocking Blue*
333 **View To A Kill** . . . *Duran Duran*
Volare
79 *Domenico Modugno*
1400 *Bobby Rydell*

W

806 **Wah Watusi** . . . *Orlons*
635 **Waiting For A Girl Like You** . . . *Foreigner*
170 **Wake Me Up Before You Go-Go** . . . *Wham!*
1704 **Wake The Town And Tell The People** . . . *Les Baxter & His Orchestra*
97 **Wake Up Little Susie** . . . *Everly Brothers*
1699 **Walk Away Renee** . . . *Left Banke*

RANK	**Title** . . . Artist
854	**Walk--Don't Run** . . . *Ventures*
240	**Walk Like A Man** . . . *4 Seasons*
1493	**Walk On By** . . . *Leroy Van Dyke*
1822	**Walk On By** . . . *Dionne Warwick*
393	**Walk Right In** . . . *Rooftop Singers*
1801	**Walking In Rhythm** . . . *Blackbyrds*
1902	**Walking To New Orleans** . . . *Fats Domino*
855	**Wanderer, The** . . . *Dion*
950	**Wanderer, The** . . . *Donna Summer*
1570	**Wanna Be Startin' Somethin'** . . . *Michael Jackson*
557	**Want Ads** . . . *Honey Cone*
216	**War** . . . *Edwin Starr*
1993	**Warrior** . . . *Scandal featuring Patty Smyth*
888	**Washington Square** . . . *Village Stompers*
1245	**Waterloo** . . . *Stonewall Jackson*
1872	**Waterloo** . . . *Abba*
1167	**Way Down Yonder In New Orleans** . . . *Freddy Cannon*
1377	**Way I Want To Touch You** . . . *Captain & Tennille*
174	**Way We Were** . . . *Barbra Streisand*
12	**Wayward Wind** . . . *Gogi Grant*
1579	**(We Ain't Got) Nothin' Yet** . . . *Blues Magoos*
757	**We Are Family** . . . *Sister Sledge*
1225	**We Are The Champions** . . . *Queen*
126	**We Are The World** . . . *USA for Africa*
1531	**We Belong** . . . *Pat Benatar*
245	**We Can Work It Out** . . . *Beatles*
1998	**We Don't Talk Anymore** . . . *Cliff Richard*
1798	**We Got Love** . . . *Bobby Rydell*
689	**We Got The Beat** . . . *Go-Go's*
1242	**We'll Sing In The Sunshine** . . . *Gale Garnett*
1957	**We're All Alone** . . . *Rita Coolidge*
539	**We're An American Band** . . . *Grand Funk*
1740	**We've Got Tonight** . . . *Kenny Rogers & Sheena Easton*
660	**We've Only Just Begun** . . . *Carpenters*
871	**Wear My Ring Around Your Neck** . . . *Elvis Presley*
211	**Wedding Bell Blues** . . . *5th Dimension*
605	**Welcome Back** . . . *John Sebastian*
1709	**Western Union** . . . *Five Americans*
	What A Feelin'...see: Flashdance
484	**What A Fool Believes** . . . *Doobie Brothers*

RANK	**Title** . . . Artist
1389	**What Does It Take (To Win Your Love)** . . . *Jr. Walker & The All Stars*
1468	**What In The World's Come Over You** . . . *Jack Scott*
1748	**What'd I Say** . . . *Ray Charles*
704	**What's Going On** . . . *Marvin Gaye*
156	**What's Love Got To Do With It** . . . *Tina Turner*
1095	**What's New Pussycat?** . . . *Tom Jones*
1763	**Whatcha Gonna Do?** . . . *Pablo Cruise*
591	**Whatever Gets You Thru The Night** . . . *John Lennon*
668	**Whatever Will Be, Will Be (Que Sera, Sera)** . . . *Doris Day*
1046	**Wheels** . . . *String-A-Longs*
1566	**When** . . . *Kalin Twins*
397	**When A Man Loves A Woman** . . . *Percy Sledge*
61	**When Doves Cry** . . . *Prince*
486	**When I Need You** . . . *Leo Sayer*
787	**When Will I Be Loved** . . . *Linda Ronstadt*
856	**When Will I See You Again** . . . *Three Degrees*
1766	**When You're In Love With A Beautiful Woman** . . . *Dr. Hook*
1529	**Whenever I Call You "Friend"** . . . *Kenny Loggins*
372	**Where Did Our Love Go** . . . *Supremes*
1691	**Where Is The Love** . . . *Roberta Flack & Donny Hathaway*
1154	**Where Or When** . . . *Dion & The Belmonts*
1397	**Where The Boys Are** . . . *Connie Francis*
770	**Which Way You Goin' Billy?** . . . *Poppy Family featuring Susan Jacks*
1758	**White Room** . . . *Cream*
2000	**White Silver Sands** . . . *Don Rondo*
836	**White Sport Coat (And A Pink Carnation)** . . . *Marty Robbins*
1588	**Whiter Shade Of Pale** . . . *Procol Harum*
426	**Who Can It Be Now?** . . . *Men At Work*
1013	**Who Loves You**. . . *Four Seasons*
1269	**Who's Crying Now** . . . *Journey*
1862	**Who's Holding Donna Now** . . . *DeBarge*
1577	**Who's Making Love** . . . *Johnnie Taylor*

RANK	**Title** . . . Artist
1261	**Who's Sorry Now** . . . *Connie Francis*
984	**Whole Lot Of Shakin' Going On** . . . *Jerry Lee Lewis*
1391	**Whole Lotta Love** . . . *Led Zeppelin*
1885	**Whole Lotta Loving** . . . *Fats Domino*
559	**Why** . . . *Frankie Avalon*
1623	**Why Baby Why** . . . *Pat Boone*
1858	**Why Can't We Be Friends?** . . . *War*
1168	**Why Can't We Live Together** . . . *Timmy Thomas*
	Why Do Fools Fall In Love
1734	*Frankie Lymon & The Teenagers*
1965	*Diana Ross*
1157	**Wichita Lineman** . . . *Glen Campbell*
659	**Wild Boys** . . . *Duran Duran*
865	**Wild One** . . . *Bobby Rydell*
410	**Wild Thing** . . . *Troggs*
1020	**Wildfire** . . . *Michael Murphey*
280	**Will It Go Round In Circles** . . . *Billy Preston*
310	**Will You Love Me Tomorrow** . . . *Shirelles*
214	**Winchester Cathedral** . . . *New Vaudeville Band*
141	**Windy** . . . *Association*
832	**Wipe Out** . . . *Surfaris*
1754	**Wishin' And Hopin'** . . . *Dusty Springfield*
189	**Witch Doctor** . . . *David Seville*
1876	**Witchcraft** . . . *Frank Sinatra*
324	**With A Little Luck** . . . *Wings*
1209	**With You I'm Born Again** . . . *Billy Preston & Syreeta*
1596	**Without Love (There Is Nothing)** . . . *Tom Jones*
122	**Without You** . . . *Nilsson*
1882	**Wolverton Mountain** . . . *Claude King*
682	**Woman** . . . *John Lennon*
167	**Woman In Love** . . . *Barbra Streisand*
1257	**Woman Needs Love (Just Like You Do)** . . . *Ray Parker Jr. & Raydio*
1241	**Woman, Woman** . . . *Gary Puckett & The Union Gap*
1207	**Wonderful Time Up There** . . . *Pat Boone*
1454	**Wonderful World** . . . *Herman's Hermits*
200	**Wonderland By Night** . . . *Bert Kaempfert*
560	**Wooden Heart** . . . *Joe Dowell*
759	**Wooly Bully** . . . *Sam The Sham & The Pharaohs*
1593	**Words Of Love** . . . *Mamas & The Papas*
732	**Working My Way Back To You/Forgive Me, Girl** . . . *Spinners*
619	**World Without Love** . . . *Peter & Gordon*
1093	**Worst That Could Happen** . . . *Brooklyn Bridge*
1636	**Would I Lie To You?** . . . *Eurythmics*
750	**Wreck Of The Edmund Fitzgerald** . . . *Gordon Lightfoot*
1599	**Writing On The Wall** . . . *Adam Wade*

Y

RANK	**Title** . . . Artist
670	**Y.M.C.A.** . . . *Village People*
549	**Yakety Yak** . . . *Coasters*
1439	**Yellow Bird** . . . *Arthur Lyman Group*
	Yellow Rose Of Texas
46	*Mitch Miller*
1141	*Johnny Desmond*
913	**Yellow Submarine** . . . *Beatles*
	Yes, I'm Ready
740	*Teri DeSario with K.C.*
1686	*Barbara Mason*
150	**Yesterday** . . . *Beatles*
889	**Yesterday Once More** . . . *Carpenters*
978	**Yo-Yo** . . . *Osmonds*
546	**You Ain't Seen Nothing Yet** . . . *Bachman-Turner Overdrive*
1955	**You And I** . . . *Eddie Rabbitt with Crystal Gayle*
1281	**You Are** . . . *Lionel Richie*
1888	**You Are My Love** . . . *Joni James*
1556	**You Are So Beautiful** . . . *Joe Cocker*
538	**You Are The Sunshine Of My Life** . . . *Stevie Wonder*
1797	**You Belong To Me** . . . *Carly Simon*
1831	**You Can Depend On Me** . . . *Brenda Lee*
389	**You Can't Hurry Love** . . . *Supremes*
1172	**You Can't Sit Down** . . . *Dovells*
329	**You Don't Bring Me Flowers** . . . *Barbra Streisand & Neil Diamond*
1187	**You Don't Have To Be A Baby To Cry** . . . *Caravelles*

RANK	**Title** . . . Artist
428	**You Don't Have To Be A Star (To Be In My Show)** . . . *Marilyn McCoo & Billy Davis, Jr.*
1431	**You Don't Have To Say You Love Me** . . . *Dusty Springfield*
909	**You Don't Know Me** . . . *Ray Charles*
1444	**You Don't Know What You've Got (Until You Lose It)** . . . *Ral Donner*
719	**You Don't Own Me** . . . *Lesley Gore*
1118	**You Give Good Love** . . . *Whitney Houston*
500	**You Haven't Done Nothin** . . . *Stevie Wonder*
	You Keep Me Hangin' On
408	*Supremes*
1875	*Vanilla Fudge*
4	**You Light Up My Life** . . . *Debby Boone*
734	**You Make Me Feel Brand New** . . . *Stylistics*
464	**You Make Me Feel Like Dancing** . . . *Leo Sayer*
1482	**You Make My Dreams** . . . *Daryl Hall & John Oates*
1975	**You May Be Right** . . . *Billy Joel*
1971	**You Might Think** . . . *Cars*
1716	**You Must Have Been A Beautiful Baby** . . . *Bobby Darin*
431	**You Needed Me** . . . *Anne Murray*
1058	**You Ought To Be With Me** . . . *Al Green*
1976	**You Really Got Me** . . . *Kinks*
162	**You Send Me** . . . *Sam Cooke*
946	**You Sexy Thing** . . . *Hot Chocolate*
492	**You Should Be Dancing** . . . *Bee Gees*
1474	**You Should Hear How She Talks About You** . . . *Melissa Manchester*
1934	**You Showed Me** . . . *Turtles*
1189	**You Talk Too Much** . . . *Joe Jones*
1161	**You Were On My Mind** . . . *We Five*
749	**You'll Never Find Another Love Like Mine** . . . *Lou Rawls*
226	**(You're) Having My Baby** . . . *Paul Anka*
1228	**You're In My Heart (The Final Acclaim)** . . . *Rod Stewart*

RANK	**Title** . . . Artist
1928	**You're My Everything** . . . *Temptations*
243	**(You're My) Soul And Inspiration** . . . *Righteous Brothers*
570	**You're No Good** . . . *Linda Ronstadt*
1963	**You're Only Lonely** . . . *J.D. Souther*
585	**You're Sixteen** . . . *Ringo Starr*
201	**You're So Vain** . . . *Carly Simon*
789	**You're The First, The Last, My Everything** . . . *Barry White*
996	**You're The Inspiration** . . . *Chicago*
1443	**You're The One** . . . *Vogues*
437	**You're The One That I Want** . . . *John Travolta & Olivia Newton-John*
1068	**You're The Reason I'm Living** . . . *Bobby Darin*
1099	**(You're the) Devil In Disguise** . . . *Elvis Presley*
598	**You've Got A Friend** . . . *James Taylor*
1230	**(You've Got) The Magic Touch** . . . *Platters*
347	**You've Lost That Lovin' Feelin'** . . . *Righteous Brothers*
716	**You've Made Me So Very Happy** . . . *Blood, Sweat & Tears*
705	**Young Girl** . . . *Gary Puckett & The Union Gap*
	Young Love
45	*Tab Hunter*
462	*Sonny James*
1951	**Young Lovers** . . . *Paul & Paula*
1464	**Young Turks** . . . *Rod Stewart*
1700	**Young World** . . . *Rick Nelson*
	(Your Love Has Lifted (Keeps Lifting) Me) Higher And Higher
835	*Rita Coolidge*
1833	*Jackie Wilson*
1384	**Your Mama Don't Dance** . . . *Loggins & Messina*
1583	**Your Precious Love** . . . *Marvin Gaye & Tammi Terrell*
1249	**Yummy Yummy Yummy** . . . *Ohio Express*

MISCELLANEOUS

THE TOP 50 ARTISTS OF THE TOP 2000

RANK	TOP 2000	
1)	34	Elvis Presley
2)	30	The Beatles
3)	18	Stevie Wonder
4)	16	Paul McCartney
5)	16	Elton John
6)	15	The Supremes
7)	14	The Rolling Stones
8)	14	Olivia Newton-John
9)	13	Daryl Hall & John Oates
10)	13	Pat Boone
11)	13	Ricky Nelson
12)	12	Bee Gees
13)	12	Donna Summer
14)	11	Michael Jackson
15)	11	Carpenters
16)	11	The Temptations
17)	11	Neil Diamond
18)	11	Brenda Lee
19)	10	The Four Seasons
20)	10	Barbra Streisand
21)	10	The Jackson 5
22)	10	The Beach Boys
23)	10	Chicago
24)	10	Aretha Franklin
25)	9	Marvin Gaye

RANK	TOP 2000	
26)	9	Three Dog Night
27)	8	Diana Ross
28)	8	The Everly Brothers
29)	8	Frank Sinatra
30)	8	Connie Francis
31)	8	Kenny Rogers
32)	8	Creedence Clearwater Revival
33)	8	Commodores
34)	8	Air Supply
35)	8	Herman's Hermits
36)	7	KC & The Sunshine Band
37)	7	Lionel Richie
38)	7	The Eagles
39)	7	Bobby Vinton
40)	7	Rod Stewart
41)	7	Ray Charles
42)	7	Foreigner
43)	7	Spinners
44)	7	Perry Como
45)	7	Gladys Knight & The Pips
46)	7	Bobby Darin
47)	7	Dion
48)	7	Dionne Warwick
49)	7	Fats Domino
50)	6	Paul Anka

Top 2000: Artist's total records making the Top 2000.

For artists with the same number of Top 2000 hits, ties are broken by totaling the final ranking of each record by these artists, and the artist with the lowest total ranks first, and so on.

SONGS WITH MORE THAN ONE HIT VERSION

Peak Position/Year (Top 2000 Rank)

1. Young Love
Tab Hunter 1/'57 (45)
Sonny James 1/'57 (462)

2. Butterfly
Andy Williams 1/'57 (188)
Charlie Gracie 1/'57 (331)

3. Go Away Little Girl
Donny Osmond 1/'71 (215)
Steve Lawrence 1/'63 (334)

4. The Loco-Motion
Grand Funk 1/'74 (301)
Little Eva 1/'62 (561)

5. Please Mr. Postman
The Marvelettes 1/'61 (445)
Carpenters 1/'75 (544)

6. I Heard It Through The Grapevine
Marvin Gaye 1/'68 (27)
Gladys Knight & The Pips 2/'67 (697)

7. MacArthur Park
Donna Summer 1/'78 (187)
Richard Harris 2/'68 (902)

8. Light My Fire
The Doors 1/'67 (178)
Jose Feliciano 3/'68 (981)

9. Sukiyaki
Kyu Sakamoto 1/'63 (232)
A Taste Of Honey 3/'81 (938)

10. The Lion Sleeps Tonight
The Tokens 1/'61 (217)
Robert John 3/'72 (962)

11. The Yellow Rose Of Texas
Mitch Miller 1/'55 (46)
Johnny Desmond 3/'55 (1141)

12. Grazing In The Grass
Hugh Masekela 1/'68 (406)
The Friends of Distinction 3/'69 (1149)

13. Da Doo Ron Ron
Shaun Cassidy 1/'77 (459)
The Crystals 3/'63 (1188)

14. Rockin' Robin
Bobby Day 2/'58 (745)
Michael Jackson 2/'72 (811)

15. Volare
Domenico Modugno 1/'58 (79)
Bobby Rydell 4/'60 (1400)

16. Moonglow and Theme From "Picnic"
Morris Stoloff 1/'56 (157)
George Cates 4/'56 (1356)

17. I'm Leaving It Up To You
Dale & Grace 1/'63 (366)
Donny & Marie Osmond 4/'74 (1401)

18. Dedicated To The One I Love
The Mamas & The Papas 2/'67 (723)
The Shirelles 3/'61 (1008)

19. Sea Of Love
Phil Phillips 2/'59 (764)
The Honeydrippers 3/'85 (1121)

20. Puppy Love
Paul Anka 2/'60 (801)
Donny Osmond 3/'72 (1191)

21. Tammy
Debbie Reynolds 1/'57 (56)
The Ames Brothers 5/'57 (1476)

22. Memories Are Made Of This
Dean Martin 1/'56 (39)
Gale Storm 5/'56 (1663)

23. Party Doll
Buddy Knox 1/'57 (443)
Steve Lawrence 5/'57 (1628)

24. Hooked On A Feeling
Blue Swede 1/'74 (531)
B.J. Thomas 5/'69 (1563)

25. He'll Have To Go (Stay)
Jim Reeves 2/'60 (679)
Jeanne Black 4/'60 (1334)

26. I Hear You Knocking
Gale Storm 2/'55 (693)
Dave Edmunds 4/'71 (1330)

27. Handy Man
Jimmy Jones 2/'60 (852)
James Taylor 4/'77 (1278)

28. Proud Mary
Creedence Clearwater Revival 2/'69 (710)
Ike & Tina Turner 4/'71 (1421)

29. Raunchy
Bill Justis 2/'57 (848)
Ernie Freeman 4/'57 (1374)

30. Shop Around
The Miracles 2/'61 (867)
Captain & Tennille 4/'76 (1386)

SONGS WITH MORE THAN ONE HIT VERSION
Peak Position/Year (Top 2000 Rank)

31. California Girls
The Beach Boys 3/'65 (1098)
David Lee Roth 3/'85 (1155)

32. Bridge Over Troubled Water
Simon & Garfunkel 1/'70 (54)
Aretha Franklin 6/'71 (1924)

33. You Keep Me Hangin' On
The Supremes 1/'66 (408)
Vanilla Fudge 6/'68 (1875)

34. Crying
Roy Orbison 2/'61 (864)
Don McLean 5/'81 (1485)

35. Yes, I'm Ready
Teri DeSario with K.C. 2/'80 (740)
Barbara Mason 5/'65 (1686)

36. Memphis
Johnny Rivers 2/'64 (822)
Lonnie Mack 5/'63 (1696)

37. Marianne
The Hilltoppers 3/'57 (1144)
Terry Gilkyson & The Easy Riders 4/'57 (1367)

38. The Letter
The Box Tops 1/'67 (132)
Joe Cocker 7/'70 (1982)

39. This Guy's (Girl's) In Love With You
Herb Alpert 1/'68 (143)
Dionne Warwick 7/'69 (1978)

40. Ivory Tower
Cathy Carr 2/'56 (837)
Gale Storm 6/'56 (1787)

41. Your Love Has Lifted (Keeps Lifting) Me Higher And Higher
Rita Coolidge 2/'77 (835)
Jackie Wilson 6/'67 (1833)

42. The Shifting, Whispering Sands
Rusty Draper 3/'55 (1044)
Billy Vaughn 5/'55 (1469)

43. Silhouettes
The Rays 3/'57 (1007)
Herman's Hermits 5/'65 (1698)

44. Seventeen
The Fontane Sisters 3/'55 (1156)
Boyd Bennett & his Rockets 5/'55 (1646)

45. Canadian Sunset
Hugo Winterhalter/Eddie Heywood 2/'56 (726)
Andy Williams 7/'56 (1989)

46. Heat Wave
Martha & The Vandellas 4/'63 (1312)
Linda Ronstadt 5/'75 (1674)

47. Dark Moon
Gale Storm 4/'57 (1351)
Bonnie Guitar 6/'57 (1851)

48. Paper Roses
Marie Osmond 5/'73 (1560)
Anita Bryant 5/'60 (1650)

49. Angel Of The Morning
Juice Newton 4/'81 (1216)
Merrilee Rush & The Turnabouts 7/'68 (1973)

50. Only You
The Platters 5/'55 (1481)
Ringo Starr 6/'75 (1922)

51. How Sweet It Is (To Be Loved By You)
James Taylor 5/'75 (1573)
Marvin Gaye 6/'65 (1899)

52. Why Do Fools Fall In Love
The Teenagers featuring Frankie Lymon 6/'56 (1734)
Diana Ross 7/'81 (1965)

SAME TITLES - DIFFERENT SONGS

The following Top 2000 songs have the same titles, but are not by the same composer(s). The titles are listed according to their Top 2000 ranking, along with the year each peaked.

Banana Boat (Song)
Harry Belafonte ('57)
The Tarriers ('57)

Band Of Gold
Don Cherry ('56)
Freda Payne ('70)

Best Of My Love
Emotions ('77)
The Eagles ('75)

(An) Everlasting Love
Andy Gibb ('78)
Carl Carlton ('74)

Fame
David Bowie ('75)
Irene Cara ('80)

Fire
Ohio Players ('75)
Pointer Sisters ('79)
The Crazy World Of Arthur Brown ('68)

I'll Never Fall In Love Again
Tom Jones ('69)
Dionne Warwick ('70)

I'm Sorry
Brenda Lee ('60)
John Denver ('75)

Lady
Kenny Rogers ('80)
Styx ('75)

Let's Dance
David Bowie ('83)
Chris Montez ('62)

Lonely Boy
Paul Anka ('59)
Andrew Gold ('77)

Magic
Olivia Newton-John ('80)
Pilot ('75)

My Love
Paul McCartney & Wings ('73)
Petula Clark ('66)
Lionel Richie ('83)

Patches
Clarence Carter ('70)
Dickey Lee ('62)

Shining Star
Earth, Wind & Fire ('75)
Manhattans ('80)

Shout
Tears For Fears ('85)
Joey Dee & The Starliters ('62)

Stuck On You
Elvis Presley ('60)
Lionel Richie ('84)

Tragedy
Bee Gees ('79)
Thomas Wayne ('59)

Venus
Frankie Avalon ('59)
The Shocking Blue ('70)

Walk On By
Leroy Van Dyke ('61)
Dionne Warwick ('64)

The Wanderer
Dion ('62)
Donna Summer ('80)

RE-CHARTED SINGLES

The Top 2000 singles which hit the charts more than once.

RANK **Peak Position/Year(Weeks Charted)**

11) Rock Around The Clock...Bill Haley & His Comets
1/'55(24); 39/'74(14)

12) The Wayward Wind...Gogi Grant
1/'56(28); 50/'61(9)

66) All I Have To Do Is Dream...The Everly Brothers
1/'58(17); 96/'61(2)

94) The Chipmunk Song...The Chipmunks
1/'58(13); 41/'59(5); 45/'60(3); 39/'61(3); 40/'62(4)

119) Ode To Billie Joe...Bobbie Gentry
1/'67(14); 54/'76(6)

151) The Twist...Chubby Checker
1/'60(18); 1/'62(21)

178) Light My Fire...The Doors
1/'67(17); 87/'68(6)

252) Monster Mash...Bobby "Boris" Pickett & The Crypt-Kickers
1/'62(14); 91/'70(3); 10/'73(20)

273) I Honestly Love You...Olivia Newton-John
1/'74(15); 48/'77(8)

640) Louie Louie...The Kingsmen
2/'63(16); 97/'66(2)

666) Honky Tonk...Bill Doggett
2/'56(29); '57/'61(10)

832) Wipe Out...The Surfaris
2/'63(16); 16/'66(14)

849) Last Kiss...J. Frank Wilson & The Cavaliers
2/'64(15); 92/'74(5)

931) I've Never Been To Me...Charlene
97/'77(3); 3/'82(20)

1008) Dedicated To The One I Love...The Shirelles
83/'59(4); 3/'61(16)

1064) Alvin's Harmonica...David Seville & The Chipmunks
3/'59(12); 73/'61(2); 87/'62(1)

1108) Surfin' U.S.A. ...The Beach Boys
3/'63(17); 36/'74(8)

1203) They're Coming To Take Me Away, Ha-Haaa!...Napolean XIV
3/'66(6); 87/'73(4)

1506) Get Together...The Youngbloods
62/'67(8); 5/'69(17)

1770) I'll Never Fall In Love Again...Tom Jones
49/'67(7); 6/'69(16)

1846) Dream On...Aerosmith
59/'73(9); 6/'76(20)

1855) Jingle Bell Rock...Bobby Helms
6/'57(6); 35/'58(4); 36/'60(3); 41/'61(4); 56/'62(4)

1985) She's Gone...Daryl Hall & John Oates
60/'74(8); 7/'76(20)

1986) On The Dark Side...John Cafferty & The Beaver Brown Band
64/'83(9); 7/'84(18)

THE TWIST

"The Twist" is the only record of the rock era to peak at position #1, drop off the charts, and then return to the charts and again peak at position #1. #1-'60(1 week); #1-'62(2 weeks)

2-SIDED HITS

Don't Be Cruel/Hound Dog...Elvis Presley
Come Together/Something...Beatles

The above two records are rare instances of a #1 record in which Billboard had a hard time determining the side that deserved to be listed first. Both sides received heavy airplay, and both sides were equally requested at record shops, therefore, in both cases the records flip-flopped during their peak weeks on the charts - in other words, one week Elvis Presley's hit was listed as "Don't Be Cruel/Hound Dog", and another week it was listed as "Hound Dog/Don't Be Cruel".

BREAKDOWN BY YEAR

Total records making the Top 2000 year-by-year

YEAR	TOP 2000	
55	27	
56	50	
57	68	
58	67	
59	62	
Total	274	(14%)
60	60	
61	72	
62	70	
63	77	
64	74	
65	69	
66	81	
67	71	
68	66	
69	73	
Total	713	(35%)

YEAR	TOP 2000	
70	64	
71	62	
72	69	
73	68	
74	80	
75	82	
76	68	
77	70	
78	54	
79	58	
Total	675	(34%)
80	59	
81	55	
82	48	
83	59	
84	64	
85	53	
Total	338	(17%)

R OTHER POP HITS!

Joel Whitburn's BUBBLING UNDER THE HOT 100 1959-1981

Lists over 4,000 hits that never made the "Hot 100". The only reference book of its kind.
240 pages. Softcover $25.00

UP AND COMING!

POP MEMORIES 1890-1954

Here, for the first time, is the complete story of American recorded popular music . . . unmatched in scope and depth.

BILLBOARD'S TOP VIDEOCASSETTES 1979-1985

The over one thousand hottest videos from the past 7 years, researched and ranked for the first time.

TOP BLACK 1942-1985

The definitive listing of every R&B single and album to ever hit Billboard's Black charts, dating back to the days of the "Harlem Hit Parade".

For more information on the complete Record Research line of books, write for a free catalog. When ordering the above books, please include a check or money order for full amount plus $3.00 for postage and handling. Overseas orders add $3.00 per book. All Canadian orders must be paid in U.S. dollars.

P.O. Box 200
Menomonee Falls, Wisconsin 53051